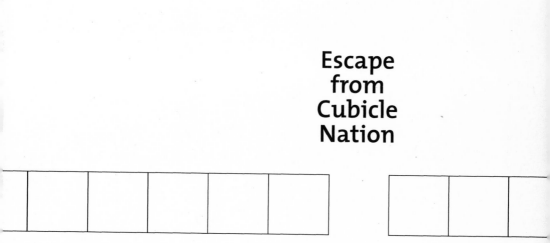

Escape
from
Cubicle
Nation

Escape from Cubicle Nation

FROM CORPORATE
PRISONER
TO THRIVING
ENTREPRENEUR

Pamela Slim

PORTFOLIO

PORTFOLIO

Published by the Penguin Group

Penguin Group (USA) Inc., 375 Hudson Street, New York, New York 10014, U.S.A.

Penguin Group (Canada), 90 Eglinton Avenue East, Suite 700, Toronto, Ontario, Canada M4P 2Y3
(a division of Pearson Penguin Canada Inc.)

Penguin Books Ltd, 80 Strand, London WC2R 0RL, England

Penguin Ireland, 25 St. Stephen's Green, Dublin 2, Ireland (a division of Penguin Books Ltd)

Penguin Books Australia Ltd, 250 Camberwell Road, Camberwell, Victoria 3124, Australia
(a division of Pearson Australia Group Pty Ltd)

Penguin Books India Pvt Ltd, 11 Community Centre, Panchsheel Park, New Delhi–110 017, India

Penguin Group (NZ), 67 Apollo Drive, Rosedale, North Shore 0632, New Zealand
(a division of Pearson New Zealand Ltd)

Penguin Books (South Africa) (Pty) Ltd, 24 Sturdee Avenue, Rosebank,
Johannesburg 2196, South Africa

Penguin Books Ltd, Registered Offices: 80 Strand, London WC2R 0RL, England

First published in 2009 by Portfolio, a member of Penguin Group (USA) Inc.

10   9   8   7   6   5   4   3   2

Portions of this book first appeared on the author's Web site.

The author gratefully acknowledges the individuals who have contributed their stories to this project.

LIBRARY OF CONGRESS CATALOGING IN PUBLICATION DATA
Slim, Pamela.
  Escape from cubicle nation : from corporate prisoner to thriving entrepreneur / Pamela Slim.
    p. cm.
  Includes index.
  ISBN 978-1-59184-257-6
  1. Entrepreneurship.   2. New business enterprises.   3. Success in business.   I. Title.
HB615.S62 2009
658.1'1—dc22   2008050022

Printed in the United States of America
Designed by Chris Welch

To Dad, who, when given a photography assignment two decades ago to take pictures of cubicles, turned to his colleague and said, "Charley: twenty years from now, some expert will be discussing the detrimental effects of these things on employee mental health."

Little did you know it would be me.

□

FOREWORD

have not worked for a large company for ten years. Even when I did, it was for Apple which is hardly what you'd call typical. However, I know enough to tell you that is unfair to characterize all large companies as difficult places and all start-ups as Shangri-las, but for some people start-ups and small companies are the only way to go.

Clearly, you don't have to spend much time in many large companies today to see that, as Steve Jobs would say, "there must be a better way." Meetings are long and painful, decision making is as much about politics as about doing what's right, and the inability to control your destiny is enough to make most people walk around with their teeth on edge.

And that's a well-run large company.

Many people go nuts in these environments and fantasize about getting out. If you're one of these people, you've come to the right place. However, the mystique of entrepreneurship is more sexy than the reality. No one wants to hear about how hard it is to finish a product, make a sale, or collect the money. Everyone wants to think they are joining the next Google, and the German and Italian cars are a few months away.

Pamela Slim is not afraid to tackle the thorny parts of the journey from employee to entrepreneur. Her pragmatism will calm your nerves, and her sense of humor will help you keep moving through the tough parts. She has spent a decade inside numerous corporations and knows the fears you currently face. She's also been an entrepreneur and knows the challenges you will face.

No book can promise you your business will be a success if you follow a set of instructions. If it did, it would cost a lot more. However, *Escape from Cubicle Nation* will help you make a good decision about whether to shut up and suck up your current cubicle or strike out on your own. Think of it as a good, hard reality check.

Guy Kawasaki

CONTENTS

Escape
from
Cubicle
Nation

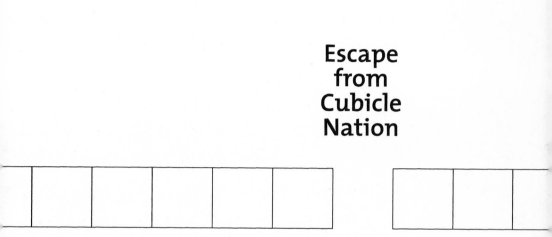

INTRODUCTION

So much of the advertising and marketing about entrepreneurship, especially on the Internet, contains exuberant exclamations like:

"Here is a picture of me cavorting with supermodels in the French Riviera in my ten-million-dollar yacht!" or

"I was an oppressed file clerk, bossed around by tyrannical managers until I spent $399 on a 12-CD training program. Now in just two short weeks I have one assistant just to paint my toes, and my former manager just called, begging to come to work for me!" or

"Here is my large car, parked in front of my large house with my large boat in the garage. None are as large as my bank account, which just keeps filling up, despite the fact that I only work three hours a week."

Am I the only one who grimaces at this picture of entrepreneurship?

If I were to inject reality into this image based on the last twelve years I have worked for myself, my commercial would be more like this:

> "Here is a picture of me at five a.m. at the Southwest terminal at the airport, pregnant and nauseated, throwing up on the curb as I prepare to fly to my client's office" or

> "Here I am at three a.m. at the copy store, on my seventh sugar/ caffeine roller coaster of the evening, near weeping as I try to get my Word document to print out as it did on my home computer so that I can finish my materials for tomorrow morning's meeting" or

> "Here I am trying to close a big deal with a senior executive, scared as hell but trying not to show it, and hoping that the spinach salad I had for lunch is not stuck to my teeth."

You see, although I think it is a tremendous idea to work for yourself and live a life of happiness and financial success, I don't believe that it is possible to become an overnight sensation with a few magic techniques or systems.

Finding work you are passionate about takes time. Building up the knowledge, skill, and experience to be truly great at this work is a labor of intense love and sweat. Creating a business out of this work and building infrastructure, customers, fans, advocates, and mentors requires patience.

And despite what a lot of hyped-up marketing material will tell you, *hating your job intensely is not a business plan.*

I spent a decade traveling all over the United States and Europe working with large corporations to improve their organizations. While I thoroughly enjoyed my work, I found a very surprising thing: some of the smartest and most successful employees inside these companies, often touted as "the best place to work," were harboring secret visions of breaking out to start their own business.

They would pull me aside after an offsite meeting or corporate training and whisper, "I would love to work for myself, but have no idea how to get started. How did you do it?"

What puzzled me about their questions is that there is a tremendous amount of information available in books and on the Internet about starting a business (77,000,000 links in Google when I last checked). So despite lots of information, corporate employees were not getting what they needed to feel comfortable making a change.

In 2005, I started a blog called Escape from Cubicle Nation with the intention of integrating information about starting a business with my experience working as a life coach helping people navigate personal change. My readership was small—I think the first month my daily visits averaged five readers, including my dad, sister, best friend, a former client, and a random person who tripped over my site while Googling for something else. But over time, the visitors increased, and I began to get a tremendous amount of questions from corporate employees all over the world.

Simultaneously, I started coaching individuals who were actually making the transition from employee to entrepreneur and got a detailed and nuanced view of what got in the way of progress. From hundreds of conversations over the years, I developed a framework and process that enabled them to make the leap successfully. And as I suspected, much of what kept them from moving forward was not lack of information, but rather self-defeating thoughts, generalized fears, and outdated notions of what it took to start a successful business in the twenty-first century.

As my blog gained popularity, I connected with some of the brightest minds in entrepreneurship like Guy Kawasaki, Seth Godin, Tim Berry, John Jantsch, and Rich and Jeff Sloan. I interviewed scores of experts on topics from personal finance to branding and learned that there is a way to structure a business that is both deeply meaningful to the entrepreneur and tremendously valuable to the market. And I witnessed a lot of hucksters and shucksters who swindled good people out of hard-earned money with fancy programs long on promise and short on results.

This book is the synthesis of thousands of these conversations over the last three years. It is my hope that it will be the answer to (real) e-mails I get every day such as this:

> I've been working in Investment Banks for almost 20 years. I have a stable job as an officer in the fixed income controller department. The problem is, I work over 14 hour days and also log into the office from home on the weekends. I feel like I have no life and never really have time for anyone. I have an opportunity to take over a pet service business—walking dogs, boarding, and day care—something closer

to what I always really wanted to do as a veterinarian. I should have tried to go to vet school but instead went to business school years ago which was always the "in" thing to do. The pet service business is risky and not as stable. My mom thinks I'm crazy. I wanted to see if you had any advice. Right now I'm torn on what to do. It's easy to just stay where I am and not give notice. I don't even want to talk to most of my friends because they'll think I'm nuts.

Like the person above, you are not nuts to want a better work life. The path from employee to entrepreneur is possible. Many people have done it successfully. You can too, if you are willing to work hard and keep your eyes wide open.

And with a good business model and smart systems, you can even get close to what Tim Ferriss promises in his *4-Hour Workweek*: escape nine-to-five, live anywhere, and join the new rich.

Potential fame, fortune, or freedom aside, there is simply no better way to learn about yourself than starting a business. And when you truly know yourself, you tend to design a business that matches your strengths. Because you are the one in charge, you care more. No longer constrained by a labyrinthine bureaucracy, you think bigger. And given the flexibility to design whatever you want, you are more likely to do something that *means* something to the world.

That is what we are all after, isn't it?

Let's get started.

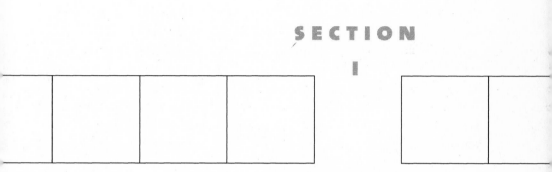

Opening Up
to the
Opportunities

1

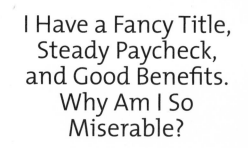

I Have a Fancy Title, Steady Paycheck, and Good Benefits. Why Am I So Miserable?

At ten o'clock in the morning, my phone rang. It was my dad calling from his twenty-ninth-floor office in downtown San Francisco. It was 1994 and we worked about a city block apart. I worked for a large financial services company and my dad worked for a public utility.

"Can you come to the office?" my dad asked.

"I'll be right there," I said. I took the elevator down thirty floors and walked through the courtyard that adjoined our buildings.

I arrived in my dad's office and was slightly puzzled. The bustling, creative office where he worked was totally empty. Desks with plants and empty in-boxes sat where there were once eleven people. My dad peeked out from behind his cube wall.

"They laid off everyone in my department this morning. I am the only one left."

My stomach dropped.

This moment, more than a decade and a half ago, was my abrupt introduction to the shift in the corporate world where solid, stable jobs were wiped off the map in a matter of minutes. Many of my dad's coworkers were career employees, who had started working for the company out of college. One woman had worked her entire career at the company, as had her father and grandfather until retirement. She came into work at 8:00 a.m., was given a cardboard box to pack her belongings, and was escorted to the exit door by 8:20.

That was the moment I stopped trusting the "stability" of corporate life.

You Aren't Crazy

I am sure that if you have worked in the corporate world for any length of time, you had your own moment when you realized that your job would never be secure, no matter how hard you worked or how long your tenure. Nevertheless, many people feel quite guilty for expressing dissatisfaction with their corporate job.

If it makes you feel better, I will sum up the advice I have given to hundreds of clients and thousands of blog readers over the years: *you aren't crazy.*

I understand your train of thought. How can you not feel a little crazy to complain about a stable job with great pay, benefits, smart coworkers, and social prestige? Isn't it selfish to want more when most people in the world would kill for the opportunity to work day in and day out in air-conditioned offices with no chance of getting calloused hands?

Logically, you are right. With all of these perks and a stable income to pay your bills, it would seem that you should be content to get up on Monday morning and go to work. So why do you feel so miserable?

The essence of the problem is two-fold:

- Large corporations have experienced tremendous change over the last twenty years, which have made them fundamentally difficult places to work, even for extremely smart and motivated employees in an "ideal" job situation.
- Some people are simply not cut out to work in large organizations. You may not have had a lot of direction when you finished school, and just followed the path put out for you by well-intentioned career counselors or managers. My former client said it well:

I realized when looking at my entire career since college that I had just fallen into jobs without thinking about them much. I had a vague interest in computer science, but never thought I would end up as a full-time programmer cranking out code in a gray cubicle. How in the world did I get here and how can I get out?

Given my entrepreneurial tendencies, you might think that I am one of those "conspiracy by the Man to keep me down" people and reject all corporate commerce. To the contrary, I loved the years that I worked as an employee. I wore my blue suit, nylons, and pearls proudly. I enjoyed the smell of freshly sharpened pencils and packs of multicolored Post-it notes more than is prudent to admit. I met tremendously smart, funny, and creative people whom I am friends with to this day.

However, since going out on my own a dozen years ago, I had the unique advantage of observing corporate culture without being part of it. That allowed me to see a number of patterns that, when put together, led me to believe that today's corporate environment has some unique challenges that make it difficult for even the most motivated employees to overcome.

Let's start with the first challenge: employees drowning in an alphabet soup of trends, programs, and processes.

Mission Statements, Outsourcing, Rightsizing, and Reengineering

Corporations today go through a tremendous amount of change and upheaval. This is necessary and by design, since market conditions continually shift, senior leadership turns over, management practices evolve, customer needs change, and competitors come out of nowhere.

I would add, somewhat cynically, that companies also go through change since management consultants need to justify their existence. If they don't cook up fancy new programs riddled with acronyms, matrices, and bulging decks of PowerPoint slides, how can they afford to send their kids to college?

In an attempt to explain organization changes to their employees, companies send out communications. Unfortunately, this often makes people more confused, as their explanations sound just like this one spun from the Dilbert Mission Statement generator:

> Our mission is to interactively facilitate enterprise-wide products and collaboratively promote long-term high-impact technology to set us apart from the competition.[1]

You could argue that in the last thirty years, a combination of market trends and corporate initiatives have improved the effectiveness and bottom line of many corporations. However, for employees who have lived in the middle of an ever-changing environment packed with all-hands meetings, whizzing acronyms, and enough binders to topple an elephant, the impact has been downright painful.

Here are some examples:

Well-intentioned trend or program	How it is supposed to work	How it often works
Offshoring	Take advantage of low labor costs and decreased regulation. Focus on "core competencies" while outsourcing the rest.	White-collar employees fear for their lives, looking over their shoulder to see if cheaper/more talented workers abroad will take their jobs.
Business process reengineering	Cut out all unnecessary steps in workflow to increase efficiency and productivity.	Increasing pressure to do more and more work with fewer and fewer resources. The stress feels like a vise slowly tightening its grip.
Mergers and acquisitions	Grow company through "buying rather than building." Gain talent without the expense or hassle of recruiting.	A hotshot manager from your acquiring company walks in with a new set of underlings and discounts the reputation you have worked hard to build for the last twenty years. You are deemed "overlap" and are out on the street.

Well-intentioned trend or program	How it is supposed to work	How it often works
Globalization	Increase market share in industry by selling in global markets. Use local staff to serve local customers. Gain overall company stability across diverse economies.	Wake up at 5 a.m. to conference call with your customers in Europe, then stay at the office until 7 p.m. to talk with your marketing team in Japan. Choosing a good time to meet with your team is like running a goat rodeo.
Pervasive mobile technology	Be available for customers 24/7; instantly responsive. Provide flexibility to telecommute or work remotely.	Your boss calls you twelve times on your family vacation and you are expected to return customer e-mails at night. Frustrated, your wife runs off with the pool boy.
Centers of excellence	Model and standardize higher performance throughout the company.	Forced to use a "standardized" process, you spend more time learning/incorporating "best practices" than doing your job or serving your customers.
Metrics-based bonuses (Individual Performance Multipliers)	Clear expectations and level of performance. Competition breeds excellence.	Your performance is measured against that of others in your "job family" who have fundamentally different jobs and by managers who hardly know you.

I want to hammer home a point here: the nature of large, global corporate organizations in today's tumultuous markets is such that they *can* and *should* change frequently to stay alive. Strategies will change. Business plans will change. Organization structure will change. Your position is not secure, no matter how well you do your job.

As long as you know this and act accordingly, you will do fine, even inside a corporate job.

Leadership Flaws

Three years ago, I was taking my son for a walk around the block in his stroller. I was reflecting on all the years I spent inside large corporations and how hard it was to change ingrained leadership behavior.

Then, in an inspired daydream, I began fantasizing what I would say in a keynote speech to top-level executives around the world.

I could hardly steer the stroller fast enough back to the house. As soon as my son went down for a nap, I started pounding at my keyboard, calling the post an "Open Letter to CXOs Across the Corporate World."

Later that evening, I sent the post to Guy Kawasaki, a prominent blogger and venture capitalist in Silicon Valley, because I thought he might find it entertaining.

He blogged about it the next morning.

I was not prepared for the response; tens of thousands of people flooded my blog within the first few days, and I got hundreds of passionate e-mails and comments.

The experience led me to believe that there are some fundamental things that are not being said by employees in corporations that need to be.

Here is the post, as it was originally written:

Open Letter to CXOs Across the Corporate World

I am writing to you as a newly minted rebel. My main purpose in life is to take your best, your brightest, most creative, hard-working and passionate employees and sneak them out the hallways of your large corporation so that they are free of the yoke of lethargy, oppression and resentment.

It hasn't always been this way. I tried for many years as a consultant to YOU to explain the importance of treating your employees with dignity and respect. I encouraged you to speak clearly and to the point, to avoid endless hours of PowerPoint, buzzwords and meaningless jargon like "our employees are our most valuable asset." I was sincere in my efforts as I coached your managers and explained the importance of providing objective, developmental feedback to employees that was based on observable behavior, not personal generalizations. I encouraged you to be open with your business strategy so that your employees could contribute ideas to grow your company.

After ten years, I give up. I was banging my head against the wall trying to find ethical, creative ways to train your employees on the merits of your forced ranking compensation plan. No amount of creativity could overcome the fact that it is a stupid idea and does nothing but create an environment of competition, politics and resentment. Whoever sold you on that idea was wrong.

So now I want to help your employees leave and start their own business. Regain control of their life. Feel blood pumping in their veins and excitement in their chest as they wake up each day. I honestly wish that it were possible for them to feel that inside your company. But things have gotten so convoluted that I honestly don't think it is possible unless you take some drastic steps:

1. **Don't spend millions of dollars to try and change your culture.** Corporate culture is a natural thing that cannot be manufactured. No amount of posters, incentive programs, PowerPoint presentations or slogans on websites will affect the hearts and minds of your employees. If you want to see things change immediately, stop acting like an asshole. If you see one of your senior managers acting like an asshole, ask him to stop. If he doesn't stop, fire him. You will be amazed at how fast the culture shifts.

2. **Stop running your company like the mafia.** By now, we are all aware that no job in any industry is secure. They can be re-scoped, eliminated or outsourced at any time. And that is the way it should be—no organization can be static in today's environment. But despite this common knowledge, many of your managers act betrayed when their employees tell them they want to leave the company. This is an absolute double standard and should be stopped immediately. If you help your employees grow and develop in their career even if they plan to leave the company, you will create an extremely loyal workforce. You never know where that employee who leaves

(continued)

will go next. They could become an incredibly valuable strategic partner. Their golfing buddy could turn out to be your next huge customer.

3. **Spend a moment walking around the halls of your company and look at your employees.** I mean really look at them. Don't just pat them on the back and pump their hand while looking over their head at the exit door. Look directly in their eyes. Imagine what their life is like. Who is waiting at home for them? What are the real consequences to their health, marriages and children when they have to work yet another thirteen hour day? What kind of dreams do they have? What makes them really happy? What do their eyes tell you? Do they trust you? Resent you? Think you are full of it? I met precious few C-level executives in 10 years consulting that truly "saw" and cared about their employees. Those that did reaped gigantic mounds of good will and respect.

4. **Teach people how to get rich like you.** I don't think there is anything inherently evil with money. It would be kind of fun to have my own jet and be able to pick up and fly to New York to watch the opening of a Broadway play or zip to Mexico for a long weekend. But the kind of disparity that exists right now between your employees who do the work and you and your senior team who reap the benefits is not only absurd, it is obscene. I know you work very hard and carry a lot of responsibility for your company. Instead of hoarding your wealth, teach your employees how to make money. Show them how you negotiate large deals. Explain investment vehicles. Explain how your business works and why it is so exciting for you to run. Make them into better businesspeople so that they can grow their opportunities and net worth. And for God's sake share the profits. It is insulting to tell your managers to look a hardworking employee in the eye and say they only get a 3% raise when you take home more in a quarterly bonus than they make in 10 years.

5. **Don't ask for your employees' input if you are not going to listen to it.** I have facilitated offsite meetings that lasted for days where well-intentioned managers brainstormed and argued and edited and wrote flip charts until their hands turned blue. They sweated over creating

something that was relevant and for a brief period of time actually were proud of what they accomplished. Until a month later when I heard that you scrapped the whole thing in favor of a plan cooked up by an outside consulting firm. This does not only completely waste smart people's time, it guarantees that you will have hostility and resentment the next time you ask for creative input.

6. **Don't train people until you know what problem you are solving.** I would be rich if I took up all the offers I got to "design and teach a 5-day course on people skills for all of our managers worldwide." Most often, I would get the call from a VP of Human Resources that received the request from their pissed off CEO. And what were the pressing business problems that caused the request? Often it was the threat of a lawsuit based on one manager's egregious behavior. Take the time to analyze what is causing the problems in your business such as high turnover, plunging sales or a huge increase in employee complaints. Usually it is something that will not be resolved by training everyone. Most often it involves firing a person or two who are causing havoc in a department. If you really want your managers to learn how to manage people, put them in tough situations with great mentors nearby. Keep an eye on them. Provide feedback and coaching exactly at the moment that they need it (like before they have to fire someone for the first time and are scared to death). There is a time and a place for training, but it should not be your first course of action.

7. **Ditch the PowerPoint when you have town hall meetings.** No one is excited to see another boring graph or 20-part building slide that describes all the components of your new strategy. If they are interested, they can read the slides at their desk. Your employees want to hear your opinions on things that they think about all the time. Your PR team may have a heart attack, but invite tough questions about the things that you know are really on their mind. Are you going to take over another company? Outsource the Help Desk to the Philippines? Why did you get a huge bonus this quarter when the rest of the employees are on a salary freeze? Did the VP of Sales really get caught with his pants down at the

(continued)

sales meeting in Vegas? Just because people ask the questions doesn't mean you have to answer them all. Know what you can and can't talk about and be direct about that (no, you can't talk about the VP of Sales or you may get sued). You will do wonders for your credibility and I guarantee no one will be sleeping in the back of the room.

8. **Focus on the work people do, not how or when they do it.** Some positions require people to be at their desk at an appointed hour to answer customer calls or to participate in live meetings. But others can do their work from home, early in the morning, late in the evening or dialing in from the local Starbucks. The turnover magnet you have for losing great employees is not the competitor down the street, it is the idea of freedom and flexibility for the self-employed. Your employees have different biorhythms and working styles and activities going on in their lives. If you provide flexible work options and don't make people sit unnecessarily at their desk, you will keep some great employees who would otherwise leave. A manager who is afraid to offer telecommuting to her employees because she thinks they will slack off is just showing her own weakness. Great managers build accountability into flexible work plans and manage performance aggressively.

9. **Watch the burnout.** Many companies measure an employee's drive and dedication by the amount of hours they work each day. I have witnessed people playing video games at their desk until their manager leaves "just so they won't think that I am a slacker." Huh? It is not a badge of honor to work 18 hours a day, it is a sure path to a heart attack or divorce. There are times when employees have to work around the clock to get critical projects done and that is part of doing business. But if they are working long hours just because "everyone does," you are creating a culture of waste, inefficiency and ill health.

10. **Forbid people to work while they are on vacation.** Of all the pet peeves that I have accumulated over the years, this is perhaps the biggest. Your employees work like pack mules all year long. They send messages via BlackBerry during dinner, take work calls during their kid's

basketball games and forgo rolling in the sheets with their spouse to finish a PowerPoint presentation on Saturday morning. When they go on vacation, let them relax. The only way to get the health and stress-relieving benefits of a vacation is to completely unplug from work. As long as they are checking e-mail each morning from the hotel lobby or fielding "urgent" calls in the evening, they might as well be in the office. The worst thing is seeing their kid's eyes as they observe once more that Dad or Mom values work more than family, even on vacation. Shame on you for making this acceptable behavior.

I won't entice anyone out your door that does not want to come willingly. Many people will choose to stay in the comfort of your oppressive predictability. But if you lose some smart, creative, entrepreneurial and positive minds, you can't say I didn't warn you.

Do any of these issues hit home for you? Based on the 100,000-plus people who read my post and vigorously agreed, you are not alone.

Many, perhaps most, corporate leaders are decent, ethical people. But some of you may have had the misfortune to work in a place so rampant with greed and devoid of ethics that it would fit what my college international studies professor Francisco Vazquez said about the "melting pot" of American culture: "Those on the bottom get burned and the scum floats to the top."

You Aren't Meant to Have a Boss

Noted software engineer and venture capitalist Paul Graham goes so far as to say human beings aren't meant to work in large corporations. In his post "You Aren't Meant to Have a Boss," he makes this comparison:

I was in Africa last year and saw a lot of animals in the wild that I'd only seen in zoos before. It was remarkable how different they seemed. Particularly lions. Lions in the wild seem about ten times more alive. They're like different animals. I suspect that working for oneself feels better to humans in much the same way that living in the wild must feel better to a wide-ranging predator like a lion. Life in a zoo is easier, but it isn't the life they were designed for.[2]

The Ill-Fitting Shoe

Complex corporate trends, leadership flaws, and the fact that humans may not be meant to work in large groups might be enough reason to confirm your suspicion that you are not crazy for feeling unhappy in your corporate job. But there may be a simpler answer: *You may not be cut out for corporate life, and don't realize it.*

In the late nineties, I conducted career development classes inside network giant Cisco Systems, which at that point was experiencing the benefits of an insane stock price increase. As follow-up to the classes, I had one-on-one sessions with the participants to discuss their personal career aspirations and goals.

One meeting in particular stuck with me, as I talked with an extremely successful young woman who had been with the company for a long time. I had remembered in class that she was a little "numbed out," meaning that it was hard to get a real reaction out of her besides superficial comments. In the individual session, it was very different. She started talking:

> Before I took this class, I had a strange, nagging feeling that something was not right about my current situation, but I couldn't figure it out. . . . I had achieved all my personal career goals and had a situation that most people would envy. . . . But despite these things, I was still unhappy. When we did the exercise about defining personal values in the class, I had an intense reaction. I went home and compared this list to the list of values currently represented in my work environment.

Then she started crying.

> And I found that not one of my top ten values was represented in my current work situation. Suddenly, I understood why I was not happy! It was a big relief.

What she described is a very common feeling among people inside corporate jobs. Each of us has natural, organic preferences for how we feel the most alive, relaxed, happy, and passionate at work. These can include things like:

- **Physical work environment:** type of building, color scheme, how desks are laid out, natural vs. artificial lights, etc.
- **Type of business:** for-profit, nonprofit, retail, established, start-up, your own business
- **Business culture:** how people treat each other, values displayed by actions of all employees (not just words), policies and procedures or lack thereof
- **Communication styles of managers, clients, and coworkers:** direct or indirect, confrontational vs. relaxed and open
- **Size of business:** number of employees
- **Type of work content:** what the company is in the business of selling, e.g. financial services, retail, consulting, consumer products, software, etc.
- **Skills and talents used in work:** which skills you are using in your day-to-day work activities

I liken it to wearing a shoe two sizes too small:

- Your ideal situation is like wearing a pair of size eight wide shoes of a stylish, comfortable brand that feels custom-made for your foot and looks sexy too.
- Your current situation is like wearing a pair of size six narrow shoes, in an unflattering material, with a heel that is both ungainly and unattractive.

So why in the world do we try to jam our foot into an unattractive, uncomfortable shoe, otherwise known as our day job?

Because our social self (shaped by family, educational institutions, the media, and religion) is so strong that we believe that our "great job at an investment bank where I have an outstanding reputation, many years' experience, and an amazing salary" should make us happy. Even if we know that it is in direct contrast to the picture of our ideal life!

So, in a chilling similarity with many well-intentioned parents who steer their kids to corporate jobs that don't match their true nature, Cinderella's stepmother instructs her daughters:

> "Listen," said the mother secretly. "Take this knife, and if the slipper is too tight, just cut off part of your foot. It will hurt a little, but what harm is that? The pain will soon pass, and then one of you will be queen." Then the oldest one went to her bedroom and tried on the slipper. The front of her foot went in, but her heel was too large, so she took the knife and cut part of it off, so she could force her foot into the slipper. Then she went out to the prince, and when he saw that she was wearing the slipper, he said that she was to be his bride. He escorted her to his carriage and was going to drive away with her. When he arrived at the gate, the two pigeons were perched above, and they called. The prince bent over and looked at the slipper. Blood was streaming from it. He saw that he had been deceived, and he took the false bride back.[3]

As much as you want to make yourself feel good about a situation that is not right for you, it will feel awkward, uncomfortable, and downright painful after a while. The blood will drip from your ill-fitting shoe, and making it to the ball with Prince Charming will be the least of your worries.

Miles from Meaningful Work

One of the disconcerting parts of working in a large company is that you often get caught up in a frenzy of activity doing things that don't have a direct bearing on the real world.

The epitome of meaningless corporate work is the 1999 movie comedy *Office Space*. The main character Peter is increasingly frustrated, and eventually pushed to the brink of sanity, by the amount of time and management effort used to ensure he uses a certain cover sheet on his "TPS Report."

The larger organizations get, the greater their capacity for doing work that is not directly related to anything in the real world. Or, in an equally frustrating outcome, months of work are scrapped as a new company is acquired, or changes vendors, or gets a new CEO with a different vision from his predecessor.

One of my favorite examples of meaningless work comes from a blog reader, Laura:

> My company had actually gotten so far away from their customers (calling them "names," as in "we need more names") that eventually management announced an ambitious program called "Customers First." Over the next year, countless global manpower hours were spent as bulging binders were handed out, launch meetings were called, task forces were assembled, brainstormings were held (and copious notes typed up), progress was benchmarked, etc. It all resulted in the startling recommendation that "we should put our phone number on the order forms in case people want to call us," which was quickly trumped by "no, that would make it easier for people to just cancel the service." That was 8 years ago. This year, new management just announced an exciting new initiative called "Putting Customers First." They are currently in the throes of a careful year-long test of what happens if you put the website address on the order form.

People who spend a lot of time on task forces, leading multiple-day offsite meetings and generating enormous binders and decks of PowerPoint slides, often have sober moments when they think, "What in heaven's name does this have to do with the real world?"

That Gray Fabric Really May Cause Brain Damage

While "cubicle nation" could be considered as much a state of mind as a physical environment, there may be something about the physical design of cubicles that actually makes people sick.

Kathy Sierra, known for her interest in brain research and learning, wrote in her blog post "Brain Death by Dull Cubicle":

> You always knew that dull, boring cubicles could suck the joy out of work, but now there's evidence that they can change your brain. Not mentally or emotionally, no, we're talking physical structural changes. You could almost say, "Dull, lifeless work environments cause brain damage."

I said "almost," because it depends on your definition of brain damage. What the research suggests is that in unstimulating, unenriched, stressful environments, the brain STOPS producing new neurons. But it's only been the last few years that scientists have finally realized that the human brain can build new neurons. For most of the previous century, it was believed that we were born with all the neurons we'd ever have.

Scientists who believed in and studied the idea of "neurogenesis" were dismissed, criticized, ignored. But Princeton's Elizabeth Gould has picked up the neurogenesis ball and run with it. She is almost single-handedly changing the face of neuroscience and psychology.

From a fascinating article in an issue of *Seed Magazine* (my new favorite):

"Eight years after Gould defied the dogma of her field and proved that the primate brain creates new cells, she has gone on to demonstrate that the structure of the brain is incredibly influenced by one's surroundings."

One of the most interesting (and, in hindsight, "doh!") discoveries was that one of the main reasons researchers kept finding NO evidence of new neuron development in their test primates is because they kept them in an environment which shut that process down. In other words, it was the caged-living that stopped the neurogenesis process. By giving her animals a rich, natural environment, Gould "flipped the switch" back on, allowing their brains to work normally, and sure enough—the happier, more stimulated animals showed a DRAMATIC increase in neurogenesis as well as dendrite density.[4]

Whether or not the design of cubicles actually makes you sick is up for scientific study. But ask just about anyone who has worked in a cubicle for a long time how it feels and they are likely to say something like this comment by a blog reader:

No fresh air, no windows, no exercise. I feel like life is coasting by while I sit and rot. My eyes are dry and my wrist aches. When I see announcements for retirement parties here (cheap sheet cake, sugary punch, some kind of tacky appreciation plaque) I'm pretty sure I'd rather jump off a bridge.

Blood from a Turnip

Since you have read this far, I hope you realize that there is a reason why you feel cranky in your corporate job. The icing on the cake for many corporate employees is an overwhelming amount of information to process within a limited time frame.

Meetings, useful when conducted the right way, turn into agonizing wastes of time as the same problems are hashed over and over by the same rambling people for months on end without any resolution or decisions. At times, they seem to mock Tim Ferriss's insight from *4-Hour Workweek*: "Slow down and remember this: Most things make no difference. Being busy is a form of laziness—lazy thinking and indiscriminate action."[5]

E-mail, originally intended to make us more productive and connected, has turned into a three-headed monster that grows back twice as big as soon as you slay it. Many employees spend up to six hours a day trying desperately to respond to hundreds of e-mails that clog their in-box.

There is nothing wrong with appreciating every paycheck, benefit, doughnut in the break room, fresh pencil, free copy, and paid vacation that comes with a corporate job. Seeing the good in what you have is one of the keys to living a happy life.

But if despite this you still don't feel great, you are really not an ungrateful curmudgeon. And you aren't crazy, as I alluded to at the beginning of the chapter.

Some of you feel much, much worse than "not great," like "ready to slam my head into the wall" or "so emotionally dead that I have no idea what I feel anymore" or "about to have a stroke from all the stress."

I found a lot of despair hidden behind smiling faces of smart people in cubicles over the years. Gut wrenching, tears, confusion, sadness, anger, you name it, I heard it. So why don't people just leave? Read on.

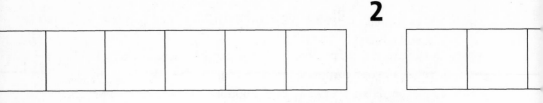

2

If It Is So Bad, Then Why Am I Afraid to Leave?

Let's get this out of the way: the kind of fear that catches in your throat and wakes you up at three in the morning with your heart pounding in your chest most likely doesn't have to do with insecurity about your business model or stress over the color palate of your Web site or concern that you don't know how to use Internet marketing to your advantage.

Your biggest fear is *living in a van down by the river.*

I Am 35, Divorced, and Live in a Van Down by the River

If you never watched Chris Farley on the television show *Saturday Night Live,* you missed his over-the-top depiction of "Matt Foley, Motivational Speaker." (You can look up the clip on YouTube.) In the clip, he says, "My name is Matt Foley and I am a motivational speaker. I am thirty-five, divorced, and live in a van down by the river."

Part of what made this clip so funny is that he expressed a situation that strikes fear in the hearts of most corporate employees: losing all social status, family, and money.

My clients openly admit that fears like this worry them the most when they are considering quitting their corporate job to start a business. Variations on the *van down by the river* theme include:

- Ending up homeless on the street and eating garbage out of a Dumpster
- Losing their wife and children after they ruin their credit and have to pawn all their worldly possessions on eBay
- Being laughed out of their high school reunion by wealthy, successful classmates who have fancy cars and job titles.

When I wrote a blog post on this topic, I got a wonderful response from a reader named Becky who shared:

> Wow. I actually DID live in a van down by the river. (Video is still online from the reality show that filmed it.) I confronted my "I'm going to end up a bag lady" fears, quit my $50,000 a year job at age 50 right after my dad died and moved into a van—in Colorado . . . down by the river sometimes, but usually in a Wal-Mart parking lot the rest of the time. I shared the van with my rottweiler and a house cat. I worked—writing and doing freelance photography and working a temp job at Camping World. It sucked. But it was fun too. I have NEVER felt so free in my life and I'm constantly drawn to do it again someday—from an RV . . . with money. I lived in the van for a year—winter, summer, spring and fall. I won a pretty prestigious journalism award while doing it too . . . near the end I went back into journalism. I moved into an apartment, got another job—and am transitioning into yet another phase of my life—as a ghostwriter. I'm working with a celebrity on a fitness book and have seven other books in the hopper for other clients. Wow. But the best part—I confronted my lizard fears that I'd end up living in my car and die in a van down by the river. I didn't and I won't. I proved to myself that your thoughts and fears *can* be confronted and changed.

Don't worry, I am not advocating that you follow Becky's experiment and move into your own van down by the river.

But in order to get the energy and motivation to move out of your corporate job, you will have to identify both the fears that are holding you back as well as a plan to overcome them.

The most pervasive and powerful fears come right from our reptilian ancestors.

Lizard Fears

One of the deepest layers of the human brain is a neural structure that evolved in early vertebrates. It is wrapped around the cortex of your brain and blasts signals on a regular basis intended to keep you fed and out of danger. Martha Beck says in *Steering by Starlight*:

> The entire purpose of your reptile brain is to continually broadcast survival fears—alarm reactions that keep animals alive in the wild. These fears fall into two different categories: lack, and attack. On one hand, our reptile brains are convinced that we lack everything we need: we don't have enough time, money, everything. On the other hand, something terrible is about to happen. A predator— human or animal—is poised to snatch us! That makes sense if we're hiding in a cave somewhere, but when we're home in bed, our imaginations can fixate on catastrophes that are so vague and hard to ward off that they fill us with anxiety that has no clear action implication.[1]

Animals will live longer when obsessed with getting more resources and avoiding danger. Corporate employees, on the other hand, sometimes have fears that are totally disproportionate to their level of risk.

How Do You Know If Your Fear Is of the Lizard Variety?

- **It is very extreme.** You worry about failing so badly that your wife leaves you, you lose your house, car, and boat and end up homeless and eating trash out of a Dumpster.
- **It crumbles with a critical eye.** I asked a client who was seriously worried about losing everything and never working again if he quit his job if he

had ever faced a situation before where he was out of work and had to find a new job.

"Oh yeah, that happened when I got laid off from my last company with no notice."

And what happened? I asked.

"I got another job right away, which was a better position at a higher salary."

- **You feel it very strongly in your body**, with typical physical reactions to anxiety like shallowness of breath, tightness in your chest, muscle contraction in your neck or shoulders, or headaches.

Lizard fears are not bad: they help alert us to danger and make sure that we don't put ourselves at unnecessary risk. But given free rein, they will cloud your judgment and ensure that you never take a step toward your budding dreams.

How Do You Tame Your Inner Lizard?

Martha Beck tells clients to name their lizard and toss him a grape when he gets particularly panicky. She also encourages them to get a physical representation of the reptile, like a small statue or pin. This will make him easier to talk to and mock at will.

Habits expert Havi Brooks imagines her fears as wooden ducks, and observes them as they trail dutifully behind her as she walks through her day.

EXERCISE

Assess Your Fears and Identify Antidotes

INSTRUCTIONS:

Create a page with four columns. Label the first column "Belief." Label the second column "Underlying assumption." Label the third column "What I need to find out." Label the fourth column "Where I can find it."

(continued)

Belief	Underlying assumption	What I need to find out	Where I can find it

COLUMN 1: BELIEF

List all the thoughts and fears related to leaving your corporate job. They can be things like:

- I will never be able to support my family if I go out on my own.
- I don't have what it takes to be a successful entrepreneur.
- I am afraid that this job is as good as it gets, and I am going to be disappointed by my next effort.
- I am afraid of losing my house and leaving my finances in ruins if I go out on my own.

Take your time and create a good list. Put down absolutely all of your concerns so that you get them out of your head, and you have the opportunity to examine them.

COLUMN 2: UNDERLYING ASSUMPTION

Starting with your first belief, try to identify the assumption that underlies this thought. So if we take the first belief example, which was "I will never be able to support my family if I go out on my own," some assumptions could be:

- There is not enough financial opportunity in the businesses I am considering to support my family.
- I don't know how to get new clients, so I will not bring in enough money.
- I really don't know what I am doing, so I am bound to make mistakes.

COLUMN 3: WHAT I NEED TO FIND OUT

Once you have listed as many assumptions as you can, identify the information you need to either refute or validate your underlying assumption. So using the first one, "There is not enough financial opportunity in the business I am considering," what you need to find out are things like:

- What is the financial opportunity in this business?
- Who is financially successful in this business?
- What specific things did they do to get successful?
- How long does it take to ramp up in this business and meet my financial goals?
- What are the investment and cash flow considerations?

The more specific you are with your questions, the more likely you are to find evidence that will either support or refute your belief.

COLUMN 4: WHERE CAN I FIND IT?

Brainstorm as many sources of information as you can for answering your column 3 questions. Following our example of finding the financial opportunity in a new business, you may want to list things like:

- Google a similar business and contact the owners in this business.
- Ask colleagues, friends, or relatives who may have experience or contacts.
- Read information about the industry online and in trade publications.

As you learn more information, you will find that your level of anxiety and fear decreases because you are moving from a vague and hypothetical understanding to an informed one.

Status, Routine, and Recognition

No matter how intriguing your new venture is, there are some big things that you would give up if you left your corporate career:

- **Status.** I don't care if you detest every day you enter the office. If your business card says "Lorraine Sanchez, Vice President of Business Development, IBM," you carry a lot of weight in our society. Try explaining to your mother why you would give up a six-figure salary with a well-known company to try your hand at starting a faux-finish painting business. It may feed your soul, but will it impress your neighbors? So much of what you learn in a corporate setting is that status matters and that your self-worth increases as you make your way up the career ladder. In your right mind you know this is ridiculous, since how can a job title bestow self-worth? But if you have any leaks in your confidence tank, your subconscious will believe the hype and make you feel very uneasy at giving it up.

- **Routine.** You may have a comfortable routine that includes a stop at your favorite café to get a latte in the morning, or a workout in the gym next to your office at lunchtime. Even if you work long hours, your body is accustomed to a familiar routine and will resist any change, regardless of whether it is good for you or not. If you are married with kids, you may have a carefully choreographed dance between you and your spouse for who gets the kids ready, drops them at school, drives them to various activities, and gets them ready for bed. When you start your business, you will not have a predictable schedule and this can wreak havoc on your family life.

- **Recognition.** If you have been working for a good number of years in a corporate setting, most likely you have developed some great skills and have a breadth of experience in your field. Peers recognize your expertise, and even partners and vendors acknowledge that you know what you are talking about. If you were to chuck all this for a new, untried venture, you would put yourself back to a beginner stage where you feel incompetent in what you are doing. A few people enjoy this feeling. Most people hate it.

Essential vs. Social Self

Even if you are very excited about your business idea, you may get riddled with fears about what "everyone" will think about your decision. This can start a game of Pong in your head:

> *Ping:* I cannot stand this job, and if I stay one minute longer my head will explode.
> *Pong:* You should be happy to have a job in this economy, why are you complaining?
> *Ping:* I want to sell homemade cookies, not practice law.

Pong: Are you freaking serious? How many snickerdoodles will you have to sell to pay off $100K in student loans? Why would you waste your education like that?

Ping: I cannot stand this incessant travel. I miss my wife and kids so much it physically hurts.

Pong: Welcome to the real world, Whiny Boy. In order to provide long-term security for your family, you must sacrifice.

A good way to decipher the competing voices in your head is to understand the essential self versus social self, described by Martha Beck in *Finding Your Own North Star*:

> Your essential self formed before you were born, and it will remain until you've shuffled off your mortal coil. It's the personality you got from your genes: your characteristic desires, preferences, emotional reactions and involuntary physiological responses, bound together by an overall sense of identity. It would be the same whether you'd been raised in France, China, or Brazil, by beggars or millionaires. It's the basic you, stripped of options and special features. It is "essential" in two ways: first, it is the essence of your personality, and second, you absolutely need it to find your North Star.
>
> The social self, on the other hand, is the part of you that developed in response to pressures from the people around you, including everyone from your family to your first love to the pope. As the most socially dependent of mammals, human babies are born knowing that their very survival depends on the goodwill of the grown-ups around them. Because of this, we're all literally designed to please others. Your essential self was the part of you that cracked your first baby smile; your social self noticed how much Mommy loved that smile, and later reproduced it at exactly the right moment to convince her to lend you the down payment on a condo. You still have both responses. Sometimes you smile involuntarily, out of amusement or silliness or joy, but many of your smiles are based purely on social convention.[2]

It is a good thing to respect the opinions of your family, friends, and mentors. But if they give you advice that makes your inner voice scream in resistance, you may want to remember my mantra: *I am the only one who lives in my skin. I trust my instincts.*

He'll Change His Cheating Ways

I am a very optimistic person. I believe anyone is able to change if given a strong enough motivation and opportunity.

But I no longer believe that corporations are going to fundamentally change the way they treat employees, regardless of how many of their PowerPoint slides say "People are our most important asset." There is too much talent in the world, they are too big, and the global marketplace is too competitive.

Employees can learn from the long-suffering girlfriend of a confirmed "player." The more she tries to please her man, do the right thing, wear the right clothes, and demonstrate the right behavior, the more she gets burned.

Her heartbreaking error, of course, as with trusting employees, is believing he will change when given no evidence he ever has in the past nor will he do so in the future. Perhaps both of them should follow the advice of Maya Angelou: "When people show you who they are, believe them."

This is not personal. It doesn't mean that the managers or executives who have been overseeing your career for years don't think you are a great person. It doesn't mean your work has not been valuable, or appreciated. It doesn't mean that all the executives in your company are greedy or cruel or corrupt. Those you have known for years may well be your greatest supporters (and first customers) when you venture out on your own.

It just means that employees who treat *companies* like old, loyal friends will die of heartbreak.

Corporations can no longer promise lifetime employment. They may try hard to get you to support their brand, wear their T-shirts, and care deeply about their customers. But if they say something like "we demand absolute employee loyalty," take a good hard look at your employment agreement, which states that they can terminate you at will, with or without cause.

Instead, view your corporate time as a wonderful opportunity to meet smart, creative people, develop new skills, learn how business works, and get funding for top-notch educational experiences (many companies still pay for university-level certificate programs or advanced degrees).

Fear of Failing

One of the biggest concerns I hear from aspiring entrepreneurs is the fear of failing. Fear is a natural part of trying something new. If you didn't feel any fear, you would likely get hit by a car (since you wouldn't bother looking when crossing the street), scammed by a telemarketer (since you would believe that the free trip to Florida truly had no strings attached), or have to bail out your teenage daughter (since you would believe her when she says "Mom, I swear, no one will be drinking beer at the homecoming party, and parents will be there to chaperone").

Fear is simply nature's way of telling us that there is some risk involved in a situation. Here is how to face it head-on so that you work with it, not against it:

1. **Examine the truth in the fear.** "What if no one buys my product?" This could be an extremely legitimate fear if you have not taken time to clearly define and research your market, identify competitors, develop a compelling marketing strategy, and define a sales process. If you have done all that and received positive and encouraging feedback from smart and successful people in your field, I say move forward. Mitigate your risk by taking it slow and watching the results carefully. You will find lots of lies among the truths in your fear, and these you can expose and leave by the roadside. (Byron Katie's "The Work" is an excellent tool for doing this—see sidebar, p. 35.)

2. **Get comfortable with being uncomfortable.** It is a huge lie that successful people feel no fear and skip effortlessly from one challenge to another. They experience the same digestive distress, sleepless nights, and trembling hands as you do when they try something very different in their life or business. The only difference between them and you is that they feel it and do it anyway! They know that fear is an essential part of growth. So purposefully put yourself in some situations that push your limits a bit and get you out of your comfort zone. This is like sit-ups for the psyche. The more you practice, the more "fear fit" you will be.

3. **Develop a strong safety net.** Surround yourself with encouraging people who take smart risks themselves. You need cynics and skeptics around when you are doing your competitive market analysis and research. But when you have done all that and are ready to make a scary leap into unknown territory, invite your globe-trotting, skydiving, and hair color–changing friends to hold your hand. They will enthusiastically encourage you to close your eyes and *jump*.

Barry Moltz, who wrote a whole book on failure called *Bounce! Failure, Resiliency, and Confidence to Achieve Your Next Great Success* says this about failure:

> How do we take ownership for our mistakes without wallowing in shame? By accepting and learning to recognize how each experience, positive or negative, has value in helping us decide what to do next.
>
> We can spend some time figuring out our part in every mistake and perhaps what others contributed as well. Many times the forces beyond our control (and yes, there are many) play a part in the mistake. In total the universe may not make mistakes. What is supposed to happen happens with a sort of natural flow and consequence, and in the interest of that big picture, sometimes some of us have to fail.
>
> Each outcome is like randomly climbing or descending the stair. Your particular goal may be at the top or the bottom of the stairs. It may be to the side at one particular landing. Treat all the outcomes you label as "failure" with an open mind and appreciative attitude, and learn from them. When we are finally able to let go, we are ready for the next experience.[3]

A lot of our view of failure in popular American culture is romanticized. The fact is, while you are failing, it feels really awful and does not become the enlightened lesson that you receive until you have some distance between you and the excruciating experience.

As Martha Beck once told me at a particularly difficult point in my life, "Someday, you will see that this was being done for you not to you."

Keeping that perspective, combined with Moltz's advice to learn from every mistake, will greatly improve your ability to bounce back from failure.

Break the Grip of Destructive Thoughts

Learning to objectively examine your thoughts is one of the most powerful things you can do as a budding entrepreneur. Byron Katie's pioneering book *Loving What Is: Four Questions That Can Change Your Life* describes a simple process for deconstructing pesky thoughts. The Four Questions from "The Work" are:

1. **Is it true?**

2. **Can you absolutely know that it is true?**

3. **How do you react when you think that thought?**

4. **Who would you be without that thought?**

   and
   Turn it around.
   Here is an example of how to use it, from a typical coaching session with my clients.

Me: You said, "If I quit my job and start a business I will end up on the street." Is it true?
Client: Well, technically it could be true; if I really screw up and spend all my savings, I could end up on the street.

Me: Can you absolutely know that it is true?
Client: Well, I suppose if I take small steps and test my idea to make sure it is viable before quitting my job that it would not be true. Or if I define a dollar amount in my savings account that I will not go under, and will take up a side job if things get tight that it will not be true. Or maybe I could get another job.

Me: How do you react when you think the thought "If I quit my job and start a business I will end up on the street"?

(*continued*)

Client: I feel scared. A lack of confidence creeps in. My brain shuts down and I want to run back to safe ground.

Me: Who would you be without that thought "If I quit my job and start a business I will end up on the street"?
Client: I would be strong and confident. I would not be afraid to start testing my idea to see if it works.

Me: Okay, so if we wanted to take your original statement and turn it around, what might it be?
Client: "If I stay in my job, I will end up on the street."

Me: Is there another way you could turn this around?
Client: I will never allow my entrepreneurial plans to land me into the street. As soon as I get close to financial worry, I will implement my backup plan to ensure that I take care of my family.

Me: Is this belief as true as or more true than your original statement?
Client: It is more true.

Me: Which of the two thoughts is going to give you more courage and success as an entrepreneur, "If I quit my job and start a business I will end up on the street" or "I will never allow my entrepreneurial plans to land me in the street. As soon as I get close to financial insecurity, I will implement my backup plan to ensure that I take care of my family"?
Client: Duh!

Going through the four questions allows you to examine thoughts that cause you excessive worry and view them from an entirely different perspective. This does not replace all the other things you need to do to ensure that your business is a success, like building a business model, testing and prototyping, marketing like crazy, and organizing your finances. What it does do is release you from the grip of paralyzing thoughts that keep you from moving forward. Try it!

As Good as It Gets

It is exciting to work with someone who finally makes a breakthrough and realizes that they have a deep, burning passion for a business idea. But inevitably, after exploring the idea for a couple of weeks and getting really excited, they call me in somewhat of a panic.

"Pam, what happens, after all of this hard work, if working in my new business is not any better than my current situation as an employee?"

"Ah," I reply. "You are afraid that your current life may be *as good as it gets.*" While I understand this concern, I would share the following perspective:

- What was it that drove you to spend a lot of time investigating self-employment? Be sure to tune in to the original emotion that spurred your quest. If you find that your fire to do something new has burned out since viewing the reality, great! Make it easy on yourself and don't change more than you need to.
- Life does not stand still. So while your "perfect" situation today as an employee feels pretty comfortable, can you guarantee it will always stay this way? What might be some of the vulnerabilities in your position, department, company, or industry?
- The qualities that make up a great employee include curiosity, drive, initiative, and creative thinking. Working for yourself, even for a short period of time, is a great way to develop skills that will make you more attractive to employers down the line. It is the equivalent of being an exchange student in high school: when you return home after your year away, you will never look at your family, community, or country in the same way. It forces you to grow up, truly know yourself, and become self-reliant.
- You do not have to, nor should you, adopt an "all or nothing" stance with your business ideas. The best way to find out if you are really cut out for self-employment is to spend some time doing it. After that, you can decide whether or not to pursue it full-time.

I had the tremendous gift of writing this chapter right in the middle of the Lehman Brothers public bankruptcy in September 2008. As I watched formerly high-flying corporate employees slink out of their offices with their personal effects in cardboard boxes, I asked myself: "Who feels better today, those employees who put all of their effort into their job, or those who took the time to develop a wide social network, invest in self-development, and pursue a small business on the side?"

Your day-to-day happiness doesn't have much to do with your form of employment. Working for yourself will not magically make all your problems go away and lift your mood. It is the exact same thing as believing that finding the perfect spouse will make you happy. *Being* happy by yourself will make you happy, and make you more likely to attract a mate who is happy, healthy, and without the tendency to try to "fix" you.

3

Detox from
Corporate Life

In my twenties, I was what some of my friends and family called a "martial arts maniac," training, teaching, and performing the Afro-Brazilian style of capoeira for up to thirty hours a week (all while working a full-time job). One of the best parts of this experience was doing performances at local schools, because the enthusiasm and excitement of the kids was infectious.

One morning, we did a show at Sanchez Elementary School, located in the Mission District of San Francisco. We performed for a full school assembly of about five hundred kids. The standard school performance format was to do our show, then invite a few volunteers from the audience to learn some basic moves and practice them onstage with a professional performer. The kids got a big kick out of it, and it was a great way to include a bit of instruction.

A few kids did the practice performance, and then we asked if there were any more volunteers. A very small boy shyly raised his hand and approached us with trepidation. I assumed by his demeanor and body language that he was going to be very ginger and timid in his movements.

I was wrong.

From the moment he stepped onstage, he exploded. He jumped, leaped, spun, kicked, and flipped around like a beautiful tiger. The audience was squealing in delight, and all of us performers were clapping wildly to see such a magnificent display of courage and talent.

After the show, the principal of the school came over to me and said in hushed tones: "I think that was the most amazing thing I have ever seen." She explained that the little boy who had shown such fire and passion onstage had emigrated from Vietnam a year earlier, and was painfully shy and withdrawn in school. The teachers were worried that he had learning or behavioral problems and had no idea how to get through to him. "I was totally shocked to see such power and creativity come out of that little boy!" she said.

This little boy, for many reasons that could have included trauma at leaving his home country and difficulty with a new language, had his inner tiger on a short, choking chain. If he had not had the opportunity to show what was inside of him, no one would have known that he contained such inner power.

Do you walk around the same way?

Find Your Inner Tiger

I believe that each of us is born with a strong, creative spirit that wants to jump, dance, learn, and grow. I call it the "inner tiger," and it is the life force that propels us toward an active, open, engaging, healthy, and fulfilling life. It can also be called your higher calling or life purpose. So why do we often chain it up and not let it roam freely?

- **We are told at an early age that our fire and passion is not "appropriate."** We hear things like "nice girls from the suburbs don't start punk rock bands," or "well-educated Indian men do not start scrappy entrepreneurial businesses," or "corn-fed farm boys from the Midwest do not join the New York City Ballet," or "spending your life traveling is a lazy and meaningless way to use your life."
- **We see others around us conforming to "safe" lives and we don't want to stand out.** So we go to the "right" schools, take a job at the "right" company, and buy a house in the "right" neighborhood, even if we have to walk around with a suppressed scream in our throat.
- **We tell ourselves lies to feel better.** Lies include: "I never wanted to

choose this career path, but my parents made me," or "I hate my job, but I have to stay in it until my kids are in college since there is no other way to make money," or "I really want to start a business, but I am too young (or old) and no one would ever take me seriously."

Keeping an active tiger chained up inside you takes a lot of energy. It saps your life force to continually pretend to be motivated, to feign enthusiasm for your life or job, to grind through another day at the office when you can feel that it is strangling your spirit. Releasing it allows you to create a life that thrives from your creative energy and utilizes the best of your strengths. So how do you cut the chain?

- **Acknowledge that it is there.** Verbalizing the fact that you feel stifled, uncreative, and unfulfilled in your life is the first step in doing something about it. Stop pretending that everything is okay if it isn't.
- **Pay attention to your body.** Tense muscles, stomach problems, anxiety, and trouble sleeping are all signs that you are trying too hard to control your creative impulses. Get back in touch with your body by exercising, meditating, and practicing deep breathing. This will reconnect you with your true voice that will tell you what you need to do to take care of yourself.
- **Stop with the mind-numbing substances.** Another sign that your creativity is stifled is when you have to down two glasses of wine when you get home from work just to calm your nerves. A funny thing happens when you remove all mood-altering substances from your diet (including excessive caffeine or chocolate, whatever your vice is): you bring a new sense of clarity to your life.
- **Agree to take action.** If you have been living an unfulfilling life, you may feel stuck, unmotivated, and overwhelmed. But staying stagnant is not going to keep things the same—it will get much worse. So begin to do something, anything, to get your creative juices flowing. Take an art class. Take an afternoon off and paint a picture. Strike up an interesting conversation with a total stranger. Run through a field of flowers or jump in a pile of leaves. When you begin to feel a bit more like your two-year-old self and have your energy back, take concrete steps to improve your life.
- **Own up to your lies.** Whenever you find yourself saying "I have to do this," or "so-and-so made me do this," or "I am like this because . . ."

stop, look in the mirror, and say very clearly: "Up to this point, I have chosen to create a life that isn't fulfilling. It isn't working. Now I am choosing something different."

Some of you know that your inner tiger is chained up, but are so tired, or stuck, or scared, that you need some extra help releasing him. Do you find yourself agreeing with any of the thoughts below, expressed by my faithful blog readers?

> I describe my office job and cubicle as toxic to my spirit. Before I graduated, I was ambitious, excited and had big dreams. My work sucks all the creativity and fun . . . and is starting to sap my spirit too. It has dampened my will and motivation and has just made me stop caring. I'm . . . no longer excited about projects or making a difference. I'm just going through the motions . . . it's hard to keep the lethargic work energy from spilling over to other aspects of my life.
>
> —*Laura* (now touring Europe)

> I feel as if I don't have a soul anymore . . . mostly machine and all traces of humanity have been pounded out of me. As my wife says "You used to be fun, but now you suck!"
>
> —*Richard*

Finally, my favorite:

> I felt as if the blood was being siphoned out of my body. Not enough to put me out of my misery, just enough to take away my will to live!
>
> —*Barbara*

In order to have the creativity, energy, motivation, and endurance to start a business, you absolutely need to thaw out your soul. Here is how to do it:

Step 1: Clear Your Plate

If you are serious about starting a business, you will need to completely reorganize your schedule so that you have time to work on your ideas.

Here are some areas to "trim fat" out of your schedule and free up time to plan your new venture:

- **Meetings, committees, and task forces.** We all know that meetings take up at least 50 percent of your time in a corporate job. Look at each of your appointments and ask yourself "Is this meeting, committee, or task force critical to get my job done effectively?" If not, find a politically astute way to back out of it. "I would love to keep attending this meeting, but I am just swamped with _____ (fill in the blank) project right now that is critical to my (boss) (customer) (VP)."

- **Outside volunteer projects.** I am 100 percent supportive of community volunteering. I spent ten years of my life volunteering at least thirty hours a week, and I learned a ton from it. But right now, you need to use all of your extra time to plan your business. So gracefully back out of as much volunteer work as you can. Don't worry, your fast-track application for sainthood will not be revoked, and you can make up your goodwill toward men (and women) once your business is successful.

- **TV zone-out time.** When I am really stressed out, I can get sucked into a bad pattern of zoning out in front of the TV to unwind and relax. One hour can turn into three or four if I am not careful (especially if I am watching one of those home improvement shows—for some strange reason, they are highly addictive).

- **Kids' activities.** I don't know if it is the same outside of the United States, but we schedule our kids like little executives. Parents frantically shuttle them between soccer, karate, and trombone lessons, play dates and extracurricular test preparation. The poor little tykes must carry electronic organizers and cell phones just to keep track of all the details of their overscheduled lives. I am not suggesting cutting out all of your kids' activities, just scale back a bit so that they are less harried and you have some time to rest or plan your business. I remember spending hours as a kid making a paper boat and sailing it in a puddle in our driveway. It was exciting and stimulating and is one of my fondest childhood memories.

You may find that a freer schedule will also clear your mind and allow you to think creatively about your new venture. Who knows—after your new business is up and running you may just choose to keep your less-harried schedule.

Step 2: Reset Your Mind to "Beginner"

We all get cocky and think we know a lot about a lot of things. This is probably true; your life experience and education have given you a rich body of experience that you should be proud to share with others.

However, if you go into entrepreneurship for the first time with an attitude that you know everything, you will miss all kinds of great information and opportunities. Great entrepreneurs see the world differently from your average person, and this is because they understand "beginner mind."

What Is "Beginner Mind"?

Beginner mind is a state of being where you approach situations with no judgment, censoring, editing, or preconceived expectations.

When you are in a state of "beginner mind," you think things like:

- Wow, this is cool! I wonder how it works.
- That is interesting! Why do you think that?
- I want to learn as much as I can about this topic!
- I really don't understand this person, but I wonder what makes him tick.
- I can't wait to get in front of customers to hear what is important to them!
- What else? Tell me more.

It is in direct opposition to its cousin "expert mind," where you think things like:

- When is this person going to stop talking so I can share what I know?
- This person is so wrong in her explanation and I can't wait to prove it to her.
- I tried that already and it didn't work.
- I can't wait to share my 152 PowerPoint slides at my first sales meeting. They will be so impressed with what I say that they will probably buy my product before I leave the building.
- This is a total waste of my time. I am learning nothing.

"Expert mind" can be very dangerous to a new entrepreneur, since you are in a phase of discovery where you need to soak up as much as possible about your new venture. Some expert-mind traps particular to corporate employees can be things like:

EXPERT MIND TRAP

"I don't need to bother learning small business marketing, because I graduated with honors in my MBA program and was the senior VP of marketing for a major company."

REALITY

The marketing you know may be very, very far removed from what you need to know to be an effective entrepreneur. Although it may sound similar in concept, in practice it is very different.

EXPERT MIND TRAP

"I know there is a need in the market, since I have studied it extensively online for the last two years and have the spreadsheets to prove it. I do not want to bother talking with someone in the market, since I know they will just confirm my research."

REALITY

Nothing substitutes for talking to real people in your target market. Many entrepreneurs see the potential of a five-billion-dollar market in their area of interest. But how many can personally name those that are ready to buy the first ten products?

EXPERT MIND TRAP

"I don't really want to talk to people who have been in this field for a long time, since they are too 'old school' and don't have half of my fresh ideas or social media savvy."

REALITY

You can learn many, many valuable things from seasoned entrepreneurs in your field. You may not agree with everything they say, but you can avoid many mistakes by listening to what they have learned through hard-won experience.

. . .

Cultivating a beginner mind as an entrepreneur will greatly increase both the depth and pace of your learning, and make the process fun and exciting. You will find that more people are willing to talk with and support you when you are open and nonjudgmental.

Step 3: Thaw Out Your Soul

I have spent lots of time in cubicles. Even as a consultant, I would often get assigned a cube to work in for a long-term project. And as much as I knew that I was not an employee and had a vibrant life outside of work, I would sometimes slip into a bit of a coma.

This is such a common feeling that I sometimes wonder if cube furniture comes with a strange chemical pheromone that actually draws your life force out of you. Maybe it is activated by fluorescent lights?

Whatever it is, I know from firsthand experience as a consultant in hundreds of corporate environments that some longtime employees, who by their nature were never meant to fit into corporate life, develop a serious rift between their emotional and intellectual selves. This manifests in:

- Not being able to identify what makes them happy
- A feeling of numbness and emptiness
- A feeling of burning rage
- A feeling of powerlessness and loss of self
- A sense of loneliness and loss of direction

Why does this happen?

As humans, we are made with both emotional urges and rational thoughts. Our emotional self, which resides in the realm of our physical body:

- Wants to be creative and playful
- Seeks out pleasure and comfort
- Is stimulated by beauty
- Recoils from unhealthy relationships

Our intellectual self, which resides in between our ears:

- Is influenced by ideas
- Wants to appear rational and reasonable, not emotional
- Can "suck it up" and bear tremendous emotional and physical pain
- Is very influenced by what is "right" and "responsible"

To make it through modern-day corporate life, you have to quash your emotional desires in order to survive. The intellectual self reigns supreme. The reality is, we are not meant to sit in meetings for hours and hours, hashing out technical details that everyone knows will be changed next week anyway. We want to run from unhealthy relationships, but when our boss (whom we often did not choose to work for) is a manipulative and political person, we choke down our feelings and stay in the unhealthy relationship for fear of backlash to our annual review or bonus. And when our job responsibilities call for us to perform a task that we find meaningless and trivial, we choke down our urge say "That is absurd, and I won't spend my valuable time that way!" and do it anyway, in order to be responsible and a "team player."

There is nothing wrong with being responsible. It is just that if you continually repress your natural desires, you will find yourself in a permanent "living dead" state, so used to choking down your emotions that you can no longer access them.

What can you do to shake up your numb soul?

- **Do not beat yourself up for feeling this way.** Remember the lessons from chapter 2: Many people feel lots of guilt for complaining about a steady job, good paycheck, and honest living. You should be thankful to have a paycheck that sustains you and your family, but don't confuse this with accepting that this job is the right fit for your creative soul.
- **Begin to reconnect your emotional and intellectual selves by exposing yourself to creative environments or activities.** Remember that your emotional self craves truth and beauty, so look for ways to express both. Nature is great for waking up the emotional self, as is music, art, and really sensuous food. See specific tips for waking up creativity in the following sections in this chapter.

- **Keep close tabs on your "inner meanie" voice.** As you brainstorm areas of interest and business ideas, the voice inside that has been shaped by your corporate life, parents, religion, and the media will say things like "You will never make money at that!" or "Only granola-eating liberals want to write poetry!" These voices are extremely unhelpful at the initial stages of brainstorming. If you find yourself blocked by such thoughts, turn to them in your gentlest of voices and say "Thanks for sharing, sweetie—I appreciate the thought!" and keep moving forward.
- **Rest.** Sometimes, what your emotional self wants most is to snuggle under the covers and take a long nap. It is tiring to repress yourself for so long, so you may need to do a bit of temporary hibernating in order to figure out what moves you.
- **Surround yourself with supportive people.** Your bitter, repressed cube mate may not be the best person to confide in if she is stuck in the complaining stage and not ready to take action. In fact, many people who finally do work up the courage to leave the cube are surprised by the negative reaction of former colleagues. You may think they would be happy for you, but many feel resentful that you actually made the step while they are still unhappily slogging away at a job they loathe. You may find more support from an enthusiastic software developer in Prague that you meet through an online forum than from your next-door neighbor whom you have known for years.
- **Make time for the creative journey.** If you really want to figure out what moves you, you need to devote time and energy to the pursuit. If you allow yourself thirteen hours a day to check e-mail and create PowerPoint slides and seven and a half minutes to think about your creative soul while you are using the restroom, guess which side will win? Take some time off from work, cut back on nonessential obligations, and make figuring out the next stage of your life a priority. You will not regret it!

Step 4: Prepare to Walk Through No Man's Land

No matter how great the ultimate benefit of a change, going from "what was" to "what will be" can be very unsettling.

One of the top authorities on change and transition, William Bridges, in his book *Transitions: Making Sense of Life's Changes*, refers to the period between "endings" (your old life) and "beginnings" (your new life) as the Neutral Zone. This term was first coined over seventy-five years ago by Dutch anthropologist Arnold van Gennep, who noticed that in most traditional societies, all ceremonies marking change involved separation, transition (which he called the neutral zone), and incorporation.[1]

To this day, many traditional societies mark significant changes with rituals that help with the transition process. In my husband's Navajo culture, for example, male and female puberty ceremonies are marked by four days of isolated reflection, sharing of wisdom between the young and elderly, time in nature, and disconnection from "modern conveniences" including electronics and all forms of media.

In today's society, if we get slowed down by a significant life transition and can't keep up a frantic level of activity and output, we question ourselves. The reality is, being in this awkward state of transition is an extremely creative and ripe period. Before doing some specific exercises to wake up your creativity, here are some hints to help you have the best experience in the Neutral Zone:

- **Embrace it.** Instead of asking yourself "When am I going to get back to normal?" be thankful that you are given an opportunity to reflect on your life and come out with a new, improved, emotionally healthier you. You may not want to do this in public, but repeat the mantra "Uncertainty is powerful and liberating!" as often as you can, and you may just begin to believe it.
- **Ask yourself "What am I afraid of?"** Your fears hold lots of information that can shape your new life. As an example, in a typical transition like getting married, you may fear losing your independence, or your prized hot car collection, or your sense of spontaneous passion. Don't choke down these fears; look at them closely and use them as the basis for good, healthy discussion with your spouse-to-be about how you can design a life to incorporate the things that are important to both of you. The same will be true for your business.
- **Tune up your health.** When I went through a slow period in my consulting business a couple of years ago, I used the free time as a way to get back into working out. I took up yoga, Pilates, and kickboxing, dropped twenty pounds and found that my overall emotional well-being skyrocketed.

- **Clear out clutter.** A period of transition is a great time to clear out junk, boxes, papers, pictures, old clothes, moldy food from the back of your refrigerator, and expired cans from the pantry. A clean environment really does contribute to a clean mind. I am also a big fan of rearranging furniture since it will get you comfortable with seeing familiar things in a new and different way.

I have done my best to suggest ways to prepare a healthy environment to support your creativity. If you are ready, let the games begin!

Step 5: Open the Creative Floodgates

I always laugh when asked for advice on reawakening creativity from extremely locked-up cubicle warriors: "I really have no idea what I want to do in life. Do you have an hour coaching session where we can figure it out?"

People in corporate environments are desperate for advice and relief, and this I can understand. But reawakening creativity is not a five-step process with a neat timeline. It is an organic, nonlinear, messy experience that needs time, space, and attention.

One of the best ways to start is by setting up a regular time to tap into your creativity.

Morning Pages

It is uncanny how many clients I talk to who have read Julia Cameron's book *The Artist's Way.* They are not all Birkenstock-wearing hippies as you may think. Software engineers, salespeople, accountants, musicians, and writers have all found her suggestions for unlocking creativity helpful. One of her cornerstone activities is doing "Morning Pages," which is a great way to get your thoughts flowing and, in her words, "quiet your inner Censor."

WHAT ARE MORNING PAGES?
In Julia's words:

> Put simply, the morning pages are three pages of longhand writing, strictly stream-of-consciousness: "Oh god, another morning. I have

NOTHING to write about. I need to wash the curtains. Did I get my laundry yesterday? Blah, blah, blah . . ." They might also, more ingloriously, be called brain drain, since that is one of their main functions.

There is no wrong way to do morning pages. These daily morning meanderings are not meant to be art. Or even writing. I stress that point to reassure the non-writers working with this book. Writing is simply one of the tools. Pages are meant to be, simply, the act of moving the hand across the page and writing whatever comes to mind. Nothing is too petty, too silly too stupid or too weird to be included.[2]

Meandering and Mindfulness

- **Spend an afternoon wandering through a new part of town.** You probably have well-worn paths from your house to the grocery store, dry cleaner, and child's school. Choose a totally new and different neighborhood that you have never explored and just wander the streets. Notice which stores or buildings are interesting. Pay attention to the people in the neighborhood.

- **Go to a local art museum and play hot-warm-cold.** Walk into the museum and pretend your body is a heat-guided missile. Try not to think, just let your body go toward the art that makes you feel hot (I mean body temperature hot based on excitement, but of course it could be *that* kind of hot, depending on what kind of museum you go to!). As you look at the art, let your body relax and soften your gaze.

- **Use your camera to document whatever you find interesting.** When you look at life through the lens of a camera, you change your perspective. Take pictures of whatever interests you, from the way a leaf sits on a sidewalk to the words of a graffiti tag on the wall to the graceful neck of a subway rider. Don't worry about the quality of each photo, just take lots and lots of shots of things that interest you.

- **Surf the Internet with a tool like StumbleUpon.** www.StumbleUpon .com is a free service you set up with your Internet browser that allows you to preselect topics of interest from a broad number of categories like "food," "photography," "health," or "business" and then click a button to see Web pages that contain information about those topics. The more popular a page is, the more likely you will see it. This is a great way to open your mind to the many different ways people approach the same topic.

- **Sit quietly in a comfortable place and pay attention to your breath.** You may notice that your mind races with all kinds of ideas. Take the role of observer and notice the thoughts without reacting to them emotionally. Close your eyes and breathe in and out slowly, noticing the rise and fall of your chest.
- **Eat a meal in small, slow bites and savor the taste in each mouthful.** Notice the taste of each item on your plate. Sense the subtle flavor in even a glass of water.

Physical Activity

While the eyes are the window to the soul, the body is the door to creative impulses. You don't need to engage in high-impact or rigorous activities, but something that makes your heart race or body sweat is a great way to shake up your mind. If your regular exercise routine feels a bit rote, try the following things:

- **Take a dance class.** By making your body move in a new way, you break old, stuck patterns and get your blood and energy moving. I spent a lot of time around Brazilian dance, and it is a very fun thing to do with lively drums and joyful, full-body expression. If that doesn't float your boat, try any style, such as ballroom dancing, free-form modern dance, or country-western two-step.
- **Take an improvisation class.** The basis of improvisation is reacting creatively to a situation with as little thinking as possible. It is an excellent way to bring fun and spontaneity into your life and learn to act from impulse, not obligation.
- **Get jiggy with it at unexpected times.** Yes, I am suggesting that you should awaken your creativity by having sex with your partner. Don't get arrested, mind you, but your sexual self has a lot of creativity, especially when you let it break out of the "only the third Wednesday of the month at nine p.m." routine. And, yes, you can tell your partner that you must do it since I told you so.

Step 6: Observe and Track Ideas

All of these creative exercises are going to start to generate all kinds of thoughts, sounds, images, and ideas. To benefit from all this creative output, you want to set up some simple systems to capture ideas. Use technology to help you track ideas, but don't get so enamored by the system that you lose the point: to capture your thoughts.

Notebooks Everywhere

I used to get very frustrated that my best ideas come late at night in the bathtub. I would sit at my computer for hours, staring at a blank screen and painfully typing out a few really bad passages. Then, as soon as I left my computer and headed for the bath, my mind would explode with ideas. A few times I actually got out dripping wet and typed ideas at the computer before going back in the water, but now I keep a notebook handy next to the bathtub. Other common places you do not often have access to a pad of paper are in the car, or a part of your house not associated with work, like the kitchen. Secret hint: the room where you do lots of sitting and thinking is a great place for a notebook (and I do not mean your parlor!).

Index Cards

Index cards are a slight variation on notebooks, except that they can be handy for tracking one idea per card, which can then be organized into sections or patterns. You can work with plain white cards, or choose a pack of different colors, which would be used to designate different topics.

Record Your Voice

Some of you may feel more comfortable recording yourself talking rather than writing down notes. This can be handy if you tend to brainstorm while driving. The relatively new service www.jott.com is also a good tool that works by leaving yourself a voicemail, which is automatically transcribed in an e-mail and sent back to you. This works well for short messages. For longer recordings, try a service like www.audioacrobat.com where you can record up to two hours of audio using your phone. You can access the voice recording later or send it to be transcribed, using one of the many cheap transcription services found at virtual assistant sites.

Computer Folder

Much like the paper folder, set up a dedicated folder on your computer that is in an obvious place, like your desktop. Each time you write or find a document that is related to your business idea, put it in the folder.

Browser

Any major browser like Internet Explorer or Firefox allows you to "bookmark" Web sites in specific categories. Try to create broad categories, since too many specific categories will make it harder for you to quickly grab and categorize something.

Del.i.cious (http://delicious.com)

This service is similar to bookmarks, but your results are public and you can also see which sites other people find interesting and noteworthy. Track and tag Web pages and blog posts that interest you over a period of time. Then, using the "cloud" feature, see which of your tags are the most prevalent.

Vision Boards

A vision board is a graphic representation of words and images related to your topic of interest. If you are a highly visual person, it can be a great way to start your brainstorming process, and to see a picture of your interests in one place. The basics are easy; just grab some magazines, scissors, and glue and get busy posting thoughts on a big board.

EXERCISE

EXERCISE

How to Create a Vision Board, by Christine Kane

WHAT IS A VISION BOARD?

A vision board is typically a poster board on which you paste or collage images that you've torn out of various magazines. It's simple.

The idea behind this is that when you surround yourself with images of who you want to become, what you want to have, where you want to live, or where you want to vacation, your life changes to match those images and those desires.

For instance, before I ever started performing music and had no idea how I'd ever get a gig, write enough songs, or assemble a press kit, I drew a picture of myself in a bar with people watching me perform (I'm a terrible visual artist, so I actually had to label the people "people"!). And though it wasn't the only factor in making it happen, I had a calendar full of bar and coffeehouse gigs by the next year.

My drawing was a kind of vision board. Vision boards do the same thing as my drawing did. They add clarity to your desires, and feeling to your visions. For instance, at the time I did my drawing, I knew I wanted to play in bars and coffeehouses. (I have since left that circuit, and I'm performing in theaters and at conferences. But in my early twenties, I wanted to play in bars and coffeehouses. I was pretty clear about that!) Taking the time to draw it out, even poorly, made it indelible in my mind.

There are several methods you can use for creating your vision board. I've written about each one below. You can choose which one works best for you, depending on where you find yourself on this path of creating your life.

SUPPLIES YOU'LL NEED FOR CREATING A VISION BOARD

- Poster board. (Target sells a really nice matte finish board. I highly recommend it.)
- A big stack of different magazines. (You can get them at libraries, hair salons, dentist offices, the YMCA.) Make sure you find lots of different types. If you limit your options, you'll lose interest after a while. When I

(continued)

facilitate my women's retreats, I always make sure we have plenty of *Oprah, Real Simple, Natural Home, Yoga Journal, Dwell, Ode, Parenting, Money, Utne*, and an assortment of nature magazines.

• Glue. Not Elmer's. (It makes the pages ripple.)

Before you begin your vision board: No matter which method you're choosing, have a little ritual before you begin your vision board. Sit quietly and set the intent. With lots of kindness and openness, ask yourself what it is you want. Maybe one word will be the answer. Maybe images will come into your head. Just take a moment to be with that. This process makes it a deeper experience. It gives a chance for your ego to step aside just a little, so that you can more clearly create your vision.

THE FIVE STEPS OF CREATING A VISION BOARD

Step 1: Go through your magazines and tear the images from them. No gluing yet! Just let yourself have lots of fun looking through magazines and pulling out pictures or words or headlines that strike your fancy. Have fun with it. Make a big pile of images and phrases and words.

Step 2: Go through the images and begin to lay your favorites on the board. Eliminate any images that no longer feel right. This step is where your intuition comes in. As you lay the pictures on the board, you'll get a sense of how the board should be laid out. For instance, you might assign a theme to each corner of the board. Health, Job, Spirituality, Relationships, for instance. Or it may just be that the images want to go all over the place. Or you might want to fold the board into a book that tells a story. At my retreats, I've seen women come up with wildly creative ways to present a vision board.

Step 3: Glue everything onto the board. Add writing if you want. You can paint on it or write words with markers.

Step 4: (optional, but powerful) Leave space in the very center of the vision board for a fantastic photo of yourself where you look radiant and happy. Paste yourself in the center of your board.

Step 5: Hang your vision board in a place where you will see it often.[3]

source: Christine Kane, www.christinekane.com

Chapter 6 will help you take the output of all your creativity dredging and see which ideas are fit enough to survive the gauntlet of a real business model. Through that process, you may find that your intense passion for hand-painted Czechoslovakian buttons is really a passing fancy, much like your lust for Ray Gonzalez in seventh grade. Or you may discover a vast marketplace of button-loving enthusiasts who will gladly pay top dollar for your rare collection. I was shocked to find that thousands of people are drawn to knitting humor. Who knew?

So if you are antsy to keep on fleshing out your business idea, go ahead and jump to chapter 6.

But if before jumping you want to know what to expect on the journey from employee to entrepreneur, read on.

4

What's Really Involved in Moving from Employee to Entrepreneur?

For most people pondering the change from employee to entrepreneur, the move feels like jumping off a cliff. You fall from a deathly boring but well-known job into a deep abyss.

I believe that this is where much of the "living in a van down by the river" terror comes from, since it makes perfect sense that you would be afraid of making a change if you have no idea what you would be doing, if there is a market for it, how you would make money, and if you have even a remote chance of success.

So let me describe the typical steps on the path from employee to entrepreneur, based on my own experience, as well as the experience of my clients.

The Moment of Reckoning

KEY

Find a good reason to spend a lot of time working on your business.

Everyone has a different reason for wanting to quit his or her job and start a business.

After plodding along in corporate life for years, sometimes decades, there is a moment that galvanizes the thought: "This is insane. I must get out!"

For my good friend Steve Darden, the moment came twelve years ago while he was heading an organization in Gallup, New Mexico, that fights substance abuse in the Navajo Nation. His wife was staying at home with their three sons and also pursuing a master's degree. "I was making the highest income I ever had in my life," Steve recalls. But his long hours in the office and weekends full of speaking engagements were taking a toll on his family.

Steve's moment of reckoning came through his youngest son, Seth. The boy woke up from a nightmare one weeknight saying, "Where is my dad? I want my dad!" Steve, who had lost his father in the Korean War when he was just three months old, didn't want his sons missing out on time with their father like he had: "I was being a father, not a daddy. I was being a provider, not a husband."

So he decided that he had to leave his job and quit on the spot. "My wife asked me, 'What are we going to do?' I honestly did not have a response. I just knew that I had to change my life."

For some people, the message to quit comes through their bodies. Symptoms include:

- **Extreme fatigue and lethargy.** One day, it feels impossible to get out of bed, even on a weekend. Energy levels are extremely low, and it is often all you can do to make it to work and back.
- **Health problems.** If fatigue is not addressed, it often turns into an illness like bronchitis, pneumonia, mononucleosis, or Graves' disease. Or muscles

act up and you have neck or back spasms. Heart problems, high blood pressure, and stroke can all be the result of stress.

- **Uncharacteristic emotional outbursts.** Emotions can range from sappy tears while watching a television commercial to deep, lashing anger at a spouse or child that is totally out of proportion to the interaction. Usually, the person feels very out of control and embarrassed by the outburst, since it comes without warning and feels out of character.

- **Depression.** Staying in an unhealthy situation for a long period of time can induce emotional reactions from slight blues to clinical depression. A blog reader who worked in a cube for years said his therapist shared that conditions in corporations are often a trigger for clinical depression.

Writer and entrepreneur Jonathan Fields was a corporate lawyer whose moment came after he was hospitalized with a severe infection after a particularly arduous three days:

> I began as an enforcement attorney at the U.S. Securities and Exchange Commission in New York, then jumped to a top New York law firm as a securities/hedge fund lawyer, before my body literally rejected my career.
>
> I'd been working nearly seventy-two hours straight, each one more excruciating than the one before. But, missing the deadline meant losing $100 million for our client, so I pressed on until we finally closed the deal. I staggered into the cab, passed out for a few hours, then headed straight to my doctor's office.
>
> His face turned ghostly white as he grabbed my hand, whisked me through a team of specialists, and sent me straight to the hospital for emergency surgery.
>
> Weeks of relentless hours had literally collapsed my immune system, allowing a softball-sized infection to ravage my intestines and eat a hole through them from the outside in. Within hours, I was in the OR. Thankfully, I made it through, battered, but on the way to a full recovery. I had plenty of time to sit around and think while I was healing. Talk about a wake-up call![1]

You may not require a soul-baring moment like Steve or a gut-busting medical condition like Jonathan to make a change.

Some people are perfectly happy with their corporate jobs, but have always had the desire to challenge themselves with a new experience like starting a business.

Whatever your reasons, in order to gather the strength for what lies ahead, you must feel deep inside that it is worth the time, energy, and money required to explore entrepreneurship.

Are you feeling it? Good.

If Not This, What?

KEY

Find out what makes you purr.

When you realize that you are not able to continue in your current line of work, the next logical question is: *What should I do?*

This strikes fear in some people's hearts since they have been on autopilot for a long time and have not considered their passions in many years. When I used to teach presentation skills to corporate salespeople all over the United States, I would always use the same practice topic: a one-minute presentation entitled "I am passionate about . . ."

I was amazed at how few people had an immediate answer to this question. Most looked at me with a blank stare. Others were annoyed and even hostile, since they could not believe that I would ask them to complete such a difficult task with so little preparation.

So a big part of your job at this stage is to reawaken curiosity, your muse and your creativity. This will require time, attention, and focus in order to get real results.

In the year 2000, in Phoenix, Arizona, at a Fast Company conference about design, I had the privilege of listening to Jim Collins, author of the best-selling books *Good to Great* and *Built to Last*. In his highly personal keynote, Jim talked about his own career path, which took him from professor of entrepreneurship at Stanford to, in his words, "an entrepreneurial professor."

He referred to the ultimate work situation as your "sweet spot." This is the intersection of three interlocking circles:

- The first circle is **"what people will pay you to do"**—marketable skills and abilities that you have developed over your working life.
- The second is **"that which you have great passion for"**—areas of interest, hobbies, ideas, or causes that make your heart race.
- The third, and most elusive, is **"that which you are *genetically encoded to do*"**—the things that you were brought on this earth to accomplish that no one else on the planet can do as well as you.

Where these circles interlock is your "sweet spot" and the place where you should spend your working life if you want to feel alive and full of joy.

Jim started his investigation by gathering data on himself much as a scientist would observe an insect in its native habitat. So when he was stuck in meetings, or listening to Brahms, or involved in a variety of other activities, he would document his behavior in a notebook he called "A Bug Called Jim." He would notice when he was engaged, or bored, or sad, or angry.

His process of discovery lasted years, and he supplemented his data gathering with personal mentors and lots of reading. After a while, he began to see patterns, and made steps each year to bring his working life closer and closer to his ideal picture.

EXERCISE

"A Bug Called You" Notebook

To start this exercise, purchase a notebook that will be easy to carry around in your bag or briefcase. It can be as simple as a lined notepad, or as fancy as a custom-engraved Moleskine. The key is to always have it handy and take note whenever you notice significant things about yourself. Here are some starter questions. Feel free to add your own:

What interests me?
What repels me?
Which topics are exciting?
Which environments make me feel open and relaxed?

Which environments make me want to crawl out of my skin?

Which kind of people do I like to be around?

What time of day do I feel most awake? Energized? Relaxed?

What do I really love to do?

What do I daydream about?

Which kinds of stores make me feel good?

Where is my favorite place in nature?

Who in my life is a bloodsucking leech?

When do I feel the most free?

When do I feel the most imprisoned?

When do I feel "in the zone," "flowing," and so preoccupied that I literally lose track of time?

Every week or so, read over your notes and pay attention to any patterns that emerge.

Through this process of introspection, you will soon begin to answer these questions:

- **Who am I?** You must get to know yourself deeply and completely if you want to act from a place of truth and self-confidence. This will include gaining insight into both your essential and social selves described in chapter 2, in addition to the part of yourself that is more creative and spiritual.

- **Who are my people?** These are not just those people who would grudgingly fork over money for your product or service; they are people who would clamor to do business with you because you are the exact answer to their problems. They are your ideal partners, clients, customers, and mentors. These are people whom you like to spend time with, who embrace you despite your perceived warts, mistakes, and flaws and who are deeply affected by your work.

- **What work do I love to do?** We often think of career development as answering the question "What do I want to be when I grow up," insinuating a job title or specific profession like lawyer, doctor, or accountant. The problem with this is that as you change, your ideal work situation can change too. So while you may revel in being a high-flying consultant

(continued)

in your unmarried twenties and early thirties, the constant time away from home can start to wear on you once you are married and have kids. A better question to understand is "What work do I love to do?" These can be things like "educate and inspire people," "write code," or "rid the world of ugliness by applying my clean and beautiful design aesthetic." You can package these basic skills and areas of interest in many different ways, depending on the nature of the market and your life situation.

Begin at the End: Create a Picture of Your Ideal Life

KEY

Design a life that will make you happy.

Once you begin to get some insight into your interests, preferred working style, and business ideas, a common inclination is to dive into business planning right away.

The danger in this is that you will become an unwitting hunting dog, following the blood of the market. You might chase a business opportunity that has great financial potential but will not match your ideal life whatsoever.

This is a very common trap for new entrepreneurs, who find that despite business success, they still are working crazy hours and aren't exactly thrilled with their life. Instead, first define the type of life that will make you happy, healthy, wealthy, and wise.

EXERCISE
Your Ideal Life

As you complete this exercise, it is important that you escort your social self out the door, since it will only get in your way. If you find yourself saying things like "but that would never work," or "no one would ever pay me to sit around talking about Dalmatian breeding," or "Brad Pitt is obviously sticking with Angelina, how could he be living with me?" kindly escort those voices to the door.

I suggest you do this exercise in an uncluttered environment, with time to daydream, and plenty of tools around you to take notes.

INSTRUCTIONS

For each of these areas, read the questions and write notes about your ideal life situation. Write in the present tense, as in "I live in San Francisco, California, in a house that overlooks the Golden Gate Bridge," or "I live in a yurt in Upper Mongolia, with a warm fire in the center of the house and a large herd of horses outside my door."

HOME

- Where do you live?
- What is your physical home like?
- What surrounds your home?
- What is the neighborhood like?
- What are the characteristics of the community? Is it an urban or rural setting? Is it a close-knit community, or does everyone live a private life?

RELATIONSHIPS

- How do you treat yourself?
- What is your relationship like with your spouse/partner?
- What is it like with your kids? (If you have them, or want to have them)
- With your pets?
- With your friends?
- With your family?
- With business partners?
- What are ideal partners like?
- What strengths do they have that complement yours?

HEALTH

- How much do you sleep?
- What exercise do you do, at what frequency?

(continued)

- What do you eat?
- How does your body feel most days?
- Write down anything else important about your ideal state of health.

WORK STYLE
- Do you work by yourself or with others?
- Do you work in an office or work from home?
- Are you home a lot, or a road warrior?
- Do you have a regular, structured schedule or do you work when you feel the muse?
- How many hours a week do you work?
- Is it the same each week, or does it change depending on what you do?

NATURE OF YOUR WORK
- Are you creating something from scratch?
- Providing a service or selling a product?
- Working with your hands?
- Inside or outside?
- Do you prefer to:
    Create something and pass it on to someone else to manage?
    Manage the details of what someone else creates?
    Both create and manage?
- Add anything else you can think of that describes the general nature of work that makes you happy.

FINANCIAL LIFE
- How much money do you make per month?
- What kinds of benefits and insurance do you have?
- What is the nature of your income stream? Do you have regular, predictable income, or does it ebb and flow depending on what you are doing?
- How much money do you have in savings?
- Write down anything else that is important to you in terms of your financial life, like levels of debt, spending habits, etc.

If you have a family, your life plan is created as a joint effort. Each person in the household (wife/husband/partner/kids/parents if you are caring for elders) should weigh in on the kind of life that would be ideal. Of course everyone won't agree with all the others' priorities, but you should be able to gain agreement on some major areas.

Once you have a life plan in place, it becomes very easy to make decisions about the kind of business you want to create. The best part is that it ensures that once your business takes off and you experience financial success, you will be happy with the life that you have created. I cannot tell you how many miserable multimillionaires I met in my years in Silicon Valley. I believe they were miserable because they got too enamored with business growth at all costs and didn't see creating a great business as a means to live a great life.

For a downloadable template of the life plan, go to www.escapefrom cubiclenation.com/book.

Find the Business Needle in the Idea Haystack

KEY

Identify a specific idea.

As you have thawed out your frozen soul, reawakened creativity, observed the kinds of things that interest and energize you, and created a snapshot of your ideal life, it is time to look for specific business ideas.

If you are like most people, when you are in brainstorming mode, you will be plagued by pesky thoughts like:

- No one will pay me to listen to music/drink Red Bull/analyze my pet's problems!
- I will never be able to make it as a writer—that is one of the most competitive fields ever!
- Artists never make money!
- Well, that is a stupid idea! Who do you think you are, Richard Branson?

At this stage, these thoughts will just get in your way. Don't get me wrong: you will absolutely need to use research, testing, and planning to find evidence that your vague business idea has some merit in the real world. But many people dismiss potential business ideas based on vague, unsubstantiated hunches before they do real testing in the market.

After lots of brainstorming, sorting, musing, research, writing, and playing around, you will start to see specific business ideas emerge. Clues that you are on the right path with your ideas at this stage are that you feel real excitement, joy, and energy when you work on your business ideas. And fear, of course—but once you see fear as a natural part of doing anything worthwhile, it will not be quite as ominous.

Figure Out the Money

KEY

Make sure you don't live in a van down by the river.

Money is a deep concern for aspiring entrepreneurs, as it should be. Before you get too far developing your idea, you want to make sure that you have the financial wherewithal to seriously consider entrepreneurship. And depending on your situation, you may need to spend considerable time saving and/or paying down debt in order to have a safe cushion when you start out. So evaluate your financial situation early.

Just about every seasoned entrepreneur I speak with says two things: if at all possible, have at least six months of living expenses saved up before you launch your business, and conserve cash like crazy when you get started. There is always risk involved when starting a business, but having a solid, realistic financial plan will give you a better shot at success. We'll go over this in greater detail in chapter 12.

Define the Spirit of Your Brand

KEY

Learn how to stand out from the crowd.

No matter the type of business you are considering, if there is a viable market, there are bound to be competitors.

If you want to be successful, you must create a compelling, authentic, and sticky brand that will draw your ideal customers to you like flies to honey. The good news is that people are hungry for real, interesting, and authentic communications with people who solve their problems.

Unlike a broad, generic corporate brand that has a vague name like "Initech" and marketing copy that aims to appeal to everyone, and therefore appeals to no one, your small business brand should hit people in the gut with its clarity or humor or utility. Some examples:

- *Legal Sanity,* advice on work-life balance for lawyers
- *Help a Reporter Out,* a free public relations service
- *Grammar Girl,* a podcast and blog with practical tips on grammar for anyone who reads or writes for a living

A great brand does a number of things:

- **Takes a stand:** Communicates a feeling, tone, personality, and spirit that is uniquely yours. Brand expert Rick Julian of QV Brands says to "zig where your competition zags."
- **Makes you feel:** Creates an inviting picture of what it will feel like to work with you by using colors, writing, images, and sounds that all communicate the spirit of your brand.
- **Invokes trust:** Makes potential customers trust you and want to work with you because you appear clear, competent, and authentic.
- **Solves a problem:** Your customer should immediately recognize what problem you are solving. *Escape from Cubicle Nation: From Corporate Prisoner to Thriving Entrepreneur* is an example of stating and solving a problem within a succinct brand name.

With today's Internet and social media tools, you do not need to pay an agency $15,000 to create your brand for you. You can start simply and polish your image as you go.

Recruit Your Tribe

> ### KEY
>
> **Identity the people who will support, guide, and partner with you.**

What I have found is that when you have the right group of people around you, you will assume less risk with more rewards, grow faster, make fewer stupid mistakes, and have a *lot* more fun.

If you are like most long-term corporate employees, your social circles have long been defined by your company connections. You might not know even one successful entrepreneur, besides those you read about in your local paper or who author the books you read. Your immediate family might be extremely skeptical about your becoming an entrepreneur, which is why I devoted chapter 15 to helping you explain your motivations to them.

So reaching out to complete strangers when you are in the midst of doing something totally new can bring up the following feelings:

- **Imposter syndrome:** Who am I to pretend that I am an entrepreneur when I have no idea what I am doing?
- **I'm not worthy:** What have I done to make anyone important want to pay attention to me?
- **Sleazy, hype-filled sales guy:** People will run screaming from me when they find out I am just trying to hustle them for some money.

Trust me, it is normal to feel these insecurities when you are first starting out. But contrary to what you may have experienced in the corporate setting, sharing honestly and vulnerably is actually celebrated and admired in entrepreneurial circles. If traditional networking strikes fear in your heart, don't worry. Chapter 7 covers specific, nonslimy ways that you can connect with people who will support you in all aspects of starting and growing your business.

Test and Prototype

KEY

Find out if you actually have a business worth quitting your job for.

Venture capitalist Guy Kawasaki says that most pitches he views from start-up founders state that "a conservative estimate for our market is 50 million people." But how many of those 50 million people will actually take out their credit card and pay you?

I once worked on a program with fantastic, smart partners who had a great reputation, raving fans, and connections with a huge market. We all "knew" that our product idea would be just what people needed. So instead of testing the idea with a small group, we designed the whole program and rolled it out.

No one bought anything. Zip. Zilch. Nada.

The funny thing was that everyone thought everyone else was buying. We got e-mails from friends and clients that said "Great idea! I can't afford it, but I am sure that you guys will kill the market."

This valuable lesson taught me that the only way to know whether or not an idea is viable is to test it in little bits in the real world.

- If you think your baked goods will make Mrs. Fields run home crying to her mommy, start selling your cookies on the corner.
- If you think you have a "space-changing, curb-jumping" application, slap together a prototype and try it out with some potential customers.
- If you think you have what it takes to be a great coach, start coaching your seatmates on the evening train on the way home from work.

Every little bit of testing will give you great information and will either validate your big projections or send you back to the planning bench to craft an entirely different solution.

Let me put it to you this way: Would you rather invest a huge amount of time, money, and energy in something that could very easily crash and burn, taking your savings and ego with it, or would you be more willing to test a little and tweak frequently and come up with a much more bankable business model?

Chapter 11 will give you lots of ideas for how to test your product or service, which will give you the data to inform your final decision: Should I stay or should I go?

Prepare to Leap . . . or Not

KEY

Make a decision.

If you feel that your current job at your current company is the *only* option you have to make money, you might want to first take some steps to shore up your employment options in general. You don't want to make a decision to start a business as a desperate move, jumping on any opportunity that is slightly less sucky than your current situation.

It is like being in a horrible relationship with an abusive, controlling, unemployed narcissist. Compared to him, just about anyone with a pulse and a steady paycheck would look good. But don't you want a little more than a man (or woman) with a pulse?

The best way to feel like the move will be a good one for you is to spend the time to really get to know yourself and the kind of business that would bring out the best in you.

If you decide to take a risk and jump, you want to be as smart as possible. At a minimum, you should have the following things in place:

- A basic business plan
- Feedback from the real world with real customers that your business idea has merit and people will pay you for your product or service
- A clear and honest picture of your finances, and at least six months' worth of expenses saved

- A clearly defined backup plan with a few options for employment if your self-employed gig doesn't work out

You must balance your desire to be thorough with the knowledge that there is no way to really know if your business is a "sure thing" until you try it. At the same time, you must realize that your "stable" corporate job may not last forever either. On many occasions, I have received e-mails from blog readers who had spent years holding back their business plans because they were worried that self-employment was too risky. Then, with no warning, they lost their jobs. Me? When pushed into a corner, I would rather have three ways out. The sooner you get moving on your plans, the more quickly you will know if you want to go full-sprint into entrepreneurship.

If You Are Going to Do It, Do It All the Way

If you make the decision to leave your job and start a business, do not hold anything back. Throw yourself into it with everything you've got. Social media favorite and TV.WineLibrary.com host Gary Vaynerchuk threw out some motivating concepts for aspiring entrepreneurs at a Web 2.0 Keynote conference in New York in September 2008 that are worth repeating:

- *Stop doing what you hate!* Gary's slogan is the sum of Jim Collins's advice to "find out what you are genetically encoded to do" plus Gary's concept of "Hustle 2.0." Basically, once you know what work you can "kill at," do it full out, every day, until you make it a viable business.
- *Work your face off!* Gary is not one who believes in working four hours a week to launch a business. He advocates doing whatever it takes to grow your brand, connect with your customers, and monetize your business, even if it means working on your side business from nine p.m. to one a.m. for a year or two.
- *Stop watching f*ing episodes of Lost!* Despite feeling like there is no extra time in the day, many people waste time on pursuits like cheesy television shows and meaningless Twitter conversations. If you want to make your business happen, you will have to be ruthless with your time.
- *Legacy is more important than currency.* How do you want to be remembered by your children and grandchildren? Will they be more excited by

their grandma who diligently trudged into her cube at 7:58 each morning and clocked out at 5:00, or by Grandma 2.0, with strong opinions, passions, and an unwaving dedication to making a difference in the world?

Now that you have a better idea of what is actually involved in your path from corporate employee to entrepreneur, I will share a few guideposts that will make your journey a bit easier.

Guideposts

Knowledge of the Learning Process Will Help You with the Stumble/Bumble of Entrepreneurship

When you transition from a "safe" corporate job to entrepreneurship, chances are you are doing a lot of new things. It is amazing how much there is to learn when you start a business for the first time, from forming new work habits to Web design to bookkeeping to product development to sales and marketing.

Based on your background, natural strengths, and experience, you might find some tasks easier than others. Regardless of what you are learning, if it is new to you, you will go through a determined set of steps that use what training and development wonks call the "conscious competence learning model."

Why should you care about an obscure model?

Because when you understand the natural stages your brain goes through to learn something new, you are more likely to relax, expect confusion and resistance, seek opportunities to practice, and give yourself lots of time to learn.

Most of us are impatient by nature, and if we don't understand something right away, think either (depending on our degree of self-esteem) "I am a lunkhead" or "this is stupid and not worth learning." Either of these thoughts may cut short critical personal and professional development.

So here is a breakdown of the stages of learning:

Stage	Example	What You Need
STAGE 1: UNCONSCIOUS INCOMPETENCE You aren't aware of what you don't know. Otherwise known as blissful ignorance.	If you are a full-time employee of a corporation and have never pondered becoming an entrepreneur, you have no real idea what is involved. The idea sounds dangerously romantic, and you spend hours in your cube, fantasizing about your carefree lifestyle.	A dose of reality.
STAGE 2: CONSCIOUS INCOMPETENCE You become painfully aware of what you don't know. This is the "hopeless klutz" phase.	You get excited about the possibility of working for yourself, so you poke around on the Web and buy a few books. You find out there are a million things to take into consideration and everyone has a different opinion about what will make your business a success. You don't feel like you have a handle on things, and it feels both uncomfortable and overwhelming.	Sound guidance, support, and information from trusted experts.
STAGE 3: CONSCIOUS COMPETENCE You are able to do the task with focus and mental effort. Think of how you felt as a kid when you were able to ride your bike without your mom or dad's hand on the back of the seat, and you didn't wipe out.	With careful planning, study, and support, you are able to start your business. You develop your product or service and begin to sell it. You start to interact with customers and handle all aspects of running your business. You still need to use instruction manuals, get expert guidance, and spend a lot of time preparing, but you are	Practice, practice, practice. And feedback from a trusted source.

Stage	Example	What You Need
	able to run your business with a decent level of comfort.	
STAGE 4: UNCONSCIOUS COMPETENCE You do the task effortlessly without even thinking about it. Very smart author Mihaly Csikszentmihalyi calls this *flow*.	You are in business for a few years and work very hard. You perfect your products and services, understand your market, and develop real expertise in your field. You learn from your mistakes. You handle all aspects of running your business without a lot of stress. People look at you as an expert and think "Man, he must have been born doing that, since he does it so well."	What you need in this phase: Not much, as you are comfortable and "at home" with your new skills. Pretty soon, however, you will need to challenge yourself with something new or focus on improving your performance, since if you stay in the "unconscious competence" stage for too long you can get bored.

Over time, you will learn that you get stuck in Stage 2 or 3 with certain tasks and it never gets better, no matter how much you practice. This is a good indication that a skill is not a natural strength, and it may be better to hire someone to do it for you.

Black Boot Moments

A few years ago, I received a call from a friend who was getting ready for a date. A hardworking single mom, she had been out of the dating pool for a long time and finally agreed to go out to dinner with a nice man. She was looking forward to the evening, and had a particular pair of black boots in mind that would go great with her outfit. The only problem was, after an hour searching high and low, she could only find one boot.

The harder she looked for her missing boot, the more anxiety she felt. She went from feeling totally confident and sexy to a shrunken violet. I imagine that her self-talk was something like this:

Where is the boot? → Why can't I ever find anything? → If I am so disorganized, why would anyone want to date me? → I never should have agreed to a date! → He will think I am hideous! → He will run away in disgust! → I will be alone forever!

By the time she called me, she was desperate. I spoke to her as only good friends can and said, "So you lost one boot, and now you will die alone in a cold room? Dust yourself off, choose another damn pair of shoes, and snap out of it!"

After a moment of silence, she burst out laughing as she realized that her fears had gotten the best of her and she had let anxiety totally destroy her self-confidence. We now call it the "Black Boot Moment."

If I told you that she made it out the door in a new pair of shoes and ended up having her lip blow up on the date as an allergic reaction to sushi, you would probably think I was making it up. I'm actually not, it really happened.

But my point is not to tell dating stories from hell, it is that *if you are going to be an entrepreneur, you will have your black boot moments.* A common situation for new entrepreneurs is something like this:

You make a plan to contact a bunch of prospective clients. You organize your information, clean your desk, and look at the phone. But then you decide that you must review your notes one more time. The more you think about talking to prospective clients, the more absurd things seem. Your self-talk goes something like this:

I hope the call goes well! → What if they don't respond to my questions? → What exactly am I offering of value? → What the hell am I doing? → Why did I ever think I was capable of doing this? → Why in the world would anyone talk to me? → Why did I leave my cushy, comfortable corporate job? → I am doomed, I am going to end up homeless on the street eating garbage out of a Dumpster.

When your emotional reaction and self-talk are totally out of proportion to the situation, you must step back. Try the following things:

1. **Call someone you trust immediately and ask for encouragement.** When you do the work on creating your tribe in chapter 7, you will have a great

    list of resources and mentors to call on when you feel yourself spiraling down an ugly hole.

2. **Get physically out of the situation.** If you are staring at your blank computer screen, convinced that a third grader could write better Web copy than you, get up, go outside, walk around, and shake it off.

3. **Pull out a folder of things that remind you of your worth.** These can be things like glowing performance evaluations, rewards for a job well done, pictures of you with your family, or a heartwarming card from a friend or family member.

Are you feeling clearer about what is involved in going from corporate employee to entrepreneur? Good. Now it is time to take your tired-as-hell, PowerPointed-to-death brain and shake things up so that you have the ideas, energy, and focus to develop a real business.

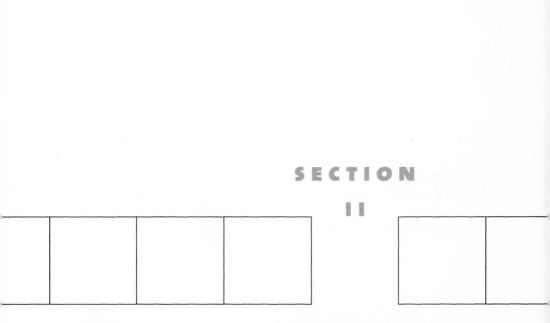

The Reality
of
Entrepreneurship

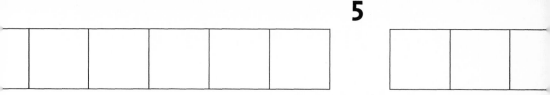

5

What Are All
the Ways to Be
Self-employed?

Living in the world of abstraction, it is easy to think that making decisions about the direction of your business will be straightforward and simple if you have done the hard work of setting life priorities, choosing a business idea, identifying a market, and creating a business plan.

Reality is much more complex.

Choosing Between a Crack Pipe and Wheatgrass Juice

One day, I had a jolt of adrenaline which I would only imagine could be equated with the rush felt by crack addicts. I was asked to facilitate a meeting of high-powered female executives, politicians, and movie stars all in support of a really good cause. It is the kind of opportunity that is the consultant's version of a P. Diddy video, elbow-rubbing with Gucci-clad female executives and exchanging gold-plated business cards.

My social self, driven by status, power, and external validation, was in overdrive as I considered the long-range implications of the experience.

Then I learned that in order to do it, I would have to devote a big chunk of time organizing the event. And I would have to fly to Washington, D.C., for two long trips. And I would be in the ultimate support role for movers and shakers.

Thankfully, my essential self spoke up. None of the activities described above were related to my life plan or business vision of helping oppressed corporate employees escape Cubicle Nation. Spending weeks of time away from my baby, then under a year old, not only would have been a logistical nightmare, it would have made me feel like a crappy mom. I didn't wait thirty-eight years to have a baby to spend it whispering goodnight through a phone. And taking time away from the current steps to build my business would have delayed my goals and dreams. What I really needed to do was to back away from the crack pipe and take a big swig of wheatgrass juice.

Wheatgrass juice, for those who don't know, is a soupy green liquid made by grinding blades of wheatgrass together. It is full of vitamins and turbocharges your blood with antioxidants and other life-enhancing nutrients. I love the taste, although I have heard others equate it to chewing cud.

Keeping clear with my life purpose and business vision, which I call drinking wheatgrass juice, will give me long-term physical, emotional, and spiritual satisfaction. It is not a fast high, it is a lifetime of making smart, healthy choices.

Succumbing to the seduction of a high-powered consulting lifestyle, which I call smoking crack, will give me a short-lived euphoric high, shortly followed by a rapid descent into the meaningless pursuit of wealth and power for its own sake. I will lose touch with myself and my family and find my life spinning out of control. Not to mention losing my teeth and many other decidedly unpleasant experiences.

Evaluating the business opportunity from my corner of suburbia in Mesa, Arizona, I realized I was meant to be at home writing blog posts, changing diapers, and slowly chipping away at my dream business. I told the client no, tossed the crack pipe in the trash, and took a big swig of wheatgrass juice.

Life First, Business Second

My "crack pipe" story is meant to illustrate a very important point: if you don't consider your life as a key part of your business model, you may find yourself outwardly successful and inwardly miserable.

The way to avoid this is to create a plan that outlines in great detail the kind of life that will make you happy and healthy. Over time, as your life changes you can adjust the plan. The important thing is to think about your ideal life *before* you make any serious decisions about your business plan.

So pull out the notes you made in the last chapter on your ideal life (you knew I made you work on it then for a reason, didn't you?) and read on. Or take some time now to turn back to page 64 and explore the possibilities.

Your life plan lays out the specific ways that your life would be structured to provide for maximum enjoyment and productivity. When done well, it is not a pie-in-the-sky vision; it is a blueprint for designing a great business.

In the process of designing a business, you will find that you may not be able to meet every single criterion of your life plan when you first start out. But you can use it as a way to prioritize, and make sure that you have clear decision guidelines for putting together your business model.

May the Force Be with You

When I recently asked successful entrepreneurs what they thought was the critical ingredient in business models, every last one of them answered: *passion.*

This overused word may annoy some of you because it seems very motivational speaker-ish, but truly, it is the key ingredient of business success.

- **When you really, really love what you do, your enthusiasm rubs off on others.** You don't have to "work yourself up" to talk to a new client, or the press or a potential partner. You come across as committed and enthusiastic, because you are! The more you work on your venture, the more energy you feel because you see the results of your efforts and they mean something to you.

- **If you are only doing something for the money, the honeymoon wears off very fast.** When you aren't inherently excited about the work you are doing, you must create energy to do it. Key activities like marketing and sales will feel awkward and forced, even downright slimy. If you are just going to work for money, why go through the hassle of working for yourself? You are better off feigning enthusiasm at a faceless corporation that will pay you retirement benefits and a steady paycheck.

A Note About Passion and Energy: Depleted vs. Spent

What many people don't realize is that when you force yourself to do something you don't want to do, you have to *deplete* the energy from your body to do it. When you make it through a week where you have forced yourself to do work you don't enjoy, you will feel exhausted, drained, and in need of martinis, industrial-strength aspirin, and/or face-planted-in-pillow rest.

When you do things you love, your body *generates energy naturally.* You may work an equal number of hours, or more, than when doing work you don't enjoy, but the difference is you will feel *spent,* not depleted.

Experiment with this concept in your own life and notice how much more quickly you bounce back from "work I love *spent* tired" than from "work I hate *depleted* tired."

Components of a Business Model

Now that you have taken a stab at defining your ideal life and understand why it is important to care about which business you choose, let's look at the key components of your business model.

What Do You Do?

This is a bit of a trick question, because the further you get into understanding your business and the value you provide, you may find, for example, that while your service is coaching, people are actually paying you for increased time, or more freedom, or reduced stress. But let's not complicate things. Start by defining "the thing" that people will trade you money for:

- Coaching
- Consulting
- Writing code
- Making ceramic pots
- Organizing rooms
- Taking pictures
- Writing
- Teaching
- Giving massages
- Walking pets
- Cooking

Why Do You Do It?

Your motivation for being in business is a key ingredient in your business model. This is a benefit that reaches beyond the immediate result of your product or service. Examples:

If you are a *coach*, you may do it to: *help people remove mental blocks that keep them from realizing dreams.*

If you are a *computer programmer*, you may do it to: *help people work at top speed, with no bugs or crashes.*

If you are an *organic chef*, you may do it to: *encourage people to eat nutritive, healthy foods.*

If you are a *masseuse*, you may do it to: *release tension in the body so that the natural immune system can fight disease without drugs.*

How Do You Do It?

Today's small business environment has many incredible advantages over prior decades. There are cheap and pervasive Internet tools and services that connect you with millions of potential customers at the click of a mouse. There are many ways to deliver services, besides meeting with live people in physical spaces. There are distribution models like eBay that allow you to sell physical products easily without investing in a brick-and-mortar storefront. Some examples of how you can deliver your services or products:

- In person
- Over the phone
- At a conference
- On video
- On the computer, using voice and video (also called a webinar)
- On television, on a home shopping network
- On the World Wide Web, via a Web site or blog

Where Do You Do It?

You certainly do not have to have your own office if you work for yourself. Home-based offices can be a great way to save costs while you get started up. There are also options for delivering your services using "third party" locations, like working at your client site, or renting a conference room at a hotel to deliver a workshop.

Whom Do You Do It With?

Defining your ideal customers is an absolutely critical part of creating your business plan. It will drive everything about your business model, as well as your brand and marketing plan. Chapter 9 will give you many specific tools for defining your ideal client. At a high level, when choosing your business model, you will want to define:

- Do you work with companies or individuals?
- If you work with companies, what is the typical size?
- What are the particular demographics of your client base? (age, income, affiliations, etc.)
- Are you planning on working by yourself, or hiring a team to work with you?
- Do you intend to have employees, or just work with independent contractors?

Answering these basic questions about your business structure is a great way to develop a foundation for your business model, as well as clearly delineate what you do and do not want to do. It is very easy to get swayed by big money or flashy clients (crack pipe!), so strengthen your resolve by defining your ideal situation first.

Ways to Sprinkle a Little More Money in Your Business Model

Would You Like Fries with That?

One of my very first clients was the computer networking company 3Com. Back in the days of the technology boom in Silicon Valley, the company was thriving and hiring scores of new employees.

I coordinated a program that taught networking basics to new employees, many of whom did not have a background in technology products. So you can imagine that eight hours of learning about the flow of data packets, Ethernet, switches, and routers would be about the equivalent of . . . purgatory.

Until I listened to a fantastic presenter named John Fritz, who liked to use colorful analogies from pop culture like fast food, the Three Stooges, and Monty Python to explain the different hardware and software associated with networking technology.

While explaining the "dangly cord thingies," otherwise known as "dongles," that were used to connect stacks of routers together, he said, "the way to think of these is French fries." When a customer buys a router, ask, "Would you like fries with that?" and watch them add ten dongles to their order.

For some reason, this analogy has stuck in my head ever since, and is an excellent way to think about making it easy to sell complementary services and products to your customers.

Some examples of ways business owners can "add fries" to their offerings:

- A coach offers a transcript of a recorded teleseminar.
- A construction contractor offers to add a few outdoor plants in addition to building a deck.

- A sales trainer offers CDs of key material covered in class for each student.
- A fitness trainer offers monthly access to a Web site with nutrition tips and meal planning in addition to one-on-one sessions at the gym.
- A conference organizer offers DVDs of presentations after workshops.

The key here is to come up with truly useful add-ons that won't be a huge price burden on your customer, but will extend and enhance the work you are hired to do. Not to mention bringing in a few extra bucks with each sale, which is never a bad thing.

Lichen as a Business Strategy

There are few things that I remember well from high school biology. For some reason, I have always remembered the lesson covering lichen:

> Lichens are composite, symbiotic organisms made up from members of as many as three kingdoms. The dominant partner is a fungus. Fungi are incapable of making their own food. They usually provide for themselves as parasites or decomposers.[1]

I was struck by the topic of lichen as a useful business strategy as I was sitting in a packed International House of Pancakes (IHOP) one Sunday morning. I was there with my own family and some friends, and between us there were four small children.

I saw a jovial man at the next table with large suspenders who was making balloon creatures for the kids at the table. He would walk around from packed table to packed table, making a sale at virtually every stop that had children. Watching him effortlessly market his services, it dawned on me:

This man has chosen a lichen business model! He has selected the perfect environment to symbiotically sell his services. The restaurant was so full that waiters took awhile to get to each table. It took some time to get food. Given unstructured time to wait, what do most small children do? Either terrorize their parents, try to run screaming through the room, eat ketchup, take the top off the salt shaker, or a thousand other disruptive things. (Those were just what my twenty-month-old son did in fifteen minutes.) What is the perfect antidote? Colorful, fancy balloon creatures!

Just imagine how much work he would have to do to sell his balloon creatures in a busy mall or park. If he was lucky, he would get one out of twenty people interested in what he was selling. That would waste his time, money, and effort.

So how can you learn from this wise IHOP balloon man and find your own lichen business model?

- **Look for businesses that are serving your target market with everything but what YOU offer.** If you are a prosperity coach, look for a multifaceted financial planning company that could offer your coaching services to its clients. If you are a massage therapist, look for places where people have to sit down and wait a long time. (If the government would participate, we could have a whole host of businesses just to support the Department of Motor Vehicles! Stress and anger management consultants, therapists, and psychologists. And that is just for the employees!)

- **Make sure that you are enhancing the experience of your "host" business, not competing with it.** If you are looking to sell your homemade jewelry in a crafts store, you may be seen as competition, not a friendly entrepreneurial parasite (if that is not an oxymoron).

- **Check out the viability of your potential business partner.** Do they have only seasonal crowds? How is their market changing? If it is an online environment, do they have a steady base of users and a good plan to continue growing? If you are going to put effort into developing the partnership, you should make sure it has a chance of surviving more than a few months.

- **Aim for exclusivity through a good agreement.** If all of a sudden IHOP allowed jugglers, clowns, and magicians into their restaurants, the balloon man would see his business rapidly decline. See if you can negotiate a business agreement that ensures you are one of the only, or few, lichen partners.

- **Subvert pure biology and make sure you offer something to your host in return.** In the scientific world of lichen, "parasites" can suck life from the hosts without giving anything tangible in return. This will most likely not fly in the human business world. Make sure you clearly articulate how your making money from your host's vast and eager market of customers will benefit them as well.

If you closely analyze lichen behavior, there are some less than glamorous attributes. Then again, is there a better description of an entrepreneur?

> Lichens grow in the leftover spots of the natural world that are too harsh or limited for most other organisms. They are pioneers on bare rock, desert sand, cleared soil, dead wood, animal bones, rusty metal, and living bark. Able to shut down metabolically during periods of unfavorable conditions, they can survive extremes of heat, cold, and drought.[2]

Mix and Match Business Models

Once you understand the core parts of your business model, you can begin to mix and match the parts to come up with a sample configuration. Here is a snapshot of the business model of a home-based entrepreneur:

Bob Walsh, 47 Hats

WHAT HE OFFERS
- Consulting
- E-books
- Hard-copy books (*Micro ISV: From Vision to Reality* and *Clear Blogging*)
- Freelance writing
- Software (Master List Professional, from his Micro ISV Safari Software)
- Training programs

WHERE HE WORKS
- Home—Sonoma, California

HOW HE WORKS
- Phone
- Webinars
- In-person for some consulting gigs
- Internet

WHOM HE SERVES

WHOM HE SERVES

- "Micro-Independent Software Vendor" programmers who want support designing, developing, and delivering software programs
- Web sites that serve an audience focused on productivity and technology
- Large corporations (like Microsoft) that serve the Micro ISV community
- Website: www.47hats.com

Profile: Real-Life Business Model

L. P. Neenz Faleafine, Pono Media

Here is a little more detailed profile of a business model used by Hawaiian entrepreneur/social media aficionado/mother/volunteer L. P. Neenz Faleafine. You can see that she has some common themes in her work, but does a number of different activities. This model can sit well with "slash careerists," a term coined by *New York Times* writer Marci Alboher in her book *One Person/Multiple Careers: How the Slash Effect Can Work for You.*[3]

WHAT DO I DO?

Chief evangelist for Alltop.com—Handle all of the online administrative duties.

Blogger—Share my thoughts and experiences with my life, family, and living in Hawai'i via photos, text, and video.

Founder of Pono Media—Implement social media strategies for organizations and individuals.

New and social media speaker to audiences new to the Internet, Web 2.0.

Volunteer:

- social media and new media services for local tech radio show
- support at Hawai'i Public Radio
- teach middle school aged children about utilizing new media tools
- coach youth basketball

WHY DO I DO IT?

Following in the footsteps of my father, my background is in property management and community building—this industry is in my blood. I have learned, and being true to myself, social and new media is in my soul.

I evangelize Alltop because it's a great resource for the majority of Internet users who do not have the time to gather feeds to build their own custom feed readers or have the time to understand how to do this at all. I am passionate about social and new media. I realize it's the future of communication, not as a replacement for traditional media—traditional media will be with us, but the two combined make a bigger impact—this is my passion, my *kuleana* as we say in Hawai'i.

WHERE DO I DO IT?

I work out of my home office and therefore much of my in-person meetings are done elsewhere. The founders of Nononina, Inc., the owners of Alltop—Guy Kawasaki, Kathryn Henkens, and Will Mayall—live in California. I live in Hawai'i, and rounding out the Alltop team is Electric Pulp, based in South Dakota. The bulk of my communications with all of them are via e-mail—and it works! My work with Pono Media is based primarily in my home office and I utilize many different forms of communication: e-mail, Skype (video, voice, and text), GTalk, Twitter, telephone, and more important, especially in building new relationships—in person!

Usually, I schedule my meetings following my morning workout in the café of the Honolulu Club. It's centrally located in Honolulu, and the risk of getting sand in my laptop protects me from the temptation of meeting at the beach!

Speaking engagement locations are set by the client (haven't been asked to have one at the beach—yet!), teaching in the classroom, and basketball practice is at the local public parks.

(Read more at ponomedia.com.)

Profile: Real-Life Business Model

Sohaib Athar, Really Virtual

Sohaib got his first computer in 1992 and has been working in the software market professionally since 1999. He considers himself lucky to be among the people who do what they love. He has been freelancing/consulting in parallel with his regular job since he started working. He has lived in Lahore, Pakistan, most of his life, though he has worked very briefly in China and the United States. He says:

More than 80 percent of my classmates from college/university have moved out of Pakistan for good and joined the corporate rat race. After weighing the pros and cons, I decided to stay in my hometown instead of going abroad to pursue a career, or a PhD.

From 2004 to 2006, I was part of the founding team of a biotech start-up—OrthoClear—and led its technology R&D team. After the OrthoClear acquisition in 2006, I decided to take a break/go solo for a few months instead of jumping immediately to a new job—probably because I was looking for the excitement of a start-up subconsciously. I rediscovered the freedom that I had given up after university and got addicted to it, and have been consulting since then.

WHAT DO YOU DO?

As a solo freelancer, a few of the areas that I enjoy working in are:

- 3D graphics programming (though it is a very tiny niche)
- Web development (I have been involved with Web-based projects for the last ten years, one way or the other)
- Optimization for performance (Web sites, databases, and complex software systems/processes)
- Desktop applications development
- Project management consulting
- R&D
- Technology planning and implementation (for clients who need to define a technology path to solve a problem, but don't have a dedicated team for it)
- Software engineering process development and implementation (for newly established small software firms)

The professional network that I have managed to develop over the years also helps me in taking up projects that require larger teams, or a different expertise, for example, designing projects for the Web, products, or the print media.

WHY DO YOU DO IT?

I have always thought of the software industry as a huge puzzle that needs to be solved—I work with computers and software mainly to help solve that puzzle, and because it is a lot of fun, and getting paid for it doesn't hurt.

I freelance because it allows me to maintain my own schedule (when allowed, my work hours tend to gravitate toward the graveyard shift), and so that I may spend time with my family when I want, and not when I am allowed.

By managing my own time, I can work on a few personal technology projects that I couldn't start with a "regular" job, and have been networking a lot more with the local technology community. For example, I have recently started writing on a couple of Pakistan-centric technology blogs. I get to work with a much larger mix of technologies, problems, and people than a typical job in a corporate culture could offer me. When I think of it, not knowing what I will be doing next month is actually exciting too.

When a project I work on contributes to making life better for people directly, or helps further our scientific knowledge, that is always an intellectually gratifying experience.

WHERE DO YOU WORK?

The Blue Brain Project, one of the larger projects that I have worked on (construction of a simulated brain to study the brain's structure; the project is a collaboration between IBM and Henry Markram's Brain and Mind Institute at the École Polytechnique), had multidisciplinary teams spread around the globe. The BBP was handled offsite by us, the client was in Switzerland, with communication taking place via Skype, phone, e-mail. We had the option to visit and meet the Swiss team if required, but it was never needed.

For the last couple of years, I have been working from home mostly. For a couple of consulting assignments recently, I did work at the clients' office twice a week for a few months, to coordinate and interact with their in-house teams and manage them, with the rest of the work done from home.

WHOM DO YOU WORK WITH?

I have worked for both large and small entities. With large companies, it is usually as a part of their in-house teams. Most of my clients have been international businesses/research institutes, though a few local clients/companies are there in the list. There are medium- to large-sized local firms that lack expertise in a particular technology but do not want to hire new resources, then there are larger multinational firms that do have the expertise but want to parallel process some projects through outsourcing.

Many of my client relationships started out on an individual level and evolved from there. I do find myself logging on to this Web site www.live person.com after every few months as an exercise in handling individual clients—it also helps in staying up-to-date with technologies that I may not get to work with otherwise.

(Read more at reallyvirtual.com.)

There are obviously endless varieties of businesses you can start. What I hope you gather from these profiles are ways to think creatively about how to structure your business so that it gives you the kind of life you want.

StartupNation, a resource-rich site for entrepreneurs, breaks down business models in seven different categories:

1. **Home-based**   Drawing upon technology, you can create a legitimate and competitive business from home. It's part of our culture now, accounting for more than half of all businesses. Home-based businesses can be run full-time or part-time, and may or may not be Web-based.
2. **Brick-and-mortar**   This is a business with a classic physical location outside of the home. It involves a dedicated facility—whether retail, wholesale, service, or manufacturing.
3. **e-Commerce**   In this model, you don't have foot traffic in your business, only traffic to your Web site. You sell your product through your Web site to consumers or to other businesses.
4. **eBay**   A subcategory of e-commerce, but one big enough to consider on its own, eBay can serve as a location for your online store, and allow you to tap into its huge marketplace.
5. **Franchising**   When you choose a franchise business model, you use someone else's proven business concept as your entrepreneurial roadmap. Typically you pay an upfront fee, as well as a portion of revenues over time, to the franchiser. (To learn more about franchising options, visit the International Franchise Association's Web site, franchise.org.)
6. **Licensing your product**   If you're working a day job and don't want to start a business, you can still take advantage of your great product idea by licensing the product to another company that has the entire infrastructure in place to properly manufacture, market, and sell the product.

7. **Multilevel marketing**   Multilevel marketing (MLM) is a marketing and distribution structure. People at the top sell to those below them, who in turn sell to those below them. The higher up you are in this structure, the more money you can make. The challenge with MLM businesses is that people at the top are frequently the winners. The vast majority of people at the bottom end up spending money and time to get involved and end up losing whatever they put in. If you're determined to choose a business with an MLM model, be sure to check with at least a handful of other people who've entered at your level, and see what they have to say. Find out their perspectives on how—and if it's possible—to be successful.

These broad categories are very helpful for understanding the broad structure of your business. But obviously, within each category there are a lot of different options. Read through the description of each of these models carefully, and highlight the one that feels the best for you. You may find that you choose more than one, such as "Home-based," "e-Commerce," and "Licensing your product." You can find information about the upside and downsides of each of these models at www.startupnation.com.

A Few Horror Stories for Good Measure

I spend a lot of time in this book telling you that you don't have to be totally terrified of starting a business, nor are you crazy for wanting more out of life than your unfulfilling job.

You can see in some of the examples I used above that it is possible to earn a good living and accomplish meaningful things by executing a carefully designed business model that supports your preferred lifestyle.

But I would be remiss if I didn't remind you of the people who have suffered at the hands of unscrupulous marketers and shaky business partners. There are literally hundreds of thousands of hucksters, shucksters, and slimebuckets on the Internet and off who view frustrated corporate employees as perfect shark bait for their nefarious schemes.

Empty Promises and Amway Dreams

Of all the business models that scare people, multilevel marketing (MLM) or network marketing has to top the list. Many, many people have reservations about participating in this business model, which often promises huge profits for very little work.

For those of you who work in multilevel marketing and have always been ethical, what I am about to say may make you angry. I truly do not mean to offend or present an exceptionally lopsided analysis, I just want to share some words of warning to overeager entrepreneurs who might get themselves into something that will not feel good at the best, and may affect family and friend relationships at the worst.

Here is an example from a longtime blog reader who was kind enough to share his own personal story about living with a parent who got involved with Amway:

> My father was a creative, intelligent, hardworking man with an entrepreneurial dream. When I was ten, his union struck the shipyard where he had worked for seventeen years. He was out of a job as the strike continued indefinitely until his job was replaced. He found work as a welder in a paper mill and built a stump-grinding machine that he used on the weekends to make extra money. Eventually, he became reemployed in the shipbuilding industry, but always as a contract employee.
>
> A coworker introduced him to Amway. It was much more than a business opportunity; it was a chance to realize our family's dream of financial freedom. For Amway we made lists . . . lists of all our friends and acquaintances that my mom was to call and invite over to our house. We were under strict instructions not to tell them it was Amway. She couldn't do it—it was humiliating and dishonest. My dad retired to his study to read endless motivational books and listen to tapes (purchased from our upline sponsor) full of people talking about their successes. He was inspired, but translating theory into practice eluded us.
>
> We attended many meetings—my dad tape-recorded many of them for later study. The meetings were a never-ending parade of people who had made their $50,000/year, quit their jobs, and bought expensive cars and jewelry. It was the 1980s and these people were living a

materialist dream—while underneath them, hundreds, like my parents, struggled to change their mindsets, to "think and grow rich," to believe in the "magic of thinking big."

As a child, I was aware of the conflict this created between my parents but I did not fully understand the costs. It was an exciting sort of game and the books were inspiring. I wanted my dad to succeed. But the business is fundamentally based on using your personal connections not only to sell a product, but to enlist those you know into a get-rich scheme where compromising your values (using people) is a fundamental prerequisite to success. It has affected my view of the world to this day—I am deeply suspicious of personal networking and have a distrust of wealth. My father's obsession with MLMs destroyed his marriage (my parents divorced during my freshman year away at college) and left him a lonely man who died alone at sixty-three with years of accumulated motivational books and tapes that I was left to literally shovel into the trash as I cleaned his house to attempt to sell it to cover his medical bills.

The Fatal Assumption

Michael Gerber has written a whole series of books based on his original book *The E-Myth*, which describes "Why most small businesses don't work and what to do about it." A cornerstone of the book is what he calls "the fatal assumption":

In the throes of your Entrepreneurial Seizure, you fell victim to the most disastrous assumption anyone can make about going into business.

It is an assumption made by all technicians who go into business for themselves, one that charts the course of a business—from Grand Opening to Liquidation—the moment it is made.

The Fatal Assumption is: if you understand the technical part of the business, you understand a business that does technical work.

And the reason it's fatal is that it just isn't true.

In fact, it's the root cause of most small business failures!

The technical work of a business and a business that does that work are two totally different things!

> To the technician suffering from an Entrepreneurial Seizure, a business is not a business but a place to go to work.
>
> So the carpenter, or the electrician, or the plumber becomes a contractor.
>
> The barber opens up a barbershop.
>
> The technical writer starts a technical writing business.
>
> The hairdresser starts a beauty salon.
>
> The engineer goes into the semiconductor business.
>
> The musician opens up a music store.
>
> All of them believe that by understanding the technical work of the business they are immediately and eminently qualified to run a business that does that kind of work.
>
> And it's simply not true![4]

Gerber explains throughout the rest of *The E-Myth Revisited* that you must study business models, learn to work on your business, not in it, and develop specific skills to run your business. I consider it required reading for anyone considering starting a business.

Passive-aggressive Revenue Streams

I mentioned earlier that there are a number of things you can do to supplement your "sell yourself by the hour" time, by creating e-books, or audio programs, or DVDs.

Often, these types of products are called "passive revenue streams," with the idea that once they are created and launched, they continue to bring in a stable, predictable income each month without a lot of additional effort.

Unfortunately, I think this is an incomplete picture, since there can still be a significant amount of ongoing work involved in supporting an online product.

Here is what you need to keep in mind with "passive revenue products":

- Typically, most products are sold with a big sales push or "launch" where most of the sales happen in a relatively short window of time.
- It takes time, effort, and energy to maintain interest in the product. You must continually drive new visitors to your site, and this takes marketing effort that is not "passive."

- Some products can become outdated quickly, especially if they have to do with technology. You need time to edit and update material.
- People will not automatically buy e-products. It takes a lot of skill and effort to create compelling marketing copy and a smooth sales process.

These kinds of products can be a fantastic part of your business model. Just make sure you plan and budget for the work it will take to sustain them.

For the Last Time, Blogging Is Not Passive Revenue!

A few months back, I wrote an article describing my feelings about certain myths associated with passive income.

Okay, so I pretty much called the whole "get rich from passive-income" thing a big, fat scam!

It is directly controverted by a bunch of research, including a fascinating study that showed how very few U.S. pentamillionaires made their money passively or inherited it. For the most part, they worked their butts off trying to solve a problem that affected a huge number of people. And, their success came after years or decades in a relatively short burst or event.

Well, I'm getting kind of tired of clicking onto websites and blogs that report online income, especially from blogging, as passive income.

Advertising income that is derived from any form of online content that needs to be created on a regular basis, whether through blogging, updating websites, populating or moderating forums or anything else is NOT passive income.

We don't need data and studies to know this. Hey, here's an interesting study, go find me 10 bloggers who earn a living blogging without working on their blogs. Okay, strike that, find me one!

Every year, millions of blogs are abandoned after 4 months. Creating and moderating content that is good enough to attract and grow a substantial readership may be fun, but . . .

Creating online content that is compelling enough to drive advertising or other revenue is hard friggin' work.

It's not even moderately passive.

What if you hire someone to manage and write your job? Still not passive, now you're not a writer, but you are a manager and employer.

What if you take a bigger step back and launch a blog-network, so you can have someone else run everything all the time. Hmmm, I wonder what Darren Rowse, Wendy Piersall or Penelope Trunk would say if you told them starting, managing, and growing a blog-network was passive?

There is no such thing as set-it-and-forget-it online content-driven revenue.

And, if there is, it comes only after an intensive, often extended "hard-work" effort to create content that is not only massively valuable, but so evergreen that its value and impact will endure. Listen . . .

I'm all for everyone earning as much as they need to be comfortable in the world.

But, if you wanna sell a fundamental philosophy, how about this one . . .

Find something you're madly passionate about, surround yourself with people you love to be around, work your buns off and make a ton of money . . . as a byproduct of the fact that you're having the time of your life and contributing value to the world along the way![5]

Jonathan Fields, *Awake at the Wheel*

The Reality of Working from Home

Much ado is made about the wonders of working from home, especially for corporate employees tired of being stuck for hours in commuter gridlock.

There are some real advantages to working from home. But the model is not for everyone, especially people who think that they can be super-parent to three kids while working full-time from home.

Here are some lessons for the entrepreneur-to-be who is fantasizing about the work-at-home lifestyle:

- **If you have young kids, you most likely will have to get a babysitter during your working hours.** Sometimes it is possible to fire out e-mails or write in short bursts with kids around, but anything requiring careful detail or professional phone demeanor needs your dedicated time. Kids deserve full attention, as do your clients. Factor this cost into your start-up plans.

- **Many of you in corporate jobs may work from home one day a week or so and relish the relaxed environment.** (I was always delighted to attend long, tedious conference calls from home so that I could fold laundry, making the meeting semiproductive.) But you may forget how easy it is to crank out a lot of work at the office when you have no home distractions. When you work from home all the time, you need to develop routines and discipline; otherwise you will never get anything done.

- **If you are married or live with someone, your non-work-at-home spouse might make the assumption that since you are at home, you don't mind taking care of a lot of tasks around the house.** This will lead to either low productivity on your part because you will do all those tasks instead of working on what you are supposed to, or resentment as you feel the injustice of a lopsided pile of domestic work. To plan for this, agree on the division of chores before you give up your office job.

So before you fall for the "You can raise five small kids at home and start your business at the same time" pitch, make sure you have really thought about what it entails.

I swear I am not trying to scare the daylights out of you by highlighting some of the potential pitfalls of self-employment. I just want you to go into the experience with your eyes open, and to understand both the opportunities and potential snake pits.

I am sure that the people highlighted in this chapter would agree that if you learn from their mistakes without risking your family, reputation, or bank account, their pain somehow served a purpose.

Keep these ideas about business models at the top of your mind as you jump into the next chapter, and try to figure out what kind of business you actually want to start.

6

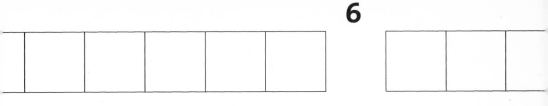

How Do I Choose
a Good
Business Idea?

A Bunch of New Age Crap?

I mean no disrespect to the career development guru Barbara Sher, who has contributed great things to the world with her books and workshops.

One of her most famous book titles is *Do What You Love, the Money Will Follow*, which has unfortunately been followed to the letter by many supremely idealistic wannabe entrepreneurs who don't bother to read her advice between the covers.

- They decide their mission is to help people color-code their closets and wonder why their phone doesn't ring off the hook with client calls when they have no Web site, marketing process, or business plan.
- They decide that traveling the world is a great passion, quit their job and wonder why they get no farther than Baltimore before running out of money.

- They get totally excited about selling used Jimmy Buffett LPs in the parking lot of a 50 Cent concert and scoff when you tell them that the total market is three people, all of whom are just briefly dropping off their kids.

Here is the problem: *intense passion for something* and *a viable business model to turn this passion into a decent living* are two totally different things.

In order to have a successful business, you must combine the creative excavation you did in chapter 4, with the business model analysis you did in chapter 5, with the business planning you will do in chapter 9.

Natural passion and interest

+

Skill and competence

+

Business model that delivers life you want to live

+

Solid business planning with well-defined market

=

Likelihood of Good Business Idea

This still doesn't mean you will actually make any money from it, but it's a start!

Sort the Results from Your Creative Brainstorm

In chapters 3 and 4, you spent lots of time tracking observations about the kinds of things that you find highly interesting and attractive. Hopefully you wrote down these observations in your "Bug Called You" journal, word processing documents, bookmarks, and vision boards.

From these general notes, start to extrapolate information and put it in categories (my examples):

- **Topics** that interest you (cars, entrepreneurship, alcoholism, quantum physics, knitting, martial arts)

- **Activities** you really enjoy doing (writing, coding, coaching, drawing, selling, running)
- **Industries** that interest you (alternative energy, high-end luxury resorts, construction, home organizing)
- **Problems you are eager to solve** (teenage pregnancy, horrible screaming sales letters that plague online marketing, broken music distribution system for independent musicians, corporate employees who feel trapped in their jobs because they don't know how to navigate the transition to entrepreneurship—sound familiar?)
- **Products you love** (the iPhone, Cold Stone Creamery ice cream, Moleskine notebooks, Sony PlayStations)

Another way to organize the information is to fill out the circles that form the "Sweet Spot" that Jim Collins described.

Circle 1

What people pay you to do: Skills you have that are natural strengths, enjoyable and marketable.

Circle 2

What you love to do: Activities that are not exactly work-related but that get you really excited.

Circle 3

What you are genetically encoded to do: Activities and/or skills that you do effortlessly, get energized by, and feel deeply competent in. This is the most elusive of the three circles, but if you ever do something and get a flashing thought like "I was meant to do this work," this can be a Circle 3 activity.

Look for Problems to Solve

Once you get the hang of it, you will see that the world is one big fantastic salad bowl of business ideas. If you are like me, as soon as you get used to seeing business opportunities in everyday situations, you won't be able to stop the flow of ideas!

Here are some examples of applying this "look for problems" approach in the hunt for a business idea:

Situation

You are stuck waiting in line at the Department of Motor Vehicles for three hours, behind two screaming babies, a member of a punk rock band who hasn't showered for a week, and a loud and frustrated corporate executive.

QUESTIONS TO ASK
- Why do I have to stand in line?
- Does my transaction require a human being?
- What would be a better way of doing this?
- Would it kill him to wear deodorant?

POSSIBLE BUSINESS IDEA
Online portal for common motor vehicle transactions.

REAL BUSINESS
Most motor vehicle departments in the United States now have Web site transactions available.

Situation

All your girlfriends complain about how hard it is to meet decent, eligible bachelors in their town.

QUESTIONS TO ASK
- Where are the eligible bachelors hanging out?
- What would be good alternatives for meeting besides a bar?
- What are ways to ensure that creeps are screened out and only the good guys get through?

POSSIBLE BUSINESS IDEA
Dating service that focuses on lunch dates.

REAL BUSINESS
www.itsjustlunch.com

Situation

You get laid off unexpectedly and scramble to track the details of your job search. You forget whom you called, which version of your cover letter you sent, and the name of the recruiter you worked with last time you were out of work.

QUESTIONS TO ASK
- How can I track my conversations with potential employers?
- Are gigantic spreadsheets the best way of doing this?
- Am I the only one who feels overwhelmed by the job search process?
- Is there an easier way to do this?

POSSIBLE BUSINESS IDEA
Tool that allows you to manage and track your job search over the course of your career.

REAL BUSINESS
www.jibberjobber.com

Use Your Interests to Narrow Your Field of Study

The work you just did in identifying things that spark your interest should guide the places you look for business opportunities.

While the examples I described above pertain to general situations in life, use the areas that interest you to look for specific opportunities.

For example, if you are passionate about martial arts and social media, spend time poring over every Web site, blog, competition, and television show that contains martial arts. Subscribe to every social media site you can find and poke around to see how they are set up, who uses them, and what purpose they serve. Then ask yourself:

- What would make this better?
- What is missing?
- What is really needed here?
- Why isn't someone already addressing this problem?
- What are people hungry for?
- What could make this experience easier?
- How could I improve this by leaps and bounds?
- Who is serving this community well?

Sometimes you are able to link all your interests together in one business, and sometimes you find that one interest or opportunity stands above the rest.

The key is to use beginner mind and be open to possibilities.

Business Problems Looking for a Solution

The more you get used to looking at the world as full of problems to be solved, the more you will start to think about particular business models that will best solve the problems.

I spend a lot of time thinking about business ideas as I am wandering around the house collecting recyclables, or burping my baby, or pulling my three-year-old off a tall chair as he prepares to fly across the room like Spider-Man. Here are some specific ideas I have for useful businesses, based on thousands of questions I get from blog readers, and things I observe in the entrepreneur/social media/coaching environments I hang out in:

ACCOUNTANT/FINANCIAL ADVISER FOR PEOPLE WITH LESS THAN PERFECT FINANCIAL HISTORIES
Business problems:

- A lot of people who are smart, creative, and motivated are scared to death of starting a business because they don't have a perfect financial history.

- Some of the financial problems faced by these people will affect their ability to secure financing, but most are crippled by a lack of confidence.
- Professionally trained financial advisers do not always understand the shame and emotional baggage that follow people in this situation and deliver financial advice and coaching in what is perceived as a judgmental and derogatory way.
- Some unscrupulous financial service providers prey on the financially uninformed and steal their money (my dear relative, who experienced a windfall of cash in the 1970s due to a good acting gig, fell under the spell of such a character, who promptly snorted her house, savings, and retirement up his nose, landing him in jail and making her penniless and heartbroken).

Sampling of key skills and experience:

- Personal or professional experience and knowledge
- Coaching skills—ability to address interpersonal issues that underlie poor financial habits

Ideas for structure:

- Teleclasses on very basic topics like "How to get a bank loan for your new business even if you don't have perfect credit"
- 1:1 evaluations and coaching in person or over the phone without hawking specific products or trying to sell anything
- Virtual work groups that provide information and support as people build their businesses one step at a time
- Referral network with good local CPAs or tax lawyers, or at least consulting services to help people find good ones

MARKETING SPECIALIST FOR CRAFTSPEOPLE AT LOCAL AND REGIONAL ART SHOWS

Business problems:

- Artists who sell at craft shows are notoriously "old school" when it comes to business, preferring to deal in-person and keep operations and techno-gadgetry to a minimum. Because of this, they miss the opportunity to

(continued)

build relationships with patrons who visit their booth once a year, or to sell other pieces online.

- Customers who purchase pieces from favorite artists never hear from them again.
- Artists miss opportunities for referrals if they only sell at local art shows.
- There is a need for "grassroots selling meets Internet marketing"

Sampling of key skills and experience:

- Love of art and appreciation of fine craftsmanship
- Knowledge of both craft show marketing and Internet marketing
- Coaching skills
- Teaching skills

Ideas for business:

- Many of the sponsor organizations are committed not just to making money marketing off the shows, but to supporting the artists with workshops before major art shows. These workshops would be peppered with specific, easy-to-implement steps like collecting business cards or names of customers, in order to follow up after the show.
- Simple do-it-yourself marketing packages, designed in an easy-to-implement and attractive manner.
- Virtual teleclasses on specific topics. Make sure instructions are clear and technology is not complicated as many craft artists are known for not liking complex technology.

Are you starting to see how these pieces fit together?

Help Your Users Kick Ass

Solving problems is a great place to start, but blogger Kathy Sierra takes things one step further and asks, "How can you help your users kick ass?" Her insights are perfect for taking your general business idea and making it a truly market-changing one:

It's not what you sell, it's what you teach that matters.

Or rather, what you help someone learn.

Too many books and businesses take users through the first steps and then leave them stranded and alone still in the frustrating and painful stage! How many readers claim they actually finished or even got halfway through a technical book? How many users ever learn anything but the most basic features of the software—even when they'd be thrilled if they could do more? But it just isn't worth it for them to struggle, so they stay with what they know, often using very inefficient steps to do something simply because that's the only "safe" way they feel comfortable with.

Kicking ass is more fun regardless of the task. It's more fun to know more. It's more fun to be able to do more. It's more fun to be able to help others do more.

I'll say more on this later, but I can think of a lot of wasted ad dollars that might be better spent teaching. Red Bull, for example, wants to be the drink of choice for late-night dancers. But rather than simply sponsoring raves and keeping popular DJs well-stocked (like anyone else would in that business) they create new and better DJs. They offer the Red Bull Music Academy:

The Red Bull Music Academy is a unique environment where musical innovators shed light on the history, the motivations and the technology behind the tunes that we love. It's a place where ideas are expanded and friendships are forged in real time. It's where sonic theorists meet up with beat junkies and communicate the best way they know how—through music.

By helping more DJs (and wanna-be DJs) kick ass, they've done more to inspire real passion than any of their freebie promotions ever can.

So . . . how are you helping your users/customers/students/guests/visitors/clients/members/readers kick ass? What are you teaching them? How are you helping them get past the painful parts and into the better-than-drugs flow state?[1]

Plastics, Young Man!

If you have ever seen the classic movie *The Graduate,* starring a fresh-faced Dustin Hoffman, you remember the scene where his parents' friend tells him "Plastics, young man!" imploring him to start his career in the latest booming industry.

I fondly recalled this quote as I dove into an issue of *Entrepreneur Magazine,* featuring "The 2007 Hot List: Best Businesses, Markets and Trends."

Before looking into some examples of trends, here is a little context:

- We all know that by the time "hot trends" are published in a mainstream magazine they are not really "hot trends" anymore.
- Any trend is set within an economic and political context. So if the stock market crashes or a significant terror strike occurs or environmental havoc is wreaked in an area where you are starting a "hot trend" business, everything can change in an instant.
- As Guy Kawasaki said in an interview at StartupNation when asked what business trends were worth examining:

> It's not like you get up in the morning and say "I want to be an entrepreneur. Should I make chips, software, a dry cleaner, desks?" That is the wrong order. The right way is you love dry cleaning or software or chips and because of that love of and knowledge of that industry, you are going to change that industry. If you want to be an artist, be an artist! But don't do it because you read in *BusinessWeek* that the market for art is getting bigger. Quite frankly, you might not have the talent.

So the best way to use market trend research in business design is to see it in two parts:

Part One: Do the work in chapter 3 to figure out the kinds of topics, ideas, people, and things that mesmerize, fascinate, light up, wake up, and energize your creative soul.

Part Two: Drink up as much information as you can about what is happening in the market and use these trends as creative springboards to "change the industry," as Guy says, or to capture a market segment that will be perfectly served by you.

Here are some examples of trends from the issue that got wheels in my mind turning.

Green Products

I know, I know, this is nothing new based on all the news coverage lately, but I distinctly remember being a passionate recycler and tree hugger in college back in 1984 and found that other than among my granola-head friends and me in Northern California, these ideas were definitely not mainstream. There is an opportunity now like no other . . . where market conditions, media awareness, and political strength are really allied behind being green. For those of you who have been hiding your leafy nature behind a cube wall all these years, the timing could be great to really move forward some great planet-saving ideas.

Creative Funerals

I was both fascinated and creeped out by this trend, explained this way: "Baby boomers who demand that things be done 'their way,' coupled with innovative entrepreneurs and a trend toward cremations are shaking life into this lifeless industry. So bid farewell to the traditional church funeral and say hello to memorial services held on golf courses, ashes scattered by skydiving and remains launched into outer space."

Minority Kids

"This segment is hotter than ever now that 45 percent of U.S. children under age 5 are part of a racial minority—Asian American, black or Hispanic. Children in these rapidly growing communities will need every sort of product imaginable—and winning their brand loyalty today is critical." I find this trend personally fascinating since I have such a vast web of diverse friends and relatives. There are so many interesting ways to approach and segment these markets, and to address problems in a culturally appropriate manner. Mainstream media tends to classify "minority" groups as a big segment . . . but if you are from a minority background or have spent any time with people who are, you know that any broad-sweep category of "Asian" or "Latino" or "Native American" has tremendously complex and nuanced elements to each market.

These are just a handful of examples of interesting opportunities arising due to social, technological, and demographic changes.

Vague to Concrete

Hopefully by now your mind is percolating some interesting business ideas. When you get a few that feel exciting and seem really interesting, it is time to define them more specifically.

Here are five steps to help you do this:

Step 1: Wrap Your Arms Around the Field

Let's say you want to start a graphic design business but don't know where to begin. First, ask "How is graphic design packaged and sold?" You will most likely find out that it can be used in high-end advertising; product design and packaging; brand identity like logos, book illustration, T-shirt design, Web-based graphic design, etc. You can start your general search by Googling the term "graphic design" or looking up the Wikipedia definition, or by looking for some large international organizations that support graphic designers to see how they segment their user base.

Then you want to look at what kinds of graphic design businesses exist. These can be everything from a one-person side business in someone's living room to large, multinational firms that handle huge contracts.

Step 2: Choose a Small Neighborhood to Explore

You decide that you'd like to work in the area of visual identity and branding for small to medium-size firms. You can focus your learning in this area by asking the following questions:

- Which kinds of services do firms like these offer?
- How are they packaged?
- What's the process they use to move clients from no visual identity to a complete set of logos and templates and graphic standards?
- What do small and medium-sized businesses look for in graphic design firms?
- What problems do these firms hope to solve with good visual identity?

There can be some specific questions like how many projects can one graphic designer take on at a time, and which tools or technology are used to create the designs. The more you learn about these firms, the more questions you'll come up with.

Step 3: Identify the Hotshots Doing This Work Successfully

By "hotshots" I don't mean arrogant people who will treat you like a gadfly in their backside, I mean people whom you personally admire, who have compatible values and interests, and whom you would consider worthy mentors or competitors. If you can set up informational interviews, you can ask the following kinds of questions:

- Of all the skills that you use on a daily basis, which are the most important?
- How do you continually produce great work?
- What advice would you give to someone like me who's starting out new in your field?
- How do you get new clients?
- What do you consider "subpar" work?
- What is the current market like for (insert field of interest)?

Pay close attention to both the *technical expertise* required to run a successful graphic design business in this area and the *business expertise* required to run a successful business.

Step 4: Carve a Niche

This is where you'll reflect on the particular kind of work you want to do with a particular group of people you want to work with. For example, you want to do logo design for import-export companies with fewer than ten employees that do business in Asia. Or you want to design Web interfaces for medium-size sports marketing companies that cater to fourteen- to eighteen-year-olds. Or you want to offer blog banner design services to life coaches and therapists. I will give some more guidance on how to narrow your market in chapter 9.

Step 5: Shake a Tree

This is where you create a marketing plan, call up potential clients, look for overflow work from your respected mentor, or do whatever you can to get some work flowing your way. By this stage, you should be serious enough about your business idea to at least get some side work started, if not having the infrastructure in place to go into business for yourself full-time. ("Shake a tree," for those who might be confused by the term, is my quaint metaphor for sales and marketing, since sometimes it feels like you have to "shake the tree" a little to get the juicy pear to fall down. Do not confuse it with the dreaded corporate term "low-hanging fruit.")

I encourage you to walk through each of these steps as you're considering a totally new field of work so that you make sure you have a good understanding of the overall field before you jump into something specific. Also know that if you get started in a specific field and find that it wasn't what you thought it would be, congratulations. You can now check it off your list of things to try and go back to the drawing board of business ideas. Entrepreneurship is really about experimentation, so have fun with the learning process. Chapter 11 will give you some suggestions for testing your business ideas before committing to a large decision like quitting your job.

I'm Just Not That into You

All this thinking about and testing business ideas may make you feel a little overwhelmed with the sheer variety of options. Some of you may have been working on business ideas for many years. If you don't start to pare down some ideas, you may get stuck trying to develop too many businesses and grind your progress to a halt.

I got inspired to think about the paring of ideas by the pop-culture hit book *He's Just Not That Into You: The No Excuses Truth to Understanding Guys.* It aimed to help single women see the brutal truth that when a suitor didn't call, was afraid to commit, or wasn't emotionally engaged, it just meant one thing: he wasn't "into" you. For centuries, women had been making up excuses for lukewarm romantic advances, thinking that either "he just wasn't ready" or "he would come around with time, patience and saintly understanding." Hogwash, said authors Greg Behrendt and Liz Tuccillo. Behavior speaks for itself, and the more time and energy you spend waiting around on a lukewarm romantic prospect, the less time and energy you have for a quality one.

This theory nicely relates to career and entrepreneurial pursuits.

How many "lukewarm" projects and endeavors have you been pursuing as if they were the ideal marriage candidates when the emotional signs all point to a temporary fling with someone of questionable character?

Here is how you can start to determine if your former "burning flame" is now a "smoldering ember":

- **When you sit down to work on it, you don't feel much of anything.** Sometimes projects that have great value and purpose elicit tremendous emotion. This is because they are so meaningful that they bring up huge fears and anxieties. Lukewarm passions, on the other hand, often bring up the emotions of detachment and apathy.
- **You find yourself justifying its value or purpose, but don't really believe your own reasons.** If your justifications are peppered with words and phrases like "should," "makes sense," "is the responsible thing to do," and "I can't back out now," this is a sign that you are fooling yourself. A quick test is to listen to your answer to the question "How do I really feel?" Trust the answer.
- **When you step back to view it in the context of your long-term strategies or goals, it either doesn't fit or has a minor role.** We spend a lot of time on "busy work" that makes us feel like we are doing the right things in our careers or business, but often is quite unimportant. Develop some rigorous criteria for what you will work on, based on being true to your essential self. Look to work on things that will leapfrog you to new creative and personal heights, not just plug along like an old, tired, and dutiful steam engine.

I am convinced that the truly successful people, those who enjoy every part of their life and have financial stability, are very picky about where they spend their time and energy. So prune relentlessly.

Lessons in Turning Your Business into a Passion: Grammar Girl Mignon Fogarty

Mignon Fogarty started her podcast on a whim, wanting to share tips and tricks about her passion for grammar. In a short time, this home-grown effort turned into a full-time business, eventually placing Grammar Girl in the top twenty podcasts on iTunes. As of this printing, she has an average of 800,000 listeners, and she expanded her single podcast into a podcast network and a book, *Quick & Dirty Tips*.

What surprised you about the reality of turning your passion (grammar) into a full-time business?

I wouldn't say it surprised me, but the hardest part of turning my passion into a full-time business is how little time I spend doing grammar-related activities and how much time I spend on general business administration. Some days I think to myself, "This is why musicians' second albums are never as good as their first." When you're doing the groundwork to get started, you get to spend a lot of your time on the parts you love; but once you're more successful—successful enough for it to be a real business—all this other stuff takes a huge chunk of your time. For musicians, I imagine it's touring that takes their time away from writing a great second album. For me, it's bookkeeping and managing people.

What advice would you give to someone who is pondering turning a natural passion into a business?

Before you start, it's important to let go of your passion enough to objectively determine whether there's a business model that will support your idea. Your passion will help sustain you when times get tough, but it won't miraculously create a business where one doesn't exist. Make a detailed financial plan, and gather as much information as you can about your market, your competition, and businesses in other areas that might be a model for what you are trying to do.

It's really important to understand how much money you need to live, and a lot of people don't have a good handle on that number. Figure out not only how much you need to survive, but how much you need to live a decent life and save for the future. It will almost certainly be necessary to make sacrifices in the beginning, but two years after you've launched, you should be making a decent living. No matter how passionate you are about your business, in the end it's still a job, and it's almost always more rewarding to spend your free time with your family and friends than to be slaving away for eighty hours a week just to make ends meet.

Probably the easiest way to turn your passion into your job is to do it gradually. If possible, don't quit your day job before launching your business. If you want to podcast, start with a monthly show or a very short weekly show and see how it goes. If you want to open a yogurt shop, take a part-time job in someone else's yogurt shop and learn everything you can about how to run the business. If you're passionate enough, it won't even feel like work. In many cases, if your idea is a good one, you'll eventually become so busy or successful in your part-time endeavor that it will be clear when you should quit your day job and become a full-time independent business owner.

Is Your Idea the Next YouTube or a Jump to Conclusions Mat?

For those of you not familiar with the sometimes vulgar but hilarious 1999 movie *Office Space*, a parody of cubicle life, let me explain the term "Jump to Conclusions Mat." One character named Tom Smykowski thinks he has the next million-dollar idea to follow the Pet Rock. Here is an excerpt from the scene where Tom shares his idea with coworkers:

Michael Bolton: You think the pet rock was a really great idea?
Tom Smykowski: Sure it was. The guy made a million dollars. You know, I had an idea like that once. A long time ago.
Peter Gibbons: Really, what was it, Tom?

Tom Smykowski: It was a "Jump to Conclusions" mat. You see, it would
  be this mat that you would put on the floor . . . and would have different CONCLUSIONS written on it that you could JUMP TO.
Michael Bolton: That's the worst idea I've ever heard in my life, Tom.
Samir Nagheenanajar (shaking his head): Yes. This is horrible. This idea.

Your friends and coworkers may not be quite as direct as Tom
Smykowski's and will let you run away with a really terrible idea out of
fear of hurting your feelings. While no one has an airtight formula for
discerning whether a business idea is good or not, here are my initial
thoughts on determining if your idea might be feasible or just an expensive hobby.

Signs Your Business Idea Might Be Feasible

1. You have a unique approach, skill, or capability that will allow you to
   serve this need better than anyone else.
2. You have the capacity, resources, and support for getting the business
   launched in a timely manner.
3. You have chosen an area in which you provide value beyond cheap pro-
   duction price.
4. Your target market not only is interested in what you have to offer, but
   has the money to pay for what you are selling.
5. You create a prototype and it generates buzz and interest.
6. You have a firm grasp of the financial metrics of your business.
7. If you require others to build your business, you have a network of
   smart and capable people who would like to work with you.
8. You welcome any and all feedback about your business idea, and use it to
   continually improve your product or service.

Signs Your Business Idea Might Be an Expensive Hobby

1. You "feel" there is a market based on hunches and a few conversations *or*,
   deep in your gut, you are not sure this is a good idea, but you are too
   proud to admit it.
2. When you discuss the idea with people who would be the target market
   for your product or service, they are either overcome by an embarrassing

silence or are direct like Michael Bolton from *Office Space* and say "That is the worst business idea I have ever heard."

3. When someone challenges your idea, you get very defensive and immediately change the subject, thinking "They obviously are not smart enough to get my brilliant idea."

4. You spend hours, weeks, months, and sometimes years working on the idea without ever bringing it in front of either a potential investor or customer.

5. You are unable to describe the true need this product or service might fill in the eyes of your customer.

6. You have never undertaken a venture like this before *and* you don't surround yourself with people who have.

7. Your personal network is very limited, and you don't think anyone you may have worked with in the past would be willing to join you in your venture.

8. You view your venture as "all or nothing" and will only consider launching one business idea, regardless of feedback from others.

These lists are just some *general guidelines* and in no way predict if your business idea will actually be successful or not. I am sure that there is someone who met all the criteria for a "feasible" idea and went broke, and there is someone with indications pointing to an "expensive hobby" who is now sipping champagne on the beach in Monaco after selling their company to Google.

Life is like that.

You Are Responsible for Your Own Experience

FROM HUGH MACLEOD, "HOW TO BE CREATIVE"

Nobody can tell you if what you're doing is good, meaningful or worthwhile. The more compelling the path, the more lonely it is.

Every creative person is looking for "The Big Idea." You know, the one that

(continued)

is going to catapult them out from the murky depths of obscurity and on to the highest planes of incandescent lucidity.

The one that's all love-at-first-sight with the Zeitgeist.

The one that's going to get them invited to all the right parties, metaphorical or otherwise.

So naturally you ask yourself, if and when you finally come up with The Big Idea, after years of toil, struggle and doubt, how do you know whether or not it is "The One"?

Answer: You don't.

There's no glorious swelling of existential triumph.

That's not what happens.

All you get is this rather kvetchy voice inside you that seems to say, "This is totally stupid. This is utterly moronic. This is a complete waste of time. I'm going to do it anyway."

And you go do it anyway.

Second-rate ideas like glorious swellings far more. Keeps them alive longer.

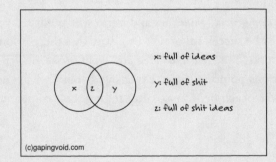

x: full of ideas

y: full of shit

z: full of shit ideas

(c)gapingvoid.com

(To read more of Hugh's creative ideas, go to www.gapingvoid.com.)[2]

Market, Management, Resources, and Competitive Edge

Entrepreneur and business plan expert Tim Berry, who founded a successful software company and who acts as adviser to countless others, says this about what will turn a good idea into a real business:

The quick answer is market, management, resources, and competitive edge. Beyond that, what I'm looking for is whether or not the idea is an opportunity. Ideas are a dime a dozen, no real value. An opportunity, however, is an idea coupled with market potential, management, and resources to get it done. There's a good potential return, a decent risk-return relationship, credibility, a team to implement, and a business to be built.

What's an opportunity for one person or group or company isn't necessarily an opportunity for the next person or group or company. General Motors can do things you and I can't. We can do things they can't. I look for the match between the scale of it and the resources to be applied.[3]

This is why I think it is important to spend some time in the business planning process, which we will do in detail in chapter 9. Don't worry, you don't have to create a gigantic Excel document or 120-slide Power-Point presentation; you will just have the opportunity to assess your market, management, resources, and competitive edge. It will be fun, I promise.

Don't Trip If You Don't Pick the Perfect Idea the First Time. Really. Don't.

A huge fear of aspiring entrepreneurs is that you will quit your job, go out and work for yourself, fail miserably, and have to slink back to the company you loathe with a huge "L for Loser" patch sewn on your sweater.

This is absurd and unrealistic.

If you remember the "conscious competence" learning model from chapter 4, it is impossible to go from "unconscious incompetence" (blissfully ignorant) to "unconscious competence" (gracefully skilled) without a lot of experience, mistakes, testing, and trying.

You can never guarantee the success of a new venture. There are too many factors out of your control, and too many new things to learn. So just do your very best to learn, plan, and test your ideas, and live by the following guidelines:

- Don't risk more than you have to.
- Learn from your mistakes.
- Build, don't burn bridges.
- Don't sweat it if you have to go back and be your own venture capitalist for a while.

7

Recruit Your Tribe

In my husband's Diné (Navajo) tribe, an important part of the culture is the clan structure, which describes the bloodlines of both your mother's and father's family. The first time you meet someone new, you introduce yourself through four distinct clans (your dad's, your mom's dad, your dad's dad, and your dad's mom).

After describing the four clans, your new acquaintance will know if and how you are related. "My mom is Minigoat clan too! You are my brother!" or "My grandpa was from the Mexican clan too. You are my uncle!"

After understanding your clan relations, introductory greetings continue (according to my mother-in-law, Angela Slim):

- Where are you from?
- Do you have a family? How many kids do you have? How old are they? How many boys or girls?
- How do you provide for your family? (What work do you do?)
- How many sisters and brothers do you have? What about your parents?

- Are your grandparents and great grandparents living? (Elders and ancestors are very revered and important in Diné culture.)

You can see why I needed flash cards when I first met my husband's relatives. In my Anglo culture, the typical introduction process is much more basic: "Hi, I'm Pam. What do you do?"

This work-focused introduction would be a very strange way to greet a traditional Diné, who finds comfort and connection in establishing clan relationships and understanding the whole family structure of the person they are talking to.

I always delight in watching Diné greet each other since invariably, after about fifteen minutes of talking, they find a common auntie from Window Rock, or have a story of how one person's grandpa performed a ceremony that cured a cousin's ailment, or how they both agree on where to find the best bowl of mutton stew and fry bread in the town of Chinlé.

That is really what we are looking for, isn't it?

As human beings, we long for a sense of place, of relation, shared history and connection.

The Outcast

When you start your journey from employee to entrepreneur, this sense of tribe, relation, and connection may be totally absent. Most adult relationships come from college or your place of employment. If all of your friends are employees, it can feel very unsafe and insecure to venture into the land of entrepreneurship. A lot of people have these concerns:

- I don't know what I'm doing, but don't know anyone else who knows either since most of my friends are employees, not entrepreneurs.
- I don't know whom to trust.
- I am so new at this that no one will want to help me.
- I don't even know where to look for people who share my interest.

These questions are perfectly normal. The entire purpose of this chapter is to learn how to connect with people who will alleviate these fears.

Why Do You Need Other People?

To some, the benefit of a robust network is self-evident. But I am always surprised to find people who think that relying on others is a sign of weakness, which somehow threatens their power or self-determination.

Based on my personal experience and that of countless other successful entrepreneurs I know, let me share some tangible benefits of surrounding yourself with supportive peers, mentors, and teachers while you build your business. Great partners will:

Talk You Down from the Edge of a Cliff

There are so many unknown and scary things that surface when you try something new. Terrors can range from losing data on a hard drive, to dealing with an extremely difficult client, to facing a period of little work and less money, to plain old self-doubt. Good people will be there for you in times of trouble, and their calm demeanor and wise words will calm you down and allow you to create a rational solution.

Save You Time

While writing this book, I was in constant, daily contact with my circle of supportive friends and mentors. When I needed a quick idea, or resource, or perspective, I sent out a Twitter message, or e-mailed the 150 ultrahelpful members of my Escape from Cubicle Nation Book Advisory Council, or posed a question on my blog. Without exception, I got quality information *twenty times faster* than if I had to research it all myself.

Share Resources

Whenever I find a product or service that I really love and think would be useful, I tell my extended circle of peers. I look for my friends to do the same thing. That is how I found a great transcription service at www.reallyvirtual.com from my friend Stever Robbins. And how I learned about a historic Mexican restaurant from About.com's Scott Allen.

Introduce You to Great People

The best possible way to build a relationship with someone is to be introduced by someone else. That makes it more "safe" for the person to talk with you, since they know that someone they trust already holds you in high regard. Think about the principles of "six degrees of separation" (capitalized on by social networks like Facebook and LinkedIn): when you meet someone new, you not only become connected to *them*, you become connected to *everyone they know*.

Spread the Word About Your Business

The age of the Internet has made "viral marketing" a real phenomenon. At its most pure, when people like what you do, they tell others about it. And because of things like blogs and Twitter, when they say they like you online, you get exposure to thousands of people.

Make You Laugh

Laughter is the immediate, all-curing remedy for any kind of entrepreneurial ailment. My most potent memory of this is when I shared on my blog that I had inadvertently offended "Million Dollar Consultant" Alan Weiss. In a post, I had encouraged my readers to check out a recorded conversation on the topic of pricing between Alan and Robert Middleton that had lots of useful information. I warned them that they might find his style a bit "crass." What I thought the word "crass" meant was direct, and no-holds-barred. But when Alan personally responded to my post greatly offended, I looked up the word in the dictionary and found it meant "So crude and unrefined as to be lacking in discrimination and sensibility." When I shared my embarrassment about my choice of words on my blog, my dear reader "Mike" shared this story:

> A number of years ago, a friend rang me up and said she was interested about a job advertised in my company. She was looking for some general background information and so on. She told me she was going to be interviewed by my boss at the time. After the interview, I asked her how it had gone, and if she was interested in the job.

She just burst out laughing. When trying to sell her on our company and how much people liked working there because we had low turnover of staff, my boss made repeated use of the term "the low rate of nutrition." He meant, of course, "attrition." After that, my friend said she couldn't consider working there because she'd never be able to look him in the eye without laughing. But truly, we were all very skinny at the time!

Alan kindly forgave my indiscretion and my blog readers were very supportive. But it was Mike's hilarious story, which made me laugh so hard I had tears in my eyes, that shook me out of a state of embarrassment and allowed me to move on with my day.

I could write pages and pages of stories of all the ways that my own "tribe" has supported and encouraged me. They are such a big part of my life and business that I know I would not be able to accomplish a fraction of the things I do without their support.

Seth Godin in his 2008 book *Tribes* says:

It's simple: there are tribes everywhere now, inside and outside of organizations, in public and in private, in nonprofits, in classrooms, across the planet. Every one of these tribes is yearning for leadership and connection. This is an opportunity for you—an opportunity to find and assemble a tribe and lead it. The question isn't, Is it possible for me to do that? Now the question is, "Will I choose to do it?"[1]

Whom Should You Have Around You?

Comadres and Compadres

I love the Spanish term *comadre* (female) or *compadre* (male) for a very close friend. It literally translates into "coparent." It is used to describe godparents of your children, but also is a special term of affection for very close friends.

When you have very special friends who are deeply supportive of you and concerned with your success, your daily tasks become much easier.

Here are examples of my *comadres* and *compadres*:

- Canadian blogger Glenda Watson Hyatt, who wrote her memoir of growing up self-determined despite her cerebral palsy, was a constant, positive force when I was writing my book. In late-night e-mails and Twitter messages, she encouraged me to keep going and not get discouraged. Due to her CP, she finished her book while typing with only her left thumb, and knowing this was hugely inspirational to me.
- Entrepreneur expert Matthew Scott shares resources, support, and information with me almost every day as he grows his own coaching business.
- Colleague Laura Back listened lovingly and patiently to eight months of whining as I struggled to survive the effects of a collapsed market in my husband's business. Her relentless optimism was crucial for navigating one of the most challenging times of my life.

The main characteristic of *comadres* and *compadres* is that they are positive, encouraging, and totally supportive of your new direction.

Mentors

There are many flavors of mentors, the major categories being:

THE TECHNICAL EXPERT

Mentors in this category are recognized in their particular industry as being the best at what they do. Sometimes, however, they don't have a well-rounded skill set. Larry Ellison of Oracle comes to mind when I think of someone who has a great capacity for creating a very successful technology company worth billions of dollars, but is known as being quite Neanderthal in his leadership style. You look to technical mentors to expose you to the smartest, most creative thinking in your field, not to bare your soul and share your personal fears (your *compadres* are for that).

THE WISE ELDER

Mentors in this category tend to have both personal and professional insight that they developed over many years. Warren Buffett comes to mind for a mentor in this category. These types of mentors are often great for big-picture advice.

Mentors in this category are peers whom you respect and admire and who have an admirable track record in your field. They make me think, "If she is doing it, then I can too!" This kind of mentor is often great for nuts-and-bolts advice such as "What are the top five things I should consider when starting a new Web site?" or "What are the best marketing strategies for reaching parents of autistic teenagers?" or "How do I register a trade name or set up a patent for a new product?"

So Where Do You Find Mentors?

The paradox of finding a good mentor is that you can't really look for them, they just show up. The process reminds me of the children's book *Are You My Mother?* A baby bird pokes out of its egg when its mother is off to find a worm, and it falls out of its perch on a tree. Since it has never seen its mother before, it goes up to every creature it can find and asks "Are you my mother?" If you look too hard for a mentor, you will force the process and find yourself asking everyone "Are you my mentor?" That is why I think so many corporate-sponsored mentoring programs struggle, since they try to manufacture what is essentially an organic process.

TIPS FOR KICKING OFF A MENTORING RELATIONSHIP

- Introduce or reintroduce yourself. If you are approaching someone for the first time or if it has been awhile since you have spoken to them, introduce yourself and get reacquainted.
- Find ways to stay connected. Find out where they "hang out" professionally and see if you can get to know them better. Invite them to coffee or lunch and find out what they are working on and what they are interested in.
- Ask for advice once, then see how it goes. This is where the organic process comes in. A natural mentor will be someone who willingly shares advice and information. Don't rush into things. Just ask for advice once and if they seem open, keep the dialogue going. If they become short or reticent, back off gently and thank them for the advice they gave.
- Offer support and advice back. When you find people, information, or resources that you feel would benefit your mentor, let them know. Send

articles of interest, make personal introductions, or let them know about good products or programs.

- You may learn about some of your ideal mentors by reading their books or hearing about them in the press. Don't be scared off if someone appears too "big" for you. I found one of my dearest mentors, Martha Beck, by watching her on *Oprah*, then reading her book. I knew that she was really busy and well known, but I just set my sights on getting to know her personally. It took a couple of years, but now we have a wonderful relationship. I have had Jim Collins on my list of "ideal mentors" for some time now, and I am sure that sooner or later our paths will cross.

Perhaps the best way to create a force field of attraction for a mentor is to be one yourself. Share what you know with others, and help them to learn and grow. Your ideal mentor will be watching you too and may just approach you first.

Characteristics of a Great Mentoring Relationship

ENCOURAGEMENT
A good mentor not only will provide you with valuable advice, he or she will also help you deal with the fear and stress involved in growing professionally and making a big change.

RECIPROCITY
Enduring mentoring relationships have mutual benefit built into them. Your mentor may have years of experience in his or her field, but you also must bring something to the table. Perhaps they are less familiar with technology so you can help them build a Web site. Whatever you do, make sure they are not the only ones offering support and advice.

CHEMISTRY
A mentoring relationship is just that, a relationship. You must truly enjoy each other's company if it is to last. If you put each other at ease and make

each other laugh, that will make your time together energizing and engaging.

GRATITUDE
Don't ever forget to acknowledge and thank your mentor for his guidance and advice. Lavish gifts or hollow praise are not necessary. Good, old-
fashioned heartfelt thanks in the form of a handwritten note or sincere
comment work the best. Let him know what his advice meant to you and
how it changed the course of your life.

MUTUAL RESPECT
Even if people are very well known in their field, they don't want to be surrounded by feet-kissing grovelers who deem themselves "not worthy." Let
me rephrase that. The mentors *you* want do not want to be surrounded by
arse-kissers. Be confident and present yourself as a humble, less-experienced
equal.

High Council of Jedi Knights

Do you ever have moments in your life when you wish that you could
tune into the Force, use your telepathic powers, and call Yoda for advice?
I do.

Comadres, compadres, mentors, and partners are all critical to your success
and happiness. But when you want to do something really bodacious, like
start a nonprofit organization or open a business or write a great novel or
radically change your life, you need to think bigger. You need a High Council of Jedi Knights.

This wise council is made up of people you really respect and admire and
see as symbols of who you want to be when you grow up. They don't have
to be powerhouses or stars, or old in age, they just need to be highly evolved
people in business and in life. I see this group as in addition to your immediate family, who obviously also play a huge role in supporting and encouraging you.

How do you identify your own High Council?

- Notice the kind of people in the world who get you really excited. Are they authors, musicians, doctors, computer programmers, spiritual figures? Scan through your bookshelf and determine your favorite books. Examine the blogs that are at the top of your RSS reader. Note the kind of people who really interest you when you read about them in the newspaper or watch them on television.

- Pay attention to how you feel when you think about these people. Some smart people have lots of knowledge but make you feel a bit inferior when you read their work or interact with them. The feeling of positive connection reserved for High Council members is what Martha Beck calls "the urge to merge," where you feel an unexplainable desire to be in their presence.

- Ask: Do they use their superpowers for good? This is a favorite expression of my dear friend Marilyn Scott-Waters, who creates free paper toys on her Web site www.thetoymaker.com (over 3 million downloads and counting!). Someone can be brilliant, charismatic, and accomplished, but how are they using their life? In *Star Wars* terms, do they lean toward the light or dark side of the Force? Are they involved in activities that solve problems, heal wounds, increase happiness, and bring people together?

- Imagine that you are in a critical stage of your bodacious goal and you feel really awful. You want to cry and give up. Who would immediately make you feel better? Who has faced a similar challenge and moved through it with success? Who would be gentle and loving while at the same time pushing you very hard to live up to your highest potential?

Creating this list is certainly an exercise in positive visualization. If you imagine a circle of highly accomplished, creative, productive people who have designed lives that you admire, you will feel increased motivation to move forward with your plans. Unlike fictional characters like Yoda, these are real, live human beings who faced the same fear and doubt as you, but moved forward anyway.

The exercise can also be something more: you may actually find that by identifying the best in your field, you meet them in real life. When I read Martha Beck's book *Finding Your Own North Star* seven years ago, I never dreamed that I would actually work with her. But because I connected so strongly with her ideas, our paths eventually crossed. Guy Kawasaki started out as a blogging hero of mine, and has since become a friend. You may be very surprised to find that those people who seem out of reach are actually very open to connecting with you.

Fantastic 4 × 4

The only side benefit to watching some really bad children's television programs with my kids is that I take away some useful business metaphors.

When I was watching *The Fantastic Four* with my son Josh, I got a flash of inspiration for how to get support from über-talented people without demanding too much time or energy.

Without getting too far-fetched with the Fantastic Four analogy, you can see how these "superpowers" can be very effective partners:

- The "scientific genius" with a gigantic stretch can share all kinds of smart ideas and expand your thinking.
- The "powerful force field" can tell you how to trust your intuition and make sure you don't do anything foolish.
- The "human torch" can set your marketing and branding on fire (pardon the pun).
- The "monstrous thing" can plow through difficulties and make sure you build a rock-solid infrastructure.

The basic idea of a Fantastic 4 × 4 is this:

1. Form a group of four fantastic people (including yourself).
2. Each person shares four pieces of information about their business (sample below).
3. Four hour-long calls are scheduled (one for each person).
4. Four questions are answered on each call (sample below).

4 × 4 PREP SHEET

Each person chooses four pieces of information to share with the group, depending on what they think is important background. About a week before the call, the hot seat person will send the 4 × 4 Prep Sheet to the rest of the group. My suggestions are below—use these, or create your own.

What I LOVE and do well:	SWOT analysis of business idea: Strengths Weaknesses Opportunities Threats
What I HATE and suck at:	Who are "my people?"
Core questions for the 4 × 4 hot seat conversation:	
What should I do?	How can I supercharge the flow of money to my business?
Which limiting thoughts do I need to zap and which stupid things do I need to stop doing?	Whom should I be working with to enhance and accelerate my business?

I know the temptation here is to make this document a lot more complex and add a bunch of additional questions.

If you feel this way, go for it. It is your Fantastic 4 × 4 and you should make it work for you.

Where Do You Find Them?

I am hoping at this point that you are getting excited about connecting with all kinds of people in order to feel support and accelerate your learning. Here are some suggestions for where to find them:

Social Networks

There are many social networks that are online gathering spots for like-minded people. Some of the most popular include:

TWITTER

Twitter is a microblogging service where you share thoughts, ideas, and information in no more than 140-character posts. The term used on Twitter is that you "follow" people who interest you, and people who are interested in you become your "followers." After spending some time on Twitter and building up your network, I think you will find it is an amazing place to talk directly with people you admire, learn about all kinds of information and events related to your area of interest, and share more personal details about your life with a supportive community.

FACEBOOK

Online marketing expert Shama Kabani equates Facebook to "coffee shop culture." It is a great place to come in, have a friendly conversation with interesting people, then if there is a good feeling about the conversation, you can agree to continue it in more depth through e-mail, on the phone, or in person.

LINKEDIN

LinkedIn is often viewed as the more "professional" social media network, and a good research tool.

Jason Alba, CEO of JibberJobber and author of *I'm on LinkedIn, Now What???*, offers the following tips for using LinkedIn as an entrepreneur:

> Think about who should know about your venture, and what decision makers might be able to help you. Strategically grow your network so you can get closer to those key people. For example, if I'm building something for the printing business, I want to connect with key players in the printing space. This might include print shop owners as well as their vendors, and those who market services to either group. As I get more contacts in this industry I'll have more reach to their contacts, who would be my second and third degree connections. Now, when I do advanced searches, or when I browse my contacts' connections, I should be able to find new people, companies and opportunities that I can reach out to.
>
> Make sure you take your LinkedIn relationships offline, or at least outside of LinkedIn. You should be able to communicate with your contacts through a newsletter, or have some kind of direct communication with them. Just being connected could be valuable, as it adds to your search capability, but nurtured relationships might be what really helps your business move forward.[2]

CONFERENCES

I have found the best way to identify interesting in-person events is to pay attention to what people talk about on blogs, Twitter, and Facebook.

Conferences can be a great way to connect in person with those you have formed relationships with online, as well as to hear the best speakers and experts in your field of interest. You can also contact your local convention and visitor's bureau to see which events are scheduled in your local area.

CLASSES

There are so many things to learn when you are starting a new business, and classes are excellent ways to both gain skills and network with the instructor and fellow participants. When I got started in my full-time coaching business, I took classes on all kinds of topics. My participation led to coaching clients, joint venture partners, and teaching gigs.

Many large universities have extended education departments that offer excellent in-depth classes you can take on an individual class basis, or in a batch like a certificate program.

MEDIA

I spend a lot of time scouring books, magazines, and newspapers for interesting people in the field of career development, entrepreneurship, writing, and creativity. I got guests for my radio show by reading about them in books or magazines. My husband and I wrote to successful Latino contractor Raymond Gonzales after we read the story in our local paper about his receiving a Minority Contractor of the Year award. The letter led to a meeting, which led to joint projects, as well as a wonderful and supportive relationship.

Clubs and Associations

There are hundreds of thousands of specialized meet-in-person clubs around the world, organized by topic and geography.

- In the United States, the Small Business Association is a good starting point for information about the technical side of starting a business (licenses, insurance, business structure, etc.) and also has networking events where you can meet other small business owners
- Search on Google for *"associations + your city"* for a list of every kind of association you can imagine.

A brief search on Google for my own area of Phoenix, Arizona, led to thousands of organizations including:

- Arizona Twirling Athletes (I wonder, do they twirl batons, or themselves?)
- International Bronchoesophagological Society (is there an award for the longest word in an association name?)
- Licentiate Ministers and Certified Mediums Society
- Resting Racers (do they rest before, after, or during the race?)
- Women's Professional Rodeo Association

And perhaps my favorite:

- National Association for Information Destruction, Inc. (it may have something to do with shredding, but it makes me laugh)

The key to finding a group of people that you connect with is to spend some time experimenting with different groups so that you get a feel for their members, culture, and meeting structure. You may find after hanging out in a number of groups that all of them are a total bore and are not worth the $20 meeting fee for cold, rubbery chicken, overcooked vegetables, and tasteless iceberg lettuce salad.

In that case, you have an opportunity: *start your own.*

Whether you start your own group or join an established one, the important thing is to realize that most likely, whatever you are interested in, there are other people who are too. And the sooner you connect with them, the sooner you will stop feeling like an outsider and start feeling *relation with your tribe.*

How Do You Connect with Them?

Don't try to form a network. This requires much effort and game playing. Instead, allow a network to form around you.
—*Dr. Srikumar Rao, AreYouReadytoSucceed.com*

Gathering a group of smart, enthusiastic, helpful, and resourceful people around you does not have to be an uncomfortable exercise involving painful small talk and sweaty palms. As Dr. Rao says above, you can gather a group around you by using a few magnetizing principles, which I outline here.

TAO: Transparent, Authentic, and Open

I chose to train as a life coach with Dr. Martha Beck to a great extent based on her hilarious writing, incredible brain, and no-nonsense coaching style. I liked that she admitted weaknesses, shared funny stories, and laughed at herself.

So it doesn't surprise me that one of Martha's fundamental principles in her coaching style is to be "TAO," which stands for "Transparent, Authentic, and Open."

Instead of listening to a client explain something really complicated, getting confused and thinking "I must appear smart and pretend to understand what she said!" we share the voice in the back of our head that says: "Laura, you just spent five minutes explaining something and I have no idea what you said. What do you really want to tell me?"

You don't have to pretend to act smart. You just speak your truth, and tune in to the part of yourself that is calm, loving, and curious, which is the best way to serve the client.

This exact frame of mind will make you an excellent relationship builder.

In practical terms, this is what it means to be transparent, authentic, and open when you build relationships with new people:

1. Admit what you don't know.
2. Ask for help.
3. If you can't help someone, find a good person who can.
4. Don't be afraid to laugh.
5. Mean what you say and say what you mean.
6. Don't worry about being perfect. It is an exhausting façade, and people won't believe you anyway. Admitting flaws, fears, and mistakes makes you human and likeable.

7. Apologize right away if you screw up.
8. Take responsibility for your business. If someone is unhappy or unsatis-fied, don't be afraid to ask why. If they ask for their money back, give it to them.

If you are an engineer reading this list, you may laugh at numbers 1 and 6. Technical people are notorious for challenging facts and figures and de-lighting when someone makes a mistake. In my experience, within the technical camp, there are people with high standards who still love to help others succeed. And there are others who are trolls who will tear you down if you make the slightest mistake. My best advice for you: ignore the trolls.

Networking Tips from a Nine-Year-Old Expert

A couple of years ago, I was standing in the sand of my local playground with my new baby in a snuggle pack, watching my two-year-old Josh play on the slide. He looked over to the basketball courts and noticed there was a new kid on a scooter.

Never one to be shy, Josh shouted, "Hi, kid! Want to come and play?"

Nine-year-old Austin made his way over, and started talking to Josh. He was gentle and kind, and really paid attention to what Josh was saying. This is markedly different from most kids his age, who blatantly ignore him as he stands by their side, begging to play.

Since I had never seen Austin before, I asked him if he was new in the neighborhood. He said he was, and lived with his mom, dog, and two cats just down the road.

As he was talking to me, he noticed Angela in the snuggle pack and said, "Can I see your baby?" I said sure and he came close to look at her. "She is so cute!" he said, again defying the typical nine-year-old boy who can hardly distinguish a new baby from a watermelon.

He told me about his cats, and suggested I get one for Josh, since "he gets really excited when I talk about cats."

After some more small talk, Austin said, "I am kind of lonely around here since I don't know any kids in the neighborhood. I heard that a boy my age lives in that house on the corner."

"Yes, Zach lives there," I said.

"Would you mind introducing me?" said Austin.

Impressed by his polite demeanor, I agreed and we all walked over to Zach's house.

Zach's parents answered the door, and I explained why I was there. Zach came running to the door to join them. Smiling and extending his hand, Austin said, "Hi, my name is Austin. Do you like Pokemon?" Zach's face lit up and he said an enthusiastic "Yes!"

Within ten seconds, Zach grabbed his book of Pokemon cards and the two were off to the playground, looking like Butch Cassidy and the Sundance Kid.

I was floored at the grace and ease with which Austin broke the ice and made a new friend. Here is what I learned from his natural networking ability:

- **Be interested.** Whomever Austin talked to, he looked them in the eye and immediately listened for what they were interested in. He answered questions about himself when asked, but kept the focus on his new friend. Ninety percent of new networkers focus on their own elevator pitch and on sounding important.

- **Be real.** Most people would be totally embarrassed to admit that they were lonely and in need of companionship. But this authenticity is exactly what endears you to people. Instead of puffing out your chest and trying to sound important as you connect with new people, be down-to-earth and let them know what you are feeling. Don't be afraid to say things like "I am really terrified of starting a new business. Did you feel that way when you started yours?" or "These networking events always make me feel slightly queasy. Do you want to go grab a drink?"

- **Notice what is important to the person you are networking with.** What new mom is not thrilled with a compliment to her baby? If you are communicating with someone in person or online, pay attention to what is important to them. Read their blog, their books, and note their interests. We are all creatures of ego, and it is hard to resist someone who really notices what we like. (Note to the single among you . . . this is good dating advice too!)

- **Ask for an introduction.** Austin could have spent a miserable couple of weeks cooped up at home, waiting to make some friends. Or he could ask for an introduction, reducing anxiety and speeding up his integration into the neighborhood. Don't be so polite that you miss the opportunity to shortcut a connection to an interesting person. The worst that can happen is that someone refuses to make the introduction, and you can gracefully move on to another way of connecting.

- **Be nice to everyone.** I am sure that Austin would rather play with someone his own age than talk to a two-year-old or a forty-one-year-old Mom. But because he was so nice to us, he opened the door to meet his target: a Pokemon-addicted nine-year-old boy who loves to ride bikes, spray water guns, and play video games. Too often, I see people brush anyone off who doesn't fit their "target profile." What they don't realize is that the receptionist, waiter, college student, or elderly woman at the grocery store whom they treat rudely could hold a golden key of introduction to someone they desire. Not to mention that it is just bad karma. In my corporate days, I would always get nauseated when watching a job candidate or salesperson act condescending to a receptionist, then lay on the honey when they met a senior executive. What they didn't realize is that receptionists and administrative assistants rule the world, and their rudeness forever doomed their efforts to get in with the "big people."

By using Austin's basic techniques, you can greatly reduce your anxiety about meeting new people.

How to Avoid Being a Fanboy or Fangirl

Over the years, I have developed deep respect for authors like Jim Collins, Kathy Sierra, Steven Pressfield, and Isabel Allende. I adore the wit and creativity of people like Ze Frank and Hugh MacLeod. I appreciate the down-to-earth business wisdom of John Jantsch, Rich and Jeff Sloan, and Andrea Lee.

Whomever you note on your "cool smart I wanna be like them when I grow up" list, you can and should look for ways to build relationships with them.

But, as creatures still stinging from the social dynamics of junior high, we can fall into "fanboy or fangirl traps" which not only make us feel insecure, but turn off the very people we are trying to impress.

So here are my tips, learned from the school of hard knocks:

FANBOY AND FANGIRL TRAPS TO AVOID

1. **You are the best and I worship you! Lather, rinse, repeat.**

   I often start correspondence with people I admire by telling them how great they are. I don't think there is anything wrong with that, as long as you say it sincerely and with no ulterior motive. The problem is when you continually gush in each subsequent conversation. It gets uncomfortable and tiresome for them and gets in the way of good conversation for you.

   Alternative: You are the best and I worship you. Now that that's out of the way, let's get to know each other. Have you read this book?

2. **I am a nobody.**

   In an attempt to be humble, you may write "I don't mean to bother you with my message, since I know you are doing great things and I am a nobody." This is rubbish. We are all equal. Some people have accomplished a lot in their lives, written great works, sculpted strong glutes, or whatever you consider noteworthy. But this does not make them a superior human being. You can have admiration for someone while still being proud of who you are. It goes to my theory of relationships formed in junior high: No one wants the person who needs them too much. Don't be the girl (or boy) desperate for a date.

   Alternative: You are very cool, and so am I in my own right. (Don't use those words of course, but convey it in your attitude, conversation, and body language if meeting in person.)

3. **I will convince you that I am worthy by spouting off my entire CV.**

   I just said that you are somebody worth talking to. This is true! But you don't need to reinforce this by sharing your every accomplishment since getting a gold star for "most cooperative" in preschool. Let the relationship develop naturally. As you share information and converse, each of you will develop natural interest in the other. Or not!

   Alternative: Save the marketing pitch for your evening telemarketing job. Be yourself, and trust that if you make a real connection with someone you admire, they will be interested in you. If they aren't, you can continue to admire their work from afar and pursue other mutually beneficial relationships.

4. **Nice to meet you! Please, oh please, will you be my mentor?**

   Think about the current mentors in your life. Did you like and trust them immediately? Or did your relationship grow with time and work and mutual support? Sometimes in your desire to learn as much as you can from people you admire, you ask them for specific support and guidance without having any consideration for their time. A favorite is "You are an expert in my field, would you mind reviewing my twenty-page business plan?"

Alternative: Respect your own time and that of busy people. Mentors grow naturally, they are not manufactured.

5. **You know everyone. Please link to my stuff.**

We are all familiar with the context in which the word "foreplay" is normally used. The same applies to building business relationships. Just as you wouldn't grope a potential mate the first time you meet him or her at a party, you shouldn't immediately demand an intimate business action upon meeting someone new. I think linking to someone is an intimate act. It means I like what I read, and trust the source.

Alternative: It is absolutely fine to say "This is what I'm working on. I thought you might be interested. Enjoy!" Just leave off "would you link to it?" Or even worse, "I'll link to you if you link to me." If you wrote a true gem that fits with their audience's needs, they will link to it. If not, move on.

6. **You can do no wrong.**

Everyone screws up. Sometimes we overlook glaring faults because of our cultlike devotion to the image of a person we admire. This is not helpful to you or to them.

Alternative: When someone you admire does something you don't agree with, let them know in a kind and straightforward way. "I really admire your business sense. But your latest advertising partnership with Stomp Bunnies and Puppies LLC seems really out of sync with who you are. What is your rationale for this decision?"

Here is the bottom line about building relationships: *We are all little people.*

Brownie Points

If you follow the recommendations above, very soon you should have some *comadres, compadres,* 4 × 4 partners, and mentors. Perhaps you have even identified a High Council member or two.

You may even feel like a *gigantic love magnet* that draws goodwill, clients, and financial abundance. You think I am kidding. I am not. I have no other way of describing the outrageously generous circle of people that gathers when you let your network form around you. And the most powerful tool to do that by far is to be a matchmaker.

What Is a Matchmaker?

A good matchmaker is someone who constantly looks for ways to connect good people, ideas, and institutions without the expectation of payback.

Without the expectation of payback is the part that may seem counterintuitive, since didn't I just say that being a matchmaker is the best way to further your own business goals? Yes, it is. But in order for it to really work, you have to just trust the process and not count on a direct "I scratch your back, you scratch my back" return favor.

Let me use some examples so you know more clearly what I am talking about, then I will tell you how to avoid a few common traps.

What Are Some Concrete Ways to Be a Matchmaker?

- **Introduce like minds.** This example is the *Fiddler on the Roof* definition: envision two people you know who would be a great fit together. While the result of effective romantic matchmaking is marriage, the result of "like minds" matchmaking is a business relationship that could take many different directions: business partners, mastermind peers, supportive friends, or creative catalysts.
- **Set up a Reese's Peanut Butter Cup.** I don't know if you have seen the old commercial that shows one person rounding the corner with a jar of peanut butter and the other rounding the corner with a chocolate bar. They collide, and the result is a Reese's Peanut Butter Cup. Look for the "peanut butter" friend who would be perfectly served by a "chocolate bar." Then set conditions for a collision.
- **Share a great story with the press.** If you are hooked into your market the right way, you are in conversation with your clients and prospects on a daily basis and have a keen sense of their businesses and what they are trying to accomplish. If you see a publication that you think would be

great for featuring their story, let them know. If you have a relationship with a journalist, pitch the story.

- **Link like crazy.** There is a reason blogs are so viral in nature: by including lots of links in your blog post, you send traffic all over the place. You definitely want to share your own expertise on your blog, but be generous with your referrals to other people. It will come back around!

- **Refer ill-fitting prospective clients to someone appropriate.** You should have a clear picture of who your ideal client is for your product or service. If you run across someone who clearly has a need but will not be best served by you, refer them to the best person you can think of. You never want to send someone away with a simple "Sorry, I can't help you," since you never know if they might know someone who does fit your perfect profile. If you help them find exactly who they need, they are more likely to send people your way. But don't count on it, of course, which brings up the next section.

Surefire Ways to Kill Good Matchmaking

- **Keep track of favors and expect a near-term payback.** If you keep marks on your wall of how many times you helped someone and expect them to return the favor right away, you will be very disappointed.

- **Force people into a predetermined funnel.** Often, referral or affiliate fees are involved, which makes the matchmaking financially motivated. This changes the way that you listen to the needs of the person you are trying to help. Instead of thinking, "Who would be the best resource for this person?" you are thinking, "Would Sally, José, or Thomas be the best resource for this person?" I don't think it is wrong to use a referral or affiliate relationship, just make sure it is the right fit.

- **Break the trust of your confidants by introducing the wrong people.** Just because you get the requests does not mean you have to make the introduction. Make sure you introduce people who would truly provide mutual benefit; otherwise you will soon become known as a pest.

- **Ask people you hardly know to make an introduction for you.** Martha Beck gets cornered at social gatherings, dinner parties, and speaking events all the time with people who want to meet Oprah. Just because she knows her does not make it appropriate. A much better question to ask is "How did you build up such a great platform?"

I hope you find, as I have, that the sheer pleasure of matchmaking makes it worthwhile. It also, over time, positions you as a connected, generous person. And that is exactly what will give you a screaming hot platform and supercharge your gigantic love magnet. Go ahead, laugh when you say that.

How to Avoid Hucksters and Shucksters

A smart and thoughtful blog reader, Ashton Udall, sent me an e-mail that summed up many of the concerns faced by people terrified of expanding their network and getting scammed. I told Ashton that I certainly have had my run-ins with the "integrity challenged" in my personal life and my business, and have come up with some general guidelines to both sniff them out before they do harm, and to get rid of them as soon as they show their true colors.

First, it may be useful to qualify the types of hucksters you may come across in your business dealings, especially when you are forging new frontiers as an entrepreneur:

"Make a Million Bucks in One Month with No Effort" Marketers

They can usually be spotted by marketing and advertising language laden with hype like "so easy a three-year-old could do it!", "No experience required!", and "Super secret formula for success only available to YOU!" If what they are offering were truly a great way to make money with no strings attached, everyone would be investing their money with them.

Unscrupulous Business Partners

These can be much trickier to detect, as some start out seeming to be nice, reputable businesspeople. But, as time goes on, slime begins to ooze from the side of their mouth. They can do things like "forget" agreements about poaching customers, flake on responsibilities and try to blame it on you, or, in the worst case, run away with money without completing work.

Slippery Customers

We tend to look at all customers as allies, right? But some have no intention of acting honorably, and do everything they can to take unfair advantage of money-back guarantees, accuse you of shoddy service or products in an attempt to get a discount, or try to muddy your reputation with other customers as a threat. Mind you, this is very different from legitimate customers who truly don't find value in what you offer, or who are mistreated by you in some way. They deserve full sympathy and refunds. The "integrity challenged" ones know that what you offer is high quality, they just don't want to pay for it.

Flaky Vendors and Suppliers

These folks will produce everything late, not take responsibility for mistakes, disappear from contact just when you need them the most, and claim nothing is their fault.

Online, Anonymous Meanies and Trolls

Perhaps the most frustrating and slippery creatures of all, these folks prefer "slash and run" techniques, where they attempt to inflict as much personal anguish on you as possible, in as public a forum as possible, then slip into the night undetected, leaving you and your reputation bruised and bloody.

So if you are afraid (as you should be) of some of these scary characters, what can you do to protect yourself from harm?

- **Observe them for a long time before letting them into your "circle of trust."** I got some awesome advice on this from an elder capoeira master when I was in the midst of a particularly messy situation in my martial arts days. He told me, "On the surface, show the same, smiling face to everyone. But behind your external mask, closely watch the person to see how he interacts with others. Is he nice to you, but rude to those around him? How does he treat his mother? Take a very long time to observe how someone truly behaves, not how they say they behave, before you really open yourself up to them." This rule can apply to people you hire to coach or teach you, programs you invest in, or joint venture partners you do projects with.

- **Discuss, clarify, and document expectations and agreements.** If you are going into a business partnership with someone, it is very important to discuss every aspect of that partnership. What are the expectations for sharing money? How will you interact with clients? How will you decide ownership of intellectual property? What are the common values that you have in your work? What will you do if the partnership doesn't work out for either person? The more you discuss and document these things up front, the easier it will be to resolve problems in the future.

- **Do your background research.** Talk to prior partners, customers, or contacts to get feedback on their experience with the person or company. If you are researching a vendor, check for complaints with the Better Business Bureau or its equivalent for those of you non-U.S. folks. I have had my personal "hunch" of trusting someone proved dramatically wrong in a few cases where I did *not* check references against my better judgment. The worst case was the birthing coach who simply disappeared (with my deposit) as soon as I went into labor with my son, never to be seen again.

- **For big, important partnerships or really sticky situations, consult with a lawyer.** I don't like that our society has become hyperlitigious. But there are a lot of good reasons to consult with an ethical lawyer so that you protect your assets, intellectual property, and reputation. In the case of the damage inflicted by the meanies and anonymous trolls, you must know your rights, and the appropriate course of action to protect your reputation.

- **When you see unethical behavior, cut the ties fast.** Don't wait for the person to do more damage just because you are in the middle of a project. It may be painful if you have to replace a key resource while you are busy, but it is better than letting a toxic person stir up more trouble. If it is an unethical customer, have a polite conversation, end the relationship, and drop a refund check in the mail. Some of you may disagree with me, but I would rather pay someone in full to close the door on future negotiations and litigation, even if I know I am right, than fight with them over contracts or dollars.

- **Pay by credit card, not cash or check.** I learned this the hard way when a custom furniture maker (who had created other pieces for me in the past) closed up his shop overnight and took off with $4,000 of my hard-earned cash. I had paid by check, which gave me no legal recourse. If I had paid with a major credit card, the credit card company could have refunded my money in full. That was a very painful lesson, and I felt like a fool. Learn from my mistake!

- **Do not stoop to bad behavior yourself, no matter how much someone provokes you.** No situation makes you want to lash out more than when someone is rude or slanderous in person or online. But the very worst thing you can do is to respond with your own tirade of bad words and accusations. Take the high road and hold your tongue, as much for your dignity as for your protection. Words spoken in public settings in the heat of angry passion will come back to haunt you. If you need to let things rip, do so when you are alone in the car and tell this person exactly what you think of him.

- **When they are gone, learn the lesson and let go of the emotion.** You can drive yourself crazy analyzing why you wrote a check for $4,000 to a shifty furniture salesman, or trusted a birth coach at face value without checking references, or allowed a slimy business partner to run away with your best customers. (Okay, maybe those are my problems—I am sure you have your own!) This angst will eat you up if you let it and make you afraid to ever trust anyone again. Instead, look for the lesson and realize that their bad behavior or karma will catch up to them at some point. Then move on with your life. Don't give away more of your life force by dwelling on their bad energy.

While you do your best to demonstrate respect for everyone you meet, it is okay if some people don't make it in your "tribe."

It reminds me of a favorite joke of my husband's Diné relatives:

The Lone Ranger and Tonto are sitting up on a hill watching a huge group of warriors on horseback galloping toward them with bows and arrows drawn. The Lone Ranger looks at Tonto and says, "What are we going to do?" Tonto looks back at him and says, "What do you mean 'we'?"

8

Rethink Your Life: Options for Scaling Back, Downshifting, and Relocating

I was talking to prospective client "Sarah" about her expectations for first-year earnings as an entrepreneur. She told me, "Well, at a minimum, I must earn at least $350,000 a year. I live in New York and it is an expensive place. And although I am not married yet and don't have kids, when I do, I will want to take time off to be with them. Schools can be sketchy in certain parts of town, so I need to live in a good neighborhood. And that is expensive."

In the meantime, she was totally unsure what kind of business she wanted to start. And the slightest suggestion of taking *one concrete step* toward setting up a business set her on edge. "I know you think two weeks is a long time to register my domain name, but I am really busy at work, and guests are coming in this weekend . . ."

"Have you considered selling crack?" I said.

Of course I didn't say this. But I sure thought it, as I was desperately trying to work with her expectations and be realistic at the same time.

Hope for the Best, Plan for the Worst

I may incur the wrath of Internet millionaires everywhere who started businesses in their pajamas and in two months were pulling in six figures.

But I believe that although all of us are *capable* of doing great things and kicking sales through the roof and creating a killer app and writing a best-selling book, most of us won't do it. The law of averages says that not everyone will have raging success their first year.

This is not because you aren't smart or hardworking or even because you have a bad business idea. It just means that sometimes things are harder or take longer than you think. And as my husband and I learned in 2008, market conditions can turn a good situation into a very bad one in the blink of an eye.

Even the Most Likely to Succeed Benefit from Scaling Back

By contrast with the "slightly optimistic" Sarah, my client Carmen, who was getting ready to launch full-time into New Demographic, a diversity consulting firm, said: "I think I am selling myself short by only planning on matching my salary the first year. Instead of trying to match what I currently make, why don't I try to triple it? Would the process really be that much different?"

In Carmen's case, she had a very popular blog and podcast that she had been diligently building on the side of her "day job" for three years. She had spoken at many conferences. She had prominent mainstream press coverage in CNN, *USA Today,* and *The New York Times.* And when I asked her to do something, she would almost always double the result in half the time. She would shoot for getting a $5,000 fee and get $10,000.

In her case, I encouraged her to go for it and make a plan based on an annual target of triple her current salary, but to have a backup if she fell short. Even if you are a go-getter with a great track record like my client Carmen, it makes sense to hope for the best and plan for the worst. Starting a new business is a unique opportunity to question all of your assumptions about your life.

- Do you really need a car?
- Is private school absolutely necessary for your kids?
- Are weekly manicures a necessity?

- Do you have to go on an extended tropical vacation each year?
- Do you have to pay for your kids' entire college tuition?

Do You Really Need a Big House in the City?

It is easy to think that the place you live is a nonnegotiable thing. What you don't consider is that the reason we tend to gather in large, expensive metropolises is for our jobs. Traditional jobs. Jobs that require us to be in a chair in an office during the day, in which case we need to live somewhere close enough that the commute won't kill us.

So if you are leaving behind the idea of a job, can you at least entertain the thought of scaling back some necessities? Here are some reasons:

- **The location you think you *must* live in may change dramatically once you are doing work you love.** No one was more surprised than I when I moved from the San Francisco Bay Area to Mesa, Arizona. I was a fourth-generation Californian with a deep love for my "City by the Bay" and all of its wonder: great food, spectacular hiking trails, and a wonderful, diverse, and open culture. Did it take awhile to get used to realizing that Taco Bell is the nearest thing to authentic Mexican cuisine? Of course it did. But the reality is, my life is great because I am doing work I love, am married to a man I adore, and I only have to work about a quarter of the time I would if I lived in the Bay Area.
- **Your need for expensive toys or vacations is often correlated with your level of loathing for your job.** When you can't stand your daily working existence, your need to escape rises dramatically. Often, you think you must indulge in luxurious vacations with lavish food, endless tropical drinks, and extreme extracurricular activities in exotic locations. You reason, "I must make this one week the absolute antithesis of my daily life the other fifty-one weeks of the year." The problem is, at about day three you begin to dread the return home, and your frantic need to enjoy every second can lead to disappointment. By contrast, when your everyday working life is pretty darn happy, a family Scrabble night can provide as much emotional connection, fun, and stress relief as a week-long stint in Jamaica. Minus the sun damage.

- **Focusing on the quality of your close relationships is the fastest way to increase overall happiness.** The Beatles were right: money can't buy you love. Our scarcest commodity these days is time to spend with close family and friends. When you reduce expenses or a huge home that takes all weekend to clean, you free up time to hang out with your friends and family. It makes me sad to think of the typical evening scene for many "corporate employee" working families these days: if they happen to hang out in the same room, Mom is on her laptop checking e-mail, Dad is working on a presentation, and Sister is texting her friend on her cell phone while Brother is playing video games on the Xbox.
- **Creating a slow ramp-up plan will ease the pressure to produce high sales results immediately in your new business.** Your dreams may include buying a nice new home or living in a favorite city, and there is absolutely nothing wrong with that. Our family plans include a custom-built ecological home in Sedona, Arizona, which isn't cheap. But until we are ready to handle that financial responsibility, my husband and I have manageable expenses and can grow our businesses at a reasonable pace. If you scale back your life while you ramp up your business, you will have more time and savings to experiment and fail, build relationships with new clients, and work the bugs out of your products or services.

Here are three questions to ask yourself to see if some of your "big dreams" are driven by true needs or "social self" expectations based on losing face:

- Am I worried about this change because of how it would feel to me on a day-to-day basis, or what others would think about me?
- Where does this belief come from?
- What do I truly crave?

Don't Take My Word for It

I made the choice to move from a very expensive urban area that I loved to a less ideal location, but one that allowed me to have a tremendous quality of life.

I think the best way to get a feel for what is really involved in scaling back, downshifting, and/or relocating is to hear directly from people who have done it. The three entrepreneurs featured here took specific steps to design a business that fit with their life plan.

The Ultimate in Scaling Back: Zen Habits

Leo Babauta is a smart and gentle man who runs the very popular blog Zen Habits. Up until a couple of years ago, he was an overworked and out-of-shape father of six, a smoker, stressed, and in debt over his ears. I interviewed him about his own journey simplifying his life.

You have shared a lot about your personal journey to simplify your life and strengthen your financial practices on your blog, Zen Habits. Where did it all begin?

My journey really began in November 2005, when I decided to finally quit smoking, after numerous attempts and failures. I was probably fifty pounds overweight, with no time for exercise, and was eating very unhealthily. I was deep into debt and was racking up more debt all the time. None of my dreams were becoming realized and I was constantly stressed, disorganized, and depressed.

I made a promise to my daughter and my wife that this time I would quit smoking for good. I was fully committed, and so I did a ton of researching into changing your habits. The things I learned about changing habits—things like public accountability, not allowing any exceptions, finding replacement habits, learning to identify your triggers, and especially the power of positive thinking—I decided to try to apply to exercise. I started running as a way to burn off stress, now that I wasn't smoking. And I applied those same techniques I learned while quitting smoking to my running. And I was successful!

It was a revelation to me. Soon I started learning more about changing habits, and started applying these techniques, one by one, to new habits. I started eating healthier. I started waking early. I simplified my life, became organized, got productive, started eliminating my debt, became a vegetarian, and then tackled a marathon. There seemed to be no end to what I could do, with positive thinking and some simple techniques.

What are the most important things you did to get control of your finances and simplify your life?

Simply to identify what's essential, and then eliminate as much as possible everything that isn't essential. When you want to reduce your spending, you need to figure out what your needs are, and then stop spending on everything else. That, of course, also requires a change of habits, using the same techniques I'd learned through quitting smoking and becoming a runner.

If people are overwhelmed with too much to do, where should they begin?

They should always start with one habit change at a time. Tackling too many things at once is a good way to fail. If you do one thing at a time, you can focus your entire being into that one change, and you make it more likely that you'll succeed. I think the best way to start is through exercise—it reduces stress, gets you into better shape, gives you a good overall feeling, and teaches you the power of a positive attitude. From there, you might start to simplify your life, reduce clutter, and then reduce debt.

What advice would you give corporate employees with high personal overhead who are considering starting a business?

If your personal expenses are going to take away from what you can spend on your business, you need to cut back to the essentials. Learn to control your impulse spending—create a spending plan and stick to it. Learn to do things that are fun but don't cost a lot of money. Focus your energies on creating the business rather than on shopping or eating out or entertainment. Learn to relax without spending money, through simplifying your life and through exercise and meditation or doing things you love.

How did you make the transition from corporate employee to entrepreneur? How did your simplification efforts help this process?

I started by working on my business in my spare time. I had to really identify the essential tasks and keep myself focused. I also always kept my mission in mind: to liberate myself from my day job. And that mission became central to everything I did, and kept me focused if I started to get distracted. Eventually I made enough income from my business to quit my day job.

Simplification efforts were key, as I had a lot of regular work on top of the work of starting a new business, so I could easily become overwhelmed. I had to keep things as simple and as focused as possible if I wanted to do both jobs and still have time for my family.

What are some of the biggest myths about simplifying your life and getting out of debt?

The biggest myth is that you have to live like some kind of hermit, and that it's hard and unenjoyable. Simplifying is really about doing the things you love, and getting rid of all the clutter in your life. Getting out of debt is just another facet of that process—cutting back on extraneous spending while still doing the things you love.

Another myth is that you have to try to do everything at once, in a major life overhaul. That's not how I did it—I did one little change at a time, until it became a regular part of my life. Done this way, you can make major changes over time without realizing it, because all you did was one little step at a time.

How to Evaluate Alternative Places to Live

If going into an office is not required to do your work, where would you choose to live? Would a nice suburb in Kansas compensate for the funkiness of San Francisco or the nightlife of New York? Could you give up the social network of Atlanta for the small-town charm of Americus? Would Leeds be as good as London? Would the sleepy beach town of Recife be better than Rio?

Interview with Matthew Scott, Entrepreneur and Business Coach

What was your concern about staying where you were (San Diego) to start your own business?

My first concern of starting my business in San Diego was the cost of living. Like many other entrepreneur start-ups, I did not have a new client base that matched my salary from my corporate position I was leaving. We began the search for lower cost of living places on the West Coast providing a great or even improved quality and cost of living.

What were the criteria that you and your wife developed for good places to live?

- Climate
- Most affordable West Coast locations
- Quality of public school system
- Diversity of outdoor environments and activities
- Environmental conscience
- Diversity tolerance
- Urban city usage. Would we actually make our large urban city a place that we spend time or would we never venture into the big city?
- Entrepreneur friendly? No sales tax, economic incentives . . .
- Home resale valuation
- Major airport within thirty minutes

How did you develop the criteria?

We moved extensively during my professional career. To be exact, nine moves in the past twenty years. Some of our criteria were developed as a result of living in each region of the country.

How did you go about your research? Did you visit each place?

First, we decided upon the region (West Coast) where we wanted to live based on the best all-around ranking of criteria I mentioned earlier. We

(continued)

reviewed *Money* magazine and *Outside* magazine listings. We also read books that provided a great listing of potential towns or cities based on one's preferences.

After we conducted our research, we narrowed our choice to two states. From those two states we plotted a thirty-mile radius around the desired metro cities and then began to conduct online research on various towns and cities. After this research, my wife and I took a one-week vacation and flew to both areas. We contacted various real estate agents and let them provide tour guides to answer our questions.

After we decided upon the exact area we wanted to live, we intensified our search for a home. In our case, we took a four-day vacation and ultimately found the home we were looking for in the town we wanted to live.

How did you ultimately decide upon Portland?

It met all of our criteria offering the best in quality of life and cost of living. We moved from a more expensive area so we took advantage of the equity and appreciation and purchased a much bigger home at a tremendous cost savings compared to what it would have cost in San Diego.

Also, Portland turned out to be the place my wife and I both felt was collectively our dream city with our dream home aligned with our desired lifestyle in an area very supportive of entrepreneurs.

Blowing Up the Job Model Entirely: Going Location-Independent

If you consider Leo and Matthew's experiences radical, imagine throwing out all notions of home base and taking your work on the road.

This is what Lea and Jonathan Woodward did when they left the stability of corporate jobs in London and set off for a "location-independent" lifestyle. Working from anywhere with an Internet connection, they have lived and worked in Panama, Buenos Aires, Toronto, the West Indies, Dubai,

Thailand, Hong Kong, and South Africa. They share their lessons in two books, *X Marks the Spot: The Indispensable Guide to Living and Working Wherever You Want,* and *Creating a Location-Independent Business.*

What was your work situation before you decided to go out on your own?

Both of our work backgrounds were firmly rooted in the corporate world; I was a management consultant and Jonathan was an in-house graphic designer.

I always knew I didn't want to end up as a management consultant but in the absence of knowing what else to do, not having a "big idea" for my own business, and getting trapped into that whole "big salary, couldn't possibly live without it" mindset, I didn't take the plunge until a life-changing event forced me to rethink everything. Jonathan has always dreamed of being a professional illustrator but likewise got caught up in the cycle of earning a salary and not going after his dreams.

When my mum died we both took leaves of absence, went traveling together and I hit upon the idea of becoming a personal trainer upon my return. So I duly qualified, set up my own business and was slowly growing it when Jonathan was let go from his job.

What led you to believe it was possible to "work from anywhere"?

When we first had the idea to do this, it was right after Jonathan had been laid off from his job and my business was still pretty new and not generating enough of an income to support us. Jonathan had never really thought of going freelance or running his own business, but we agreed that we no longer wanted to be at the mercy of an employer and we'd rather make our own decisions and be in control of our own future.

Having decided that, I was convinced that we didn't need to be paying such high prices for the lifestyle we were living in the UK and was very taken with the idea that if we were living somewhere with a far lower cost of living, then it wouldn't put so much pressure on our business to make much money. Once I'd convinced Jonathan that this was a great idea, we began to research where to go and how we could do it.

How did you simplify your life in order to be on the road so much?

We sold our apartment, got rid of a lot of our things, and then put the rest into as small a storage room as we could manage. We did come back to the UK after the first six months on the road and culled all our things again and moved into a smaller storage room; that passage of time helped remove some of the emotional ties to things we just didn't need anymore and couldn't see needing in our future.

After our first few destinations, we also realized that we rarely used half of the clothes or items we carried with us, so cut down that to a minimum too; we now travel as light as possible (often with no more than 30 kg between us). Our mindset these days is very much one of minimalism—if we need something, we can always buy it, but when we do, we ask ourselves how much we're likely to use it again in the future and whether we can live without it.

How do you choose where to live/work from?

At first it was determined largely by the weather and costs of living; but because the places we've lived in so far have been quite varied, we learn each time about what we do and don't like and therefore have a better idea about what to look for when we're choosing where to go next time.

From a practical perspective, there are certain things we always consider as a matter of course and priority:

- Internet access (vital for running our business)
- Language (we started off in a country where we didn't speak any of the language; we won't make that mistake again!)
- Cost of living (ideally we prefer it to be lower than we'd pay in the UK)
- Weather
- Visas and permits

How long do you plan on working this way? Ever considering "settling down"?

At the moment, we have no desire to stop what we're doing and change our lifestyle to settle down. We've thought about where we might settle but a big problem is that we don't know where we want to settle! Plus we both get bored of our surroundings easily and the nomadic lifestyle suits us way more than we thought it would.

So our standard answer is this: we'll stop when we feel like it and when we no longer enjoy it!

How has the financial side of this lifestyle been? Any lessons?

Plenty of lessons! Some of them are the usual business start-up lessons everyone probably learns; things like the importance of cash flow, learning to focus on profit, not just income, and how to set the right key performance indicators (KPIs) to measure your business performance.

Our lifestyle, however, has added some additional challenges such as having to manage the cash flow so we have the cash to pay three months' rent in advance all in one go, factoring in flight costs and the additional "setup" costs whenever you move to a new place.

Given that our initial objective of leading this kind of lifestyle was to help minimize outgoings, maintain the same quality of lifestyle and take the pressure off our relatively new business, I'd say we've largely achieved that; plus the freedom we feel to be able to move around to different countries (e.g. when the economy is challenged in one place or when our pipeline is slower and we need to live more cheaply) is a major benefit for us.

Tips for Evaluating the Location-Independent Lifestyle

Here are a few of their tips if you are considering a nomadic lifestyle:

1. Have you already done some traveling in your life and enjoyed it?
2. Do you yearn for a different culture/environment after staying in one place for too long?
3. Do you like challenging yourself?
4. Do you consider yourself to be flexible and adaptable?
5. Do you speak one or more foreign languages?
6. Do you have dependents to support or friends and family who rely on you?
7. Do you have the finances to support this lifestyle for at least six months without earning anything else?

8. Do you like your creature comforts and having your "things" around you?
9. Do you dislike constant change and always like to know where you're going to be next week?
10. Do you like routines and strict schedules?

(Lea and Jonathan share all kinds of information on their blog, locationindependent.com.)

You Can Always Stay Put

Starting your own business certainly does not mean that you have to give up your current life and move to the spare bedroom of your parents' home. But I hope that the entrepreneurs profiled here have stimulated your thinking a little bit, and given you some ideas for how to clean out, scale back, and perhaps relocate so that you have the space, time, and money required to start up your business without pressure. As my go-to Web consultant Paul Hyatt of Open Range Inc. told me after moving from San Diego, California, to Durango, Colorado, and finally settling in Wichita, Kansas:

> Decide your priorities, and where you live follows that. Now, some people believe where they live is their top priority. Obviously they would not consider moving! For the rest of us, I suggest that you do not get "boxed in" by your physical location. Do your homework before you move, make several visits. To get a jump-start on new friendships and relationships, visit churches, schools, grocery stores, parks (whatever activities you do in your current location), particularly as you narrow your list. Try to spend at least one extended visit in the worst time of the year weather-wise if you are going into an unfamiliar environment in that regard.[1]

9

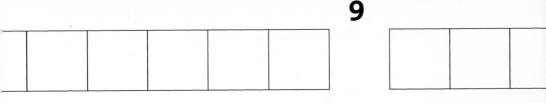

Do I Really Have to Do a Business Plan?

n 1994, while I was still an employee of a financial services firm, I took a class at the University of California at Berkeley about the business of training and development. My assignment was to imagine my dream business and write a business plan based on the Dr. Seuss book *If I Ran the Circus.*

My detailed plan was:

- Live in a cool Victorian house in San Francisco
- Sit on the back porch and sip lemonade in the summer and lattes in the winter
- Take a month off each year to travel to exotic parts of the world
- Work in the field of training and development
- Make money

I named my fictitious business Ganas Inc. *Ganas* is a word I learned in Mexico which means "the intense desire to do something, inner motivation, exuberance and drive." That was how I wanted to feel about my work, and how I wanted my clients to feel as a result of having worked with me.

Two years later when I went out on my own as a consultant, I needed to get a business license and a business name. I vaguely remembered my "business plan," so I pulled it out of the drawer and dusted it off. Wow, I thought, *Ganas*—that's a great name! So that's what I called my company. The bullet points in my "business plan" looked good, so I opened my door for business. And never looked back.

With this flimsy structure, I should have been doomed to failure and chased back into life as an employee within a month.

Ironically, my business thrived for over a decade.

I lived in a Victorian in San Francisco, drank lemonade in the summer and lattes in the winter. I led month-long tours to Brazil each year. I worked with large companies all throughout the United States and Europe in the field of training and development. I made money.

I lucked out—I had highly marketable skills in a ripe, juicy part of the world: Silicon Valley in 1996. And I was not afraid of networking and marketing, having run a highly successful nonprofit organization on a volunteer basis for ten years. I was very good at what I did, and used that to build a referral-only business.

Is a Business Plan Really Necessary?

After hearing stories like mine, many people ask: Is a business plan really necessary? Short answer: Absolutely not.

What they should ask is: Is business *planning* really necessary? Short answer: Absolutely.

Think of it in terms of this metaphor: you decide to build your own home.

Option A: You are not sure which materials to order, so you grab what you have available. You don't know any architects or professional builders, so you just wing it and build it the way that feels good. You don't worry about electrical codes or plumbing standards, since wading through lots of dense manuals feels overwhelming.

Option B: Working with trusted advisers, you put together the design of a house that matches your aesthetics and will withstand your local climate and soil composition. You don't worry about doing everything yourself, you focus on what you are good at and hire out the rest. At each stage of the project, you bring in the city inspectors and make sure your house is up to code.

Which house would you rather sleep in during a heat wave? A windstorm? A flood? An earthquake? Business planning expert Tim Berry says: "Planning isn't about writing some ponderous homework assignment or dull business memo; it's about envisioning the business that you want to create. It should be fascinating to you. What do people want, how are you going to get it to them, how are you different and what do you do better than anyone else?"[1]

The goal of planning is not to impress your old college professor. It is to bring your vague, optimistic, dreamy ideas into the land of the living.

Is There Any "There" There?

In earlier chapters, you worked hard to identify the kind of business that would be energizing and meaningful. You may have a few different ideas that you want to start to examine closely and see if there is any "there" there.

When you start to do this concrete planning and examination of your business idea, you will end up with one of two emotions:

- Growing excitement that your idea does indeed have merit in the real world
- Growing dread that your big idea is destined to be an expensive hobby

Either feeling is exactly what you want to get out of the experience of business planning. If you find once you run specific numbers that you would make a minuscule profit on your product, or that your market is so small that it would not be able to sustain an ongoing business, or that implementing your grand vision would take more money than you could shake down your relatives for, you will be able to gently put the idea to rest.

But sometimes we still resist.

I was talking with a client the other day and asked her to move forward and do some planning so she could understand if her idea would make any money. I could feel her hesitation.

"What are you afraid of?" I asked.

"I am afraid that once I see real numbers I will realize that I will not be able to make any money with this idea, and this breaks my heart since I love it so much."

I was obliged to bring out my often-used dating metaphor, even though both of us are happily married.

Dating Before Marriage

Imagine that your business idea is like the "perfect guy" that you had a mad crush on in seventh grade. You know the one, who always looked so cool in his tight jeans and T-shirt, headband and long hair (hey, I grew up in the seventies).

Flash forward twenty years and you see him sitting in a coffee shop. You are still single, and he appears to be as well, since you can't see a ring on his finger. He still has that slight rebel look, but updated with a nice watch and freshly pressed shirt. You are intrigued.

What is the best thing to do at this point? Walk up and talk to him and see if he indeed is the man of your dreams, or scurry off like an insecure teenager, fantasizing about the imaginary children you would have together?

Some people like to stay in fantasyland for a long time, imagining all the great things that will happen once they start a business. But they never look any closer, afraid to lose their dream.

This perspective will really slow you down and keep you from the adventure of pursuing a real and fruitful business opportunity.

So go ahead and date. Find out all you can about the business idea—is it interesting? Important? Useful? Practical? Dependable? Is it going to run off with your best friend after stealing your credit cards? If it isn't more than eye candy, let the fantasy go and move on.

Conversation with Business Planning Guru Tim Berry

Tim Berry is the founder of Palo Alto Software, regular columnist for entrepreneur blogs, and the author of many books about business planning, most recently *The Plan as You Go Business Plan*.

In the many decades you have worked with people trying to write business plans, what are some of the main reasons that people give for not doing them?

What people normally say is "Yes, I'm going to tomorrow," or "next month," or "six months from now." And then there's the variant on that, "Yes, I really agree it's stupid that we don't have a business plan and so-and-so has been promising to write it for years." So they pass the buck. The perception we fight is that writing a business plan is like writing a PhD dissertation. I don't blame people for thinking, "No, I'm too busy. I don't have time for that. I've got to run my business."

What should a business plan be for somebody who has never done one before?

I want to resist the temptation to say: "It starts with . . ." since I don't like the idea that a business plan has to be sequential. The core business plan is how you're different, what you're doing for the people who spend money with you. It's strategy related to target market focus and product focus and generally understanding what you're doing and what you're not doing. And I mean "strategy" with a small s not a big s. It's not academic, it's *What meaning do we make for our customers?* As our customers are walking down the street, far away from us, talking with each other, what are they going to say about us? That's the core of the business plan, what I call the "heart."

Then the flesh and the bones of the plan are a collection of what's going to happen, when, who's going to do it, how much is it going to cost, how much is it going to generate.

(continued)

For corporate employees pondering a business, where do you suggest they start with the business plan?

My first suggestion would be that they choose a place to start that suits them. People are different. I've seen people get going by starting with a mission or a mantra. But I've also known people who have done a beautiful job of planning starting with the numbers. I've seen people start a business plan with a sales forecast. The key here is to find what suits you and get going.

Let's say someone had two different business ideas: one that has a pretty good chance of making money quickly and one that was a little bit harder to sell but that inspires them greatly. How would you counsel them as to which idea they should start with?

I would ask them to look into it, pulling apart the uncertainties and seeing how they can make that second business that they believe in work better than the first. I think there are fatal flaws probably in the comparison of the two businesses and they really ought to go back to the drawing board and refocus, find another angle. If the one they love is brokering mortgages and we're in a subprime housing crisis, then maybe they can find a way to help people who are about to be foreclosed and find a different but related continuous closed market.

If they stay with what they know and what they like, that's going to give a better long-term chance of success. Sometimes you need to step away from it so you can see how you might be missing something that people really want and need a little bit more.

When people are starting a new business, often they feel uncomfortable limiting their market because they feel they are shutting down opportunities. What is your perspective on that?

There's that common reaction of "No, no, no, but everybody wants this." Well, yes, but you can't do business based on everybody. I try to talk about displacement. In small business, displacement is a critical principle that I think is poorly understood. And what that means is that everything you do rules out something else that you can't do. So you're

stuck with trying to focus on what's most important and the narrower
the market, the easier it is to get there. You want to really know your
target customer.

Why are assumptions an important part of a business plan?
Well, one of the worst myths in business planning is that there's some
value in following a plan just because you're following a plan. In fact,
there's huge value in planning even though there's constant change and
planning is frequently being corrected and reviewed and revised. So assumptions, then, are the foundation of a process of reviewing and revis-
ing. Assumptions are what you use to manage the difficult paradox that
sometimes you have to stick with the plan because it's taking more time
and the plan is fundamentally sound; sometimes you have to have the
vision to abandon what you thought you were going to do because it
isn't working and there's no algorithm, there's nothing they teach in
business schools to tell you which time is which.[2]

The Parts of a Business Plan

Here is my summary of the key parts of a business plan. The important
thing is to dig in and get more information about the viability of your idea.

Save Yourself from the Tyranny of Sequence

As Tim described in his interview, and also in *The Plan as You Go Business
Plan*, it is less overwhelming to view a business plan in "blocks." He says:
"The blocks idea also saves you from the tyranny of sequence. You don't
have to start at the beginning and work through to the end. You can jump
in and start wherever you want."

- **Mission statement maybe?** Define for yourself what your company will
  do for its customers, for its employees, and for its owners. Mission

statements are a bit last-century, perhaps doomed forever to Dilbert-related derision, but that's still where some people start.

- **Maybe you're a numbers person.** That's okay, don't apologize—business planning needs that too. I was a literature major in college but I still like to start my business planning with a sales forecast. Then I'll do some conceptual work, then go back to costs and expenses, classic budgeting work, then back to basics.
- **Business plans have hearts, like artichokes.** Their hearts are their core, the best part. I thought of this analogy when somebody I know and respect suggested that the heart of a business plan is the marketing plan, meaning its identity, positioning, differentiation, the sense of what business you're in and why people will buy from you. That's a great place to start.
- **Some plans start with a product or prototype.** Maybe your first block is a bill of materials for manufacturing the new thing. That's okay too; that's a block, you can jump in there.
- **There are lots more blocks.** The mantra. The vision. A market analysis. A market forecast. Personnel strategy. Financial strategy. Some people like to build an equity plan first, defining how many shares exist, how many the founders get and how many the investors get.[3]

The Heart of Your Plan

Element	Description
Your business identity	• How are you different from others? • What are your strengths and weaknesses? • What is your core competence? • What are your goals?
Your market	• Who are your customers? • Why do they buy from you? • What do they want and need? • What business are you really in?
Strategic focus	• Since you can't do everything well, what do you do that is unique to you? • What do you sell?

The Flesh and Bones

Element	Description
Assumptions	• All assumptions about your business including market size, conditions, constraints, and opportunities
Review schedule	• Specific times when you will review your plan to see how reality meshes with projections. The key is to make plan reviews a key part of how you run your business, not an extra chore.
Metrics	• Tangible metrics like sales, costs, expenses, taxes, interest, profitability, assets, liabilities, capital and "soft" metrics like customers, deliveries, complaints, calls, presentations, meals, people served
Who does what	• Description of organization, team, roles and responsibilities • If you will be the only person in your business, still describe your key responsibilities, and describe other ways you might use outside resources for specific tasks.
Timeline	• Milestones and associated deliverables with specific dates
Costs	• Budgets, cash flow projections

The Body

Many people get stuck when thinking about how to document the business planning process. Here are some guidelines:

- **Make it easy.** If you are a PowerPoint wizard, stick with that format and build your plan on slides. If Word or Excel are more your style, use those applications. They key is to use tools that are familiar and comfortable.
- **Use blank templates if that speeds things up.** Business planning software or books may have some templates that you can use to organize your thoughts.

- **Make it yours.** If you are more of a creative type, you may be interested in a totally different business planning format created by Laura West called The Joyful Business Guide™.

The important thing is that you start to plan, and capture your thoughts in an easy-to-understand and easy-to-update format.

Your Market

As a coach, I probably spend 50 percent of my time working with my clients on defining their target market. This is so exceptionally important since it is the area that most people get wrong when starting a business.

- They are deathly afraid of turning away anyone, so they cling desperately to the notion that their product or service would be good for anyone with a credit card and a pulse.
- They feel resistant to lock into a specific market since they enjoy working with all kinds of people on all kinds of projects.
- By trying to market to everyone, they water down their message, and in their attempt to reach everyone, end up appealing to no one.

I am not heavy-handed in most of my coaching and advice. But on this topic of choosing a niche, I draw a line in the sand. Just do it.

An Inch Wide and a Mile Deep

Branding expert Suzanne Falter-Barns once told me that you want to choose a niche an inch wide and a mile deep. I understood the general concept, but it wasn't until I stumbled upon a book one day that I saw the power of what she was talking about.

KNITTING HUMOR

A blog reader told me in a comment on one of my posts on marketing that there is a whole group of people out there that are interested in *knitting humor*. I had to read the term twice to make sure I wasn't misunderstanding it.

Read this partial description of famed writer (in knitting humor circles at least) Stephanie Pearl-McPhee's latest book, *Knitting Rules: The Yarn Harlot's Bag of Knitting Tricks*:

> The best-selling author of *At Knit's End: Meditations for Women Who Knit Too Much* and celebrated blogger and humorist of the knitting world, is back! Funnier than ever, Pearl-McPhee continues her running dialogue with her knitting compatriots—cheering them on to ever-greater heights in the climb to make knitting universally recognized as THE peak life experience.
>
> In chapters on everything from yarn needles, gauge, and knitting bag essentials to hats, socks, shawls, and sweaters, Pearl-McPhee unravels the mysteries of what it is that makes knitting click, from the inside out. She dares to question longstanding rules and uncover the true essence of what makes a hat a hat, a sock a sock, and so on. Insights into why certain techniques work encourage knitters to take control and knit in the way that works best for them. As she says, "There are no knitting police."

Wow, I never thought to question what makes a hat a hat or a sock a sock. Nor did I think of knitting as THE peak life experience. Apparently, about 300,000 people would disagree with me. I guess they like to be in stitches. (See? Knitting humor!)

Do you see now how absurd your concern would be about narrowing your market to just "women" or even "crafty women"? In the massive market of crafty women, there are probably a thousand subniches like *vegan weavers who love too much*.

I even found a subversive crafters' market: *The Anti-Scrapbooking Moms Online Magazine*.

Craft wars, knitting humor, subversive moms online. Who knew there was so much depth to a niche?

Slice and Dice

To find your particular piece of the market, you need to start narrowing down the people you want to work with.

You can call this group whatever you want. Some prefer "target market," others "my people" or "my niche." You can call them your peeps, your homies, or your crew. The term doesn't matter; defining its characteristics does.

Here are some ideas:

- **Life situation** (first job, retiring, changing career, surviving breast cancer, losing weight, etc.)
- **Demographic** (African American females, residents of New York City, gay former firefighters turned circus acrobats, etc.)
- **Psychographic** (optimistic, sassy, resilient, motivated)
- **Common interest, affiliation** (raging liberals, Ann Coulter conservatives, tree huggers, salsa dancing enthusiasts, etc.)
- **Income level** (low, middle, or high income)
- **Challenge or issue** (hopeless procrastinator, arrogant bastard, parents of ADD child, etc.)
- **Which problems do they face?**
    Want to start a business but don't know how and are afraid (sound familiar?)
    Need help raising out-of-control teenager
    Can't seem to get financial life together and have raging debt

Let's look at an example:

Broad market segment: Men

Niche: Divorced African American male entrepreneurs aged fifty to fifty-five who graduated summa cum laude from a top ten college, make more than $250,000/year, and live in the greater New York area.

The more specific you get with your niche, the better chance you have to reach them with your marketing efforts. And you can further define your niche by asking the following question: *Who would I really enjoy working with who would find my product or service extremely valuable and have the means to pay for it?*

The benefits of defining a specific niche are many:

- You can immediately think of publications that write for this market, and target your PR efforts.

- You can identify which associations might cater to this market (in my example, you could explore alumni associations of top ten colleges or entrepreneur associations that target African American professionals) and try to get speaking gigs.
- You can identify Web sites or blogs that target this market and post ads or write valuable comments on blogs.
- You can be very specific in your marketing materials about the type of problems your product or service addresses. And if you do it right, people will say things like "I read your Web site and felt like you were talking directly to me!"

Basically, if you need to start getting some clients, would you rather stare at your phone and try to figure out how you will reach "women," or how you can reach the Association of Retired Disgruntled Postmasters in Glendale, Arizona?

Planning Tricks and Tips

You can be committed to the planning process, but still struggle when it comes to defining specific products or services to add to your business model. It can also be hard to figure out the right mix of services that will match both your income expectations and your lifestyle requirements. These tips will help you with this part of the planning process.

Trick #1: The Money Game

As a new business owner, it can be kind of overwhelming to figure out how to meet your annual revenue targets.

In the midst of pages and pages of notes, research, business plan drafts, and product ideas, you can get very stuck.

So set aside your MBA and PhD-trained minds for a minute, and play along with a game of math. If you laugh mockingly in a Dr. Evil kind of way at the simplicity of the concept, I can only share the following nugget:

Common sense is rarely common practice.

My favorite coaching mentor, Andrea Lee, describes a very simple process for figuring out revenue targets in her book *Multiple Streams of Coaching Income*. This book is built on the premise that thriving coaches (and consultants, or any service-based business) need to develop multiple streams of revenue besides their hourly consulting time. These additional streams can be things like group coaching programs, electronic books (e-books), teleclasses, membership Web sites, and a whole variety of other things.

Her process is called "The Money Game." You will need the following things:

> a pad of paper
> a pencil
> or, if you are fancy, a spreadsheet

Now take the following steps:

1. Write your annual income goal at the top of the page. It doesn't matter if it is $10,000 or $100,000 this year. There is no right or wrong answer.
2. Create three columns on your page.
3. In column 1, list your products or services.
4. In column 2, list the cost of each product or service.
5. In column 3, list how many units you think you can sell of each product or service.

The game comes into play as you begin to juggle around the mixture of what you want to offer. So in example one, you imagine one mix of services and products.

Income Goal:	$100,000		
Services	**Cost**	**# Sold**	**Total**
Consulting	$150.00	20	$3,000.00
E-book	$37.00	100	$3,700.00
Monthly teleclass	$19.00	20	$380.00

Income Goal:	$100,000		
Services	**Cost**	**# Sold**	**Total**
Monthly Web site membership fee	$27.00	50	$1,350.00
		Monthly Income	$8,430.00
		Annual Income	$101,160.00

After review, you may feel like it is wildly optimistic to sell one hundred e-books a month, so you revise your estimates downward to a more reasonable number. You may also want to increase your monthly consulting hours, as you think it will be easier to sell consulting than products at first. Then you might decrease the number of new members to your paid membership site, but increase the monthly fee.

Services	**Cost**	**# Sold**	**Total**
Consulting	$150.00	40	$6,000.00
E-book	$37.00	35	$1,295.00
Monthly teleclass	$19.00	20	$380.00
Monthly Web site membership fee	$47.00	20	$940.00
		Monthly Income	$8,615.00
		Annual Income	$103,380.00

Thinking some more, you choose to add two new programs to the mix: a once-a-year live retreat for your clients, and a group telephone-coaching program held twice a year. Knowing it will take time to develop and promote these programs, you decrease your consulting hours.

Services	Cost	# Sold	Total
Consulting	$150.00	13	$1,950.00
E-book	$37.00	35	$1,295.00
Monthly teleclass	$19.00	20	$380.00
Monthly Web site membership fee	$47.00	20	$940.00
		Monthly Income	**$4,565.00**
1x/year live retreat	$1500.00	20	$30,000.00
2x/year phone coaching program	$850.00	20	$17,000.00
		Annual Income	**$101,780.00**

The possibilities are endless. The key is to keep juggling the numbers around until you reach a mix of products and services that feels comfortable and feasible for you to accomplish.

You can play the Money Game as you launch your business, and revisit it every month or quarter. You may decide to add or remove products. You may decide to launch a new program. The key is to break your large annual financial goal into realistic pieces.

The more concrete you are, the more likely it is that you will reach your goals.

Trick #2: Tips on Pricing

How do you know what to charge for your professional services?

By professional services I mean things like coaching, consulting, financial advising, writing, and Web design. Basically, any gig where you sell your knowledge for a fee.

Why is pricing so tricky?

Pricing your services is tricky because there is no magic formula or "correct" answer. I see four distinct parts of the pricing equation: psychological demons, practical needs, external market, and financial results.

PART ONE: PSYCHOLOGICAL DEMONS

To be able to charge decent rates for your services, you have to feel confident about your skills and talents. Herein lies the rub for new entrepreneurs, since you are either offering your services on a freelance basis for the first time, or doing something totally new. Suggestion: Fortify your self-esteem. However you need to, validate that you are indeed good enough, smart enough, and people like you.

- Ask trusted colleagues to give you objective feedback about your skills and past business results.
- Repeat affirmations such as "My relationship advice will create harmony in thousands of homes across the world" or "I am meant to help people overcome their shame over poor financial management" or whatever saying rings true for you. Far from just being fodder for comedians like Al Franken with his character Stuart Smalley, affirmations can truly heal a fractured self-image.
- Invest in training and advice for yourself at the same rate you plan on charging clients. This is really important! By doing so, you will feel in your bones what it is like to spend some of your hard-earned cash on professional advice. If you are not willing to invest in your own growth and development, how can you expect your clients to?

PART TWO: PRACTICAL NEEDS

A common error made by new entrepreneurs is not to take into consideration all of the expenses related to working for themselves when setting hourly rates. Most people take their annual salary and divide it into hourly increments. What this approach misses is:

- Your annual salary as an employee is based on working full-time. Unless you have excellent luck and get full-time contract work immediately, chances are you won't be working full-time your first year as an entrepreneur. Nor may you want to work full-time, as billable consulting hours tend to be much more draining than the "padded hours" you get as a salaried employee. I never worked more than two-thirds time as a consultant, since I had to spend the rest of the time catching up on administration, marketing, and relaxing.

- Your salary doesn't include your benefits like health insurance, retirement investments, vacations, and sick time. An extremely crude general estimate for these things in the United States is 30 percent of your salary.

Suggestions:

- Review your summary of the value of employee benefits.
- Create a spreadsheet to account for all of your expenses as a self-employed person. To get ideas for what to include, look at FreelanceSwitch.com's handy Rates Calculator.

PART THREE: EXTERNAL MARKET

Knowing what you need to make to cover your living expenses is only part of the equation. You also have to know the competitive range for similar services.

Early in my career, I was negotiating the salary for a new position. I asked a very seasoned female mentor for her advice. "What are you thinking of asking for an annual salary?" she said. "All I need is about $50,000 a year," I replied. She said, "The most common mistake I see females make in negotiating salary is just thinking about their basic needs and no more. You must charge what the market will bear, especially on par with your male counterparts. If you don't, they will lose respect for you."

I grimaced a little bit and said, "I don't want to become one of those greedy businesspeople who only thinks about money. I don't just work for the paycheck, I also do it to contribute something meaningful to the world."

"Here is the key," she said. "You must charge the market rate or more, but you can give it all away."

This floored me. I was raised to live modestly and to reduce, reuse, and recycle. I had the idea that anyone who made a lot of money was automatically greedy and selfish. Suddenly, I realized that the more money I made, the more I had at my disposal to invest in the community, pursue artistic passions, travel, and help others in need. It totally changed how I viewed money.

Suggestions:

- Survey your competitors to get a range of fees for similar services.
- Ask a couple of trusted colleagues about their pricing strategy. When I recently had to put together a proposal for a blogging project, I e-mailed two of the smartest bloggers I knew and asked about their pricing. Hearing both what they charged and what the fees included was extremely helpful.

PART FOUR: FINANCIAL RESULTS

I saved this for last, but it is by far the most important part of the pricing equation. People don't pay you for your time or process, they pay you for the results of your work. These results are translated into value, which can be money or time saved or earned, brand value increased or risk reduced. My friend Skip Miller summed it up well: "When clients give you money, guess what? They want it back!"

It is your job to identify and quantify metrics. This is not simply to justify your fees, it is also to make sure that what you provide is useful and will have a positive impact on your client. Here is value pricing in action:

I had a friend who did a presentation for 250 sales representatives from a large computer company. He charged $30,000 for two hours of his time. After wondering how he was able to hypnotize his client before signing the contract, I asked him how he justified such a fee. "Easy," he said. "Each rep has a minimum of $300,000 worth of business in their annual sales funnel. I have proven that by using my techniques, you can close a minimum of 10 percent more deals. So if *one* of the 250 participants does what I tell him, they will recoup their money. If 25 percent of them do, they will make nearly two million dollars. In reality, I charged too little."

Can you see how solely relying on your practical financial needs and the norms of the market can skew your pricing model? By focusing on results and value, you will not only be able to charge more, you will do better work because you will be defining and measuring the right things.

Suggestions:

- As you are discussing the project with your client, define success metrics. Ask them, "How will you know that our work together was effective?"

They should say things like "I will get more clients" or "I will deliver better presentations" or "I will improve my credit score" or "I will capture more names on my mailing list from my Web site visitors."

- From these broad results, dig deeper and ask, "And what would that mean to you in terms of money, time, or risk?" You should hear things like "If I deliver more effective presentations, I will get more referrals which will increase my income by X percent," or "If I improve my credit score, I will qualify for a loan which will allow me to start my business and make $5,000 a month." You must dig until you get some tangible metrics.

Once you have a good baseline for your prices that takes into account these four factors, you can create some standard pricing that will act as a starting point for new contracts.

Trick #3: Plotting Milestones for the Year

What activities are you going to do when? When is a product going to ship or a service launch?

An easy way to create a general timeline is to make a grid with four squares, one for each quarter of the year. You can use a piece of paper that is flipchart size and use Post-it notes to mark major milestones.

Plot the milestones in each quarter. Then step back, do some rearranging, and create your final plan.

Trick #4: Recommendations for Cash Flow Management

These tips come from Denise O'Berry, author of *Small Business Cash Flow: Strategies for Making Your Business a Financial Success.*

If you don't have cash flow in your business, you don't have a business. Yes, cash really is king for a small business. Here are five things you must do to manage the cash flow in your business.

1. Understand how cash works in your business. Know that profit does not equal cash flow because assets and liabilities play a big part in your bottom line.

2. Don't sell yourself short. Make sure you charge the best price for what you offer. Consider value based pricing and packaged services to get what you deserve. Resist an hourly fee structure; it's a dead end road. You should charge just the right price for what your target market will tolerate.

3. Remember, you are not a bank. Don't let your invoices become idle or your accounts receivable grow. You must have money coming into your business to survive.

4. Save cash for a rainy day. It's tempting to go out and make a big purchase when you collect a large amount of money that you worked so hard for. Don't do it. Maintain a cash cushion in your business to help you through the valleys.

5. Prepare (and use) a Cash Flow Budget. A budget is the financial road map for your business and will help guide your business decision making. It should project out at least six months to give you time to plan, react to, and accommodate conditions that impact your business so you can adjust accordingly.[4]

Your Marketing System

Marketing is the fuel that powers your company. Many people tend to think about marketing as a series of isolated activities: you send an e-mail to announce a workshop, then you give a talk to your local Rotary Club, then you jump on Facebook and look up a few groups that share your interests.

Each of these approaches yields a few clients and you begin to generate some business. You relax your marketing, because you are so busy running around getting work done that you don't have time for much else.

Until you finish your projects and your customers go away. So you quickly throw together another bunch of marketing activities to drum up clients.

If you approach marketing in this haphazard way, you will never get a predictable flow of clients or customers. Marketing must be structured, systematic, and consistent.

I lean on three small business marketing experts for advice, each of whom offers unique and valuable insights into small business marketing:

- **John Jantsch,** founder of Duct Tape Marketing and expert blogger—www .ducttapemarketing.com
- **Robert Middleton,** expert on independent service professional marketing—www.actionplan.com
- **Michael Port,** expert on "thinking big" and business marketing systems—www.michaelport.com

All of them have excellent, systematic approaches to marketing. Visit each site and see who fits your niche and needs best. Then move forward and do what they say.

I Don't Have Time for Marketing

JOHN JANTSCH, DUCT TAPE MARKETING BLOG

The preposterous sounding title of this post is a direct quote from the lips of many a small business owner I have encountered. The root of this problem of course can be summed up nicely in something known as Parkinson's Law.

Parkinson's Law is the adage that "work expands so as to fill the time available for its completion." It was first articulated by Cyril Northcote Parkinson, appearing as the first sentence of a humorous essay published in *The Economist* in 1955.

The Law is as alive and well in the small business as it may be in the halls of the largest bureaucracy on the planet. So, the key to effective marketing may simply be a matter of defining the right work to fill up the time available.

Marketing is and must become a habitual activity in your business. You must live by the marketing calendar or die by the lack of time available to complete the greasing of the squeaky wheel.

The only way to find time for marketing is to plan for it. Create a marketing theme for every month of the year and then build marketing activities on a daily and weekly basis around the theme.

You know you need to be sending out more press releases and building relationships with key journalists in your industry—make that September's theme and do it. You know you need to build a network of strategic partners to make your referral leads really soar—make that October's theme. You know you need a blog, you need to start blogging as a part of your Internet presence—make that November's theme.

Create the biggest, most hard to ignore wall calendar you can find and post your year of marketing themes. Then break each month down into the action steps needed to make progress on the monthly theme. Finally, assign yourself or someone on your team daily action steps, appointments really, and then complete the daily marketing action before you pass Go or return another email.

That's how you make time for marketing, that's how you build marketing momentum and that's how you make marketing expand to fill the time available for its completion.[5]

Obsession with the Competition is a Luxury of the Overfunded

Any business-minded consultant or entrepreneur will tell you that you need to know about your competition when you do your business plan. It is an important part of understanding your market and differentiating yourself from the rest of the herd.

But some business owners get so focused on every move a competitor makes that they completely lose focus on their own business. At the extreme, it is not only distracting, it is downright self-destructive.

I lived through an example of this working with a very talented artist and dance instructor in the 1990s. He was creatively brilliant and a gifted teacher. But he was completely obsessed with other instructors in the area and would fly into a rage if a student from his school left to join another school. At a certain point, he was as focused on studying, subverting, and badmouthing the competition as he was on creating new art and building his own school.

I learned a number of lessons from this experience, and many others like it, working with entrepreneurs:

- When you shift focus from understanding who your competitors are to spending half your time thinking about them, you have ceded your own power. In essence, you are choosing the role of follower and not leader. Focus on what is exciting, special, unique, and revolutionary about *your* own business.
- No matter how much expertise and experience you have, if your market is worth operating in, there will always be a worthy competitor. Rather than fight it, constantly look for ways that you can reshape and refine your business to match your greatest strengths and better serve your customers. If you find that there is nowhere to grow or innovate, maybe you are operating in an overripe market and should look for a new one to play in.
- No matter how secure you feel, a competitor will come along that pushes a personal button because they are smarter, younger, richer, better-looking, or more charismatic than you are. This is where you have a chance to put into practice what they say about the best lovers: they are most often not the suave and good-looking sports all-stars, they are the quiet, unassuming, average-looking people who develop their "skills" based on reading and responding to the needs of their object of affection. Don't let your own insecurities run away from you and cloud your business judgment. Celebrate your unique strengths and know that you are perfect just the way you are.
- Coercing customers to stay with you based on badmouthing competitors will always backfire. People like to feel they are free to make a choice about where to spend their time and money. And like a first date with a man who spews venom about his ex-wife, they will wonder how long it will take before you start spewing your venom at them. The more open and secure you are about your own business, the more secure your customers will feel with you and the more likely they will stick around. Remember, if you truly want to serve your customers, you have to realize that at certain times your competitors may be a better fit. As Sting says, "When you love someone, set them free."

- There will be times when a competitor does something that feels unethical or mean or just plain shifty. If it directly impacts your business or reputation, you must address the issue quickly and appropriately. But once it is handled, go back to focusing on the needs of your customers. If it involves legal matters, you must weigh carefully the return on investment of your time, energy, and money to resolve the issue in the courts. Play out the two scenarios: If you win, will it make your business stronger and better able to serve the needs of your customers? If you lose, will you have a business to salvage? I think we often engage in legal battles more to punish the offending person than to achieve a desired business outcome. Don't worry about punishment . . . karma takes care of that for you.
- There is nothing wrong with competition—it is all how you react to it. A business-building reaction to a strong competitor would be thinking, "So you want to amp up this game? Bring it on, bucko, I can handle anything you throw my way." A business-destroying reaction to a strong competitor would be: "No one does that to me and gets away with it. I will crush you and everyone who supports you to prove that I am the best."

If you are Intel, you may have an army of lawyers and consultants to track and monitor every move AMD makes. If you operate in a niche desired by Larry Ellison, you should watch your back, as you never know when he will feel like flattening your business by landing on it with one of his noisy jets.

But if you are Jane the Dog Walker with a small practice in Boise, Idaho, or Matthew the Marketing Genius in Boston, Massachusetts, your real focus should be on studying and understanding the feelings, aspirations, problems, and desires of your target audience. When you do this, you will naturally grow your business in the right direction, and serve your people in a way that makes them feel truly special. And you will enjoy your life a whole lot more.

Make Sure There Is Water in the Pool Before You Jump

Spending time planning your business, defining your market, and setting up regular marketing activities is time very well spent.

As you will find out in chapter 11, you don't need to have an extensive business plan in place before you can start testing ideas.

But getting in the habit of regular planning will give you a much clearer picture of the health of your potential business.

As my friend Skip Miller used to say to his sales training students:

"Make sure there is water in the pool before you jump!"

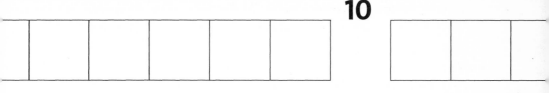

10

Define the Spirit of Your Brand

About fifteen years ago, I lived in San Francisco and owned a Honda Civic. It was my first brand-new car, and I was eager to take good care of it. So I started looking around for a mechanic.

I was not looking forward to the selection process, since my experience to date had been really unpleasant. Since I don't know a whole lot about cars, I braced myself to be sold unnecessary services by unscrupulous shop owners.

Then someone told me about Pat's Garage.

Nestled in the technology and industry-heavy South of Market neighborhood was a Honda shop called Pat's Garage. On the outside, it looked like any other auto shop, with the requisite big sign and grease spots in the driveway.

As soon as I stepped inside, I knew it was a special place. Pat and his staff were welcoming, open, and nonthreatening.

Their office walls were filled with art pieces and postcards from happy customers. The closest thing to a blonde in a bikini on the wall was a picture of Hillary Clinton in S&M garb. I don't remember the exact message behind the parody, but it was in good taste and not disparaging of either Hillary or women in general.

And the best part? Really, really great coffee. Not the watered-down Folgers crap that you find at most shops, but jet fuel grade, organic and flavorful coffee. Served in real mugs.

The more I got to know Pat, the more I was fascinated by his story of creating a totally unique and valuable business in a crowded niche. He once told me, "My business is not really about cars, it is about people. When I focus on my customers and their needs and concerns, my business thrives." He chose to service Hondas because "I like the kind of people that drive Hondas. In general, they are nice, funny, down-to-earth, and environmentally aware."

The home page of his Web site describes the spirit of his brand well: "Located in San Francisco's burgeoning Third Street Corridor, Pat's Garage is dedicated to providing the best service and advice for Hondas, Acuras, Subarus, and Hybrids. We've been in business for 28,000 years, and besides cultivating an obsession for the technical aspects of our work, we believe in the power of community, education, and strong coffee."

His business is offbeat, vibrant, welcoming, and delivers excellent technical and customer service. His mechanics are dreamers, poets, artists, and writers, in addition to being experts in their technical field. And Pat is one of the most talented managers I have ever met, and I have met thousands of them in every business you can imagine.

Pat embodies exactly what I mean by the *spirit of a brand:*

- He provides value to a specific, defined niche.
- His personality clearly shows up in every part of his business, from the message on his answering machine to his Web site to the quality of his work to his physical location.
- He inspires trust, enthusiasm, and evangelism in every one of his customers. You walk away after working with Pat and not only feel great having given him money, but want to tell twelve of your friends about his auto shop.
- He attracts a great team. He values and supports his employees better than most leaders I've met in entrepreneurial and corporate settings. He once told me, after explaining how he was paying for his mechanic to take a day off a week to take an art class, "When you learn what is impor-

tant to people who work for you and support that, no matter if it is related to the work they do for you, they will be happier. That translates into better work and natural loyalty."

From "All About Me" to "All About Them"

The most powerful way to connect with the people you are meant to serve is by talking in their language.

This will solve the problem of coming up with copy that makes you sound important like:

> For the last twenty years, Jim has been a leader in innovating creative solutions for his corporate clients, who all think he is the smartest consultant they have ever met. His numerous degrees from Stanford make him qualified to talk about all kinds of things....

No wonder you want to hurl when you write things like this. Instead, think about this "flash of branding insight" from author Tom Asacker:

THE FLASH OF BRAND INSIGHT

Who am I? What is my brand?

Me.

What is my promise, personality, and positioning?

Me. Me.

What do I want to say? How should I say it?

Me. Me. Me.

If only I can get the details right. If only I can discover my essence.

Me. Me. Me. Me.

■

BAM!

■

I wonder who they are.

Them.

I wonder what they're doing.

(continued)

Them. Them.

I wonder how they're feeling.

Them. Them. Them.

I wonder how I can make life better for them and make them feel better about themselves.

Them. Them. Them. Them.[1]

Common Brand Mistakes

Happy Fluffy Terms

I realize that I may offend some of my peers with my sarcastic subhead, but I simply must tell you that your "Happy! Fluffy! Be all you can be! Live your best life!" marketing copy is really irritating. It is as if you had toilet paper hanging out of the back of your pants after leaving a public restroom. It would be irresponsible for me not to mention it.

The reason it is so important is that people generally don't go searching for "how to live their best life." They look for help with problems—how to get out of debt, heal their marriage, make their computer work, spend more time with their kids.

I had a great experience with this when working with a coaching client on her brand. We started brainstorming ideas and this is the dialogue that ensued:

"I am really excited by the phrase 'stop and smell the roses,'" she said. "Is that a good brand position?"

I bit my tongue. Then I asked: "What does 'stop and smell the roses' mean to you?"

"It means taking time to be in the present, to take time to enjoy your life instead of just rushing through your life."

"And why is that important?"

"People who pause and breathe seem to feel that they are really participating in life, not just sleeping through life."

"What happens to people when they are really participating in life?"

"They get more pleasure; they seem to be happier and more fulfilled."

"And then what happens?"

"They are more successful in their life. They are happy." Then she paused. "They seem to have fewer regrets."

I suddenly got the chills. *Regret.* That is a powerful word.

She continued: "I am working with a lot of men now. Their concern is 'I don't want to be the dad in the "Cat's in the Cradle" song—I know I need to be with my kids, but I am scared, and I want to provide.'"

I sat back in my chair and my heart started beating really hard. For a forty-two-year-old person like me, and anyone who grew up listening to this song, you will know immediately what I am talking about. I cannot listen to this song without getting tears in my eyes.

The message, the emotion, the *regret* in this song shoots right through the heart of men who care about their careers *and* their kids. So I asked her: "What do you think would speak to men in their forties and fifties more, 'stop and smell the roses,' or 'not being the guy in the "Cat's in the Cradle" song'?"

Silence.

Obviously, to develop a compelling brand, she has to do some refining. www.dontbetheguyinthecatsinthecradlesong.com may be a bit bulky. But I hope you get my point: *people do not respond to generic brand names that cause no emotional reaction.* Your job is to reach out and sock your people in the gut with clear, direct language that speaks directly to them.

A Rose by Any Other Name . . .

You have gotten through the tough part of dreaming up a product or service, analyzing your market, defining your niche, and doing a first draft of your business plan. Now you are ready for the fun part: choosing a name for your business. Although certainly a creative exercise, it isn't always as easy as it seems. Branding expert Suzanne Falter-Barns breaks down the process into two parts:

1. **Brand Name:** Catchy, easy-to-understand name that says something about what you do.
2. **Unique Selling Proposition (USP):** Phrase that describes what you do more specifically, preferably addressing a key problem faced by your target market.

Examples I love:

FURNITURE THAT FITS: *SMALL FURNITURE FOR SMALL SPACES*

I saw this on a billboard here in Arizona. The URL is actually owned by a company called "A Perfect Space." But I like it as an example of directly addressing a problem faced by people living in small spaces. I think they could have raging success targeting people in New York City or San Francisco where you spend 82 percent of your salary on rent for an apartment the size of a small storage locker.

AREA 51: *TOP SECRET RESEARCH FACILITY*

I realize that this is a government-run facility more known for UFO conspiracy theories than a spunky brand name. But what if they had chosen to call it the *Nellis Air Force Range Research Center*? It hardly has the same effect. If I were a famous researcher aiming to take over the world, or build a better bomb or whatever they do inside there, I certainly would want to be part of a "top secret research facility."

GARAGE TECHNOLOGY VENTURES: *WE START UP START-UPS:*
EARLY STAGE VENTURE CAPITAL

This is a good example of a clean, clear, and crisp business and brand name. You don't have to guess what they do. The "garage" part of their brand is very pertinent to their target market, Silicon Valley technology start-ups. Those in this community would love to grow big like a few famous people who started in a garage: Bill and Dave in their Palo Alto garage (now known as Hewlett-Packard) and the Steves (Jobs and Wozniak who started Apple).

We can also learn a lot from good book titles. Granted, the titles are probably longer than you would want for a USP, but they do speak directly to their target audience and the problems they face. The bold part of the title could be considered the brand, the rest the USP.

MADE TO STICK: WHY SOME IDEAS SURVIVE AND OTHERS DIE

This book by Chip Heath and Dan Heath, which became a *New York Times* bestseller, walks its own talk as it draws in anyone who has to communicate ideas for a living with a compelling title and intriguing promise.

BOOK YOURSELF SOLID: THE FASTEST, EASIEST, AND MOST
RELIABLE SYSTEM FOR GETTING MORE CLIENTS THAN YOU
CAN HANDLE EVEN IF YOU HATE MARKETING AND SELLING
Author Michael Port works in two major problems people in his target market face: lack of clients and a deep loathing of sales and marketing.

In *The Art of the Start*, Guy Kawasaki recommends some guidelines for choosing a name (my explanations are in parentheses):

- Have a first initial that's early in the alphabet (you will be in a directory, may as well be in the top)
- Avoid numbers (too hard to know how to spell: 1 or one?)
- Pick a name with "verb potential" (think Google)
- Sound different (don't choose a name close to a competitor or other, unrelated brand which will get confusing)
- Sound logical (match your business name with what you actually do)
- Avoid the trendy (probably not a good idea to call your firm Sick and Phat Technology Services)

I would now add my two cents:

- **Choose a name with an available URL.** These days, your Web presence is critical. And you don't want to have a different URL from your brand name. If you can't find a perfect match, it isn't the end of the world. Remember, it doesn't have to be *matchy-matchy*, it just has to *go*.
- **Don't be fluffy or cute.** See example above, for coaches like me tend to go off into happy-fluffy-lala-land when choosing business names, with ridiculous results like "Be all that you can be coaching: Find the YOU in YOU!" (No, it doesn't exist yet, but just wait!)
- **Don't use a misspelled word.** Kawasaki mentions that Krispy Kreme is misspelled and sells products that are neither crispy nor creamy. I don't know if the misspelling has anything to do with their recent tanking stock, but it couldn't have helped. Please, please avoid names like "Kute Klocks and Krafts" (the USP would be fun: *Ridiculous stuff you don't need that make perfect gifts for annoying relatives*).
- **Focus on the benefits to your target market.** You may think "Anal Accounting" is clever and catchy, but your target market may care more

about "Accepting Accounting: *Cleans up your financial mess without making you feel like a loser.*"

Everything for Everyone

As the saying goes, if you don't stand for something, you will go for anything. Trying to market to everyone who could possibly buy your products or services will water down your message and actually repel potential clients.

In chapter 9, you looked at the importance of defining a niche to work with that both needs your services and has the wherewithal to pay you.

As hard as this is to do in the business planning stage, it gets even harder when it comes to developing your brand.

A common reaction I get when I work with clients at this stage is something like: "I know I said I only wanted to work with African American men aged fifty-five who graduated with advanced degrees from Columbia and work in financial services, but since I am going through the trouble of setting up a Web site, can't I also mention my interest in teenage farming entrepreneurs from eastern Iowa?"

If you want to have a clean, compelling brand that attracts your ideal clients, you have to be targeted.

And remember, just because you choose to start your business with a tight focus and specific brand, it does not mean that you have to serve this market for the rest of your life. You can grow and expand, create subbrands and complementary products.

You just have to start somewhere, and that is with a clearly identified niche served by a great brand.

It Doesn't Have to Be Matchy-Matchy, It Just Has to *Go*

I am a fool for makeover shows where frumpy housewives or people with a fashion sense stuck in the eighties get a sleek, updated look. On one of my favorites, *What Not to Wear*, stylist Stacy London always tells people who are afraid of pairing an orange purse with a black belt and teal shoes, "It doesn't have to be matchy-matchy, it just has to *go*."

The same is true for your brand. You want people to look at your overall presence on the Web, see you in person, check out the sales page for your products, read your blog, and listen to your podcast and say, "Yeah, that feels like Arnie, the Legal Sanity guy." Or "That blog has a Skellie look and voice," referring to the smart and talented Australian blogger who writes for a number of sites including FreelanceSwitch.com, Anywired.com, and Skelliewag.org. Or "that project definitely has a Seth Godin vibe."

But don't worry if not every part of your brand is perfectly integrated. It takes some time and money to harmonize the look and feel of your print and online materials, and when you are starting out, you may need that money elsewhere, like getting your product or service launched. People will forgive an inelegant temporary design as long as your content is clear, focused, and zippy.

"Grown Up" Corporatespeak

If you have come from a corporate environment, you have been taught that to earn your annual bonus, you need to take perfectly clear language and add jargon, buzzwords, and a series of legal disclaimers to make a point.

This approach will repel real customers in the real world faster than your teenager will leave the room if you try to discuss sex education.

I have a suggestion: get a gang member coach.

When I recruited for the martial arts program that I mentioned in chapter 3, I walked the streets of the Mission District of San Francisco, talking to kids to encourage them to join our program. Some were pretty hard-core, either in or on the verge of joining gangs. I learned very quickly that they had zero tolerance for touchy-feely language, and preferred to "keep it real."

So one day, as I was sitting in a conference room listening to an excruciatingly obtuse presentation by a senior manager, it dawned on me: *My kids could coach the b.s. right out of this presentation in five seconds flat!*

Imagine the scenario:

Joe, VP of Alliance Partnerships: "And as you can see from my deck, by creating a strategic partnership that focuses on key enablers of the new paradigm, we can leverage out-of-the-box thinking and deliver an integrated solution to our end-users."

Juan, the Gang Member Coach: "Joe, what the f**k are you talking about?"

In five minutes or less, Joe, the stammering vice president, would have to explain in clear, plain terms what he was trying to say.

Visualizing your gang member coach is a great way to ensure that you do not write marketing copy that is convoluted, dull, and boring.

Write as though your life depended on it. It does.

Keys to Building a Killer Brand

The best way to develop the elements of your brand is to review all of the information you excavated from your hard work. When you have a deep sense of what work you want to do, and which business you want to open, there are a few things you want to do that will really make you stand out from the crowd.

Be the Sharpest Knife in the Drawer

A few years ago, I hosted a holiday dinner at my house and my mom helped me cook. After riffling through my kitchen drawers, she pulled out half a dozen dull and inferior knives, all of which would pulverize a tomato instead of creating crisp and clean slices.

"Do you have a good knife?" my mom asked.

"Um—not really," I replied, realizing that my shoddy collection of ten-bucks-for-a-set-of-twelve knives would never satisfy her culinary needs.

Thankfully, the next Christmas, she bought me a beautiful and razor-sharp cooking knife that made cutting through carrots feel like slicing through butter. Soon I was using it for everything, and wondered how I ever lived without it.

As a small business owner, you should make your clients feel the same about working with you.

Because despite all the other things that you worry about when setting up your business, the most valuable and enduring asset you have is providing the absolute best service that solves not only the articulated needs of your customers, but also the unspoken ones.

So how can you make sure you are a sharp knife yourself?

1. **Choose the right business.** As hard as you try, you cannot manufacture passion. Choose a business that allows you to express your best skills, talents, and interests. This enthusiasm will permeate your brand and draw customers to you. You want to make sure that you will enjoy your business as you are growing it, not just when you get to a certain level of financial success.

2. **Be fiercely dedicated to learning.** All fields of business are rapidly growing and changing. Learn as much as you can about your profession so that you provide the absolute best service. Take classes. Read books. Surf the Internet. Connect with other professionals in your field. Your love of learning will keep you fresh and alive, and ensure that you solve new problems in new and effective ways.

3. **Always ask yourself "What would really help my customer?"** In my years as a corporate consultant, I would say that at least 50 percent of the time, clients would bring me in with a predetermined idea of what solution I should provide to solve their problems. But after a short conversation, it became clear that following their prescriptive path would not solve the problem, it would either do nothing or exacerbate it. If they were insistent on following a path I didn't agree with, I would graciously turn down the work and offer other resources. It is never worth it to take a big check for a project that you know is doomed from the start. (And since it will fail spectacularly, who will get blamed? The errant executive? Of course not. The incompetent consultant!)

4. **Avoid clients who are not a match with your ideal profile.** Martha Beck humorously calls these folks "life-sucking squids," due to their tendency to wrap their needy tentacles around you and drain your life force. You will not be of good service to someone you don't enjoy working with; it is better to pass them on to someone who can truly serve them.

5. **Check out your competition.** Regularly benchmark yourself and your company with others in your field. Find out how you stack up, and learn from the things others are doing right and wrong. You don't have to aim to crush all your rivals, you just want to honestly assess your place in the pack of people serving similar clients. Being around smart, effective competitors is great motivation for stepping up your game.

Create an *Experience* for Your Customers

Your customers evaluate your brand not just by the usability of your Web site or look of your logo, but by *the entire experience* they have with your business from the first time they make contact.

I understood this clearly with a positive experience at a retail store.

As soon as I walked in the Apple store to buy an iPod, I felt very engaged. The atmosphere was simple and stylish, and I didn't feel overwhelmed by screaming advertisements or mounds and mounds of computer equipment. A friendly and knowledgeable young man came up to me and in a very relaxed way asked what I was looking for. After I told him I was looking for an iPod, he steered me over to an easy-to-understand chart and asked a few simple questions:

What was I planning on using it for?
How much music or how many movies was I planning to download?
Did I prefer white or black?

The technically savvy among you may groan loudly at my lack of technical finesse, but I just want someone to listen carefully to what my intended use of the product will be, use their vast technical expertise to recommend what I should buy, and stick out their hand to accept my credit card.

And that is exactly what happened at the store. This cute techno sales kid got me the exact product that I wanted, put it in my hands in less than five minutes, rang my sale with a handheld remote credit card processor so that I didn't have to stand in line to pay for it, and did nothing to hype me into an extended warranty plan.

To top it off, while I was being taken care of in the aisle, my husband and baby son were sitting on comfortable, kid-sized beanbag chairs at a low table and playing educational games on Macintosh computers. My husband was so enchanted by the whole thing that he was ready to buy my son a new Mac right then and there. I had to remind him that our son had just barely started to walk and talk and that perhaps we should wait until he doesn't try to *eat* the mouse before buying him a computer.

This is just one example of a retail location that does so many things right, and takes its target customer's needs into account with its entire sales model, a key part of its brand spirit. They don't force you to buy, they *seduce* you into buying.

What are the lessons to learn from these examples as you plan your business?

- **Respect your customer's style.** Even if you are a fifth-degree black belt in Java programming and could slice electrons with your bare fists, save your technobabble for someone who cares. When you see a clueless, pressed-for-time, and credit-card-bearing customer like me walk through your door, become a consultant and help me make an informed purchase without forcing me to listen to information I don't understand or care about.
- **Make it easy for the customer to buy from you.** Analyze the steps that your customers have to take to purchase a product from you. If you have a Web-based business, how can you make it "1-Click Amazon" simple? For a retail store, how can you be like Apple and avoid the line at the cash register altogether?
- **Let people mess around with your stuff.** I learned from a savvy salesperson that the key to getting someone emotionally ready to buy is to let them "test drive" your product. Find ways to let them try on, hold in their hands, eat, listen to, and play with your products. If you are a service-based company, offer a free sample of a great audio program, assessment tool, or video.
- **Don't be afraid to be funky and use humor.** One of the appeals of the blogging world is the free speech, humor, and open communication. This medium is growing because people are hungry for real conversations with real people. Let your true self show through in your business. As mentioned before, no corporatespeak allowed. You can still be professional, smart, and fun.
- **Use color, art, and style in your brand.** We are sensual creatures! The more we see, hear, taste, touch, and feel beautiful, rich, colorful, and pleasing things, the more engaged we are with them. Make your facilities, Web site, product packaging, business cards and all other marketing collateral pleasing to look at. You don't have to spend a fortune, just engage a smart and talented artist to help you.
- **Hire genuine, caring, and knowledgeable employees.** I have no patience for gum-chewing, irreverent, and bored employees. Anywhere. Make

sure that you, and your employees if you have them, respect your customers. Care about them. Listen to them and thank them for their business. My worst pet peeve? When I politely say "thank you" after
purchasing an item in a store and a bored-looking employee rolls her
eyes and says "You're welcome." Make your customers feel like rock
stars, not lucky to do business with you.

Living Brand: Sergio Photographer

For my wedding ceremony, I was looking for a great photographer to capture pictures that we could treasure forever. I have high creative standards
when it comes to photographs because my dad is a professional photographer and I grew up in the darkroom.

So I did the usual thing, Googled "wedding photographers in Arizona."
After looking at a number of sites that had the typical boring staged shots, I
stumbled upon Sergio Photographer's site. I was really taken aback by the
photos—they had energy, color, and life, and they communicated a lot of
emotion. I was intrigued.

I called Sergio and immediately felt comfortable. He was accessible, easy
to talk to, and asked lots of good questions about what we were looking to
capture with our wedding photos. We ended up hiring him, and I soon saw
a number of things he does well that we can all learn from as we develop
our brands:

1. **He has a specific niche.** Obviously, as a talented photographer, Sergio can
   take shots of just about anything. But he chose weddings because of the
   specific emotional content of the events, as well as the workflow that fits
   with his lifestyle. Based on his portfolio, I am sure that if you asked him
   he would also say he loves to work with nontraditional, multicultural,
   creative, and family-oriented people.
2. **He has a clearly defined style.** Rather than taking posed "say cheese for
   the camera" shots, Sergio acts as a photojournalist, capturing the move-
   ment and action of a wedding. The intimate father/daughter shots in his
   portfolio are some of my favorites. I cry when I look at them, even
   though I don't know the people in the photos, because I can feel the tender emotion in the moment.

3. **He is doing the work he is meant to do.** You cannot spend one minute with Sergio and not know that he is meant to have a camera in his hand. He loves what he does, and that love shines through in every part of his business. And he is damn good at it.

4. **He has great partners.** Sergio often shoots with his partner Kelly Rashka, who also worked on our wedding. She is an amazing artist in her own right, and the two of them work really well together. Both flow seamlessly through many different situations and complement each other's strengths and shortfalls.

5. **He understands that the way he works is also part of his brand.** One of the best things about Sergio is that he gets along with anyone. When we first met, he said, "The way I want you to feel about me at your wedding is not as a photographer, but as a family member." And that is exactly what happened. He laughed and joked with my husband's relatives and my relatives, sampled the roast mutton and fry bread (it is a Navajo thing!), played with the kids, and was quietly respectful with the grandmas. This ease made everyone relax, which, of course, is the key to getting great candid photos.

6. **He has clearly defined packages.** Once we decided to go with him (which for me took about thirty seconds), he made it really easy to buy. He outlined a very clear wedding package and sent an organized contract right away. That made me feel comfortable, knowing that if he was organized in his business he was most likely going to show up to the wedding on time and deliver the photos as promised. Which he did, right when he said he would.

7. **He provides value-added services.** In addition to standard photos, Sergio creates slick slideshows and gorgeous wedding books. This not only gives him more things to sell, but cements his reputation as a high-end photographer since the books are works of art, worthy of any coffee table, even for those who are not related to the happy couple.

8. **He charges what he is worth.** He is not the cheapest person on the block, but is worth every penny. By charging a good rate, he ensures that those he works with value his services. Because he is not busy running from cheap gig to cheap gig to pay the bills, he has time to plan and prepare for outstanding events.

9. **He has a consistent look and feel in all his materials.** His Web site, printed materials, and blog all go together. They capture the spirit of who he is. He describes himself this way: "I have been a wedding photographer for about five years and I love doing this more than anything else in my life. I enjoy every single aspect of my job. From the moment I get an inquiry and everything throughout until I deliver the album after the wedding."

   Funny, that is exactly what I said about him as a customer! That is true brand harmony.

Like many of you, Sergio used to be a cog in a corporate machine. Fed up, he jumped ship to launch his business. Each of us, in our own way, can learn from Sergio about showing up in our businesses in a big way.

You can find Sergio at sergiophotographer.com. Look at his site and tell me if you don't immediately get a sense of his brand spirit.

Do You Have to Be an Expert to Have a Strong Brand?

One of the things that trips up a lot of people establishing a new brand is the concept of "expert."

If you feel like you have to have three advanced degrees and twenty years' experience to have credibility as a business owner, here are some alternative "expert" definitions:

1. **The "no one would call them an expert because they are too young but they really are an expert" expert.** Ben Zweig, a very enthusiastic "folding expert," demonstrated proper shirt folding techniques on YouTube, at the tender age of eleven years old. What he lacked in years on the planet, he made up for with exuberance, charm, and a true knack for making a great instructional video.

2. **The "low on training or formal education but high on results" expert**. Thirty minute meal cooking phenomenon Rachael Ray is a perfect example of this. She was not formally trained at an elite cooking school or five-star restaurant; she honed her skills while preparing food demonstrations in a mall. Now she perkily flings food around her kitchen on her way to a multimedia empire. It doesn't hurt to have Oprah as a

backer, but I do believe that it was a lot of her own *ganas* (inner fire, drive) that got her noticed by major media. She is a master at being open, friendly, accessible, and practical, and this adds to her appeal.

3. **The "been there done that" expert**. This kind of expert has learned a tremendous amount from real-life experience, not formal education. They often share their expertise through analogies and examples, not textbook citations. Sometimes the experts from this area gain experience in areas outside of work, for example the child abuse expert who grew up in an abusive household.

4. **The "been to the right schools and has the right advanced academic degrees" expert**. They do exist, and thank goodness. There is real value in seasoned, well-read, and analytical experts who know volumes about their subject matter. The caveat I would propose for experts with this pedigree in the business world is that they should be able to demonstrate results from all of their book smarts. All of us have probably come across a cultured genius with more letters *after* their name than *in* their name who is also a tremendous windbag. The key is not just knowing a lot about a given field, but knowing how to apply what you know in a practical business situation.

5. **The "has a combination of academic and 'been there done that' experience along with a boatload of enthusiasm" expert**. My aim in giving some texture to the definition of the word "expert" is to encourage you to expand your view of what it means to be credible. It is okay to stand up and say with pride, "I really do know and care a lot about this subject and you should listen to me!" If you have the results to back it up, you have just as much right to say this as does a postdoctorate from Stanford.

Building a Brand Case Study: Rachael Ray

2007 was the year of 30-Minute Meal perky cooking diva Rachael Ray. It seems that her brand and media presence jumped from a whisper (a few cooking shows and cookbooks) to a scream (a talk show, magazine, product line, pet advice, etc.) all in a short period of time.

I think she is kind of spunky and I admire her business growth so she doesn't bother me a lot, but I know that there are some people who feel she is the human equivalent of nails scratching on a blackboard. Maybe there is such a thing as too perky.

Regardless of how you feel about her personally, I think we can all learn a few things about building a brand from her meteoric success:

- **Find a real need in the marketplace**. So many stressed and overworked moms and dads long for a way to cook healthy and fast meals for their families. Rachael saw this need when she started out as a humble manager and cook at a food equipment store in Albany, New York, and started offering "30-Minute Meal" cooking classes as a way to increase sales. They became so popular that she realized she was on to something big, and started writing cookbooks.

- **To get national media, start local**. After her cooking classes exploded, she got some local press coverage. This caught the eye of an Albany television producer who invited her to do a weekly "30-Minute Meals" segment for the local news. As she was promoting her first book, she got booked on the *Today* show, and an interview on a public broadcasting station caught the interest of a Food Network executive who invited her to start the first of her four cooking shows. Many people want big, national media immediately. Start in your own backyard, and you may be surprised when the media heavies come calling.

- **Be yourself**. I find it hard to believe that her smiling personality is all an act (or is she really like Martha Stewart behind closed doors?). A big part of what draws people to Rachael is her unpretentiousness in the kitchen. She makes people feel that they, too, could have fun in the kitchen while preparing a quick and healthy meal—and without being a Cordon Bleu–trained chef. Her personality is her brand.

- **Build a product set around a core concept**. For Rachael, it was the 30-Minute Meals that started as a class, then moved to a cookbook, then a food network show, then a series of shows, then a magazine and a national daytime talk show. The idea is to take a great fundamental idea and build a whole set of products and services around it.

- **Align yourself with influential people who will help get you where you want to go**. I am not sure how the introduction happened, but Rachael Ray somehow connected with Oprah. After appearing on Oprah's show a few times, she struck a deal to have Oprah's Harpo Productions produce her daytime talk show. I have a feeling that aligning with Oprah was a very conscious choice on Rachael's part, given the target demographic of Oprah's viewers.

So while you may faint at the thought of ever using a term like "Yum-o" or "E.V.O.O.," don't lose the branding lessons of the most exposed cooking sensation of the year.

You should feel as comfortable in your brand as in a well-worn pair of pajamas. You are not posturing or pretending or positioning. You are sharing the best of you with your people, your market, your tribe.

Bring it on in Technicolor.

Test Often and Fail Fast: The Art of Prototypes and Samples

Perfectionists Are Losers

A few years ago, I interviewed Ramit Sethi, a young, bright entrepreneur, on my radio show. At the ripe age of twenty-six, Ramit had already started a screamingly hot blog with a huge following (*I Will Teach You to Be Rich*, a personal finance blog for college students and recent graduates), gotten two degrees from Stanford, started a company (PBwiki), and struck two book deals.

So I asked Ramit a question that I have heard from many young people who want to start a business:

"What if people won't want to hire me because I am too young?"

"Give me a break," he said. "Perfectionists are losers."

I laughed out loud at his bluntness, but immediately got what he was saying.

When you sit back and wait until you are perfectly prepared for an opportunity, it passes you by. What highly productive and successful people do is spend as little time as possible at the edge of opportunities, agonizing whether or not to move forward.

Instead, they jump in with both feet and sink or swim quickly. After lots of real-world experience, they fine-tune their understanding of the types of opportunities that will yield the most success and the kinds of situations that will best utilize their talents.

So if you think that your perfectionist tendencies are going to get in the way of making progress on your business plans, how can you overcome them?

Tip #1: Reframe Your Understanding of How Perfect Happens

There is nothing wrong with having very high standards and wanting to produce excellent work. The problem is, most people don't understand that extremely high quality work usually results from a practice my father taught me from photography: bracketing. Bracketing is a general technique of taking multiple frames of the same shot of the same subject using the same or different camera settings.

I used to think that professional photographers took award-winning shots with every click of the camera. As seasoned professionals, they surely did not have the same out of focus, finger in front of the lens, or poor lighting problems that plagued my amateur shots, right? Wrong. Great photographers might pluck one great shot in the middle of ninety-nine mediocre ones. They know that it is impossible to get the perfect shot in one try, so they take lots and lots of pictures of the same thing with the hope that one frame will come out perfect.

Writer Anne Lamott shares similar advice in her brilliant book *Bird by Bird*, which should be required reading for anyone who writes. She explains the importance of writing really, really bad first drafts:

> The first draft is the child's draft, where you let it all pour out and let it romp all over the place, knowing that no one is going to see it and that you can shape it later. You just let this childlike part of you channel whatever voices and visions come through and onto the page. If one of the characters wants to say "Well, so what, Mr. Poopy Pants?" you let her . . . If the kid wants to get into really sentimental, weepy emotional territory, you let him. Just get it all down on paper, because

there may be something great in those crazy six pages that you would never have gotten to by more rational, grown-up means. There may be something in the very last line of the very last paragraph on page six that you just love, that is so beautiful or wild that you now know what you are supposed to be writing about, more or less, or in what direction you might go—but there was no way to get to this without first getting through the first five and a half pages.[1]

So when you feel the breath of your inner perfectionist on your neck, turn to it and say, "Thanks for caring, but I am in the process of bracketing and doing really, really shitty drafts. I must do this in order to discover the perfect spots of my work, so rest assured that I will not be this bad forever."

Tip #2: Fail Fast and Move On

A "perfect" work situation for you is doing work you love and are great at with people who totally support you in an environment that rewards you handsomely. If you are in a less-than-ideal environment and with bad partners, you will always feel inferior and mediocre.

Seth Godin explains this very well in his book *The Dip*. He says: "What really sets superstars apart from everyone else is the ability to escape dead ends quickly, while staying focused and motivated when it really counts."[2]

You know you are in a situation where you have to quit and move on when:

- A client or partner continually disappoints you and makes you feel either incompetent or inferior.
- You have poured tons of time and money into an endeavor that never seems to catch fire. Despite enormous effort, you never get any real signals from the universe (or from plain old paying customers or partners) that the project is one you are meant to do. Don't be embarrassed to admit failure because of the effort and money spent—just cut the strings and move on to the next thing that is more enjoyable to do and will best leverage your talents.
- You are working in an area that has tremendous constraints, so no matter how hard you work, you are not likely to be compensated adequately.

This can involve a market that is very competitive, clients who can never afford to pay you what you are worth, or an idea so complex or difficult that it saps all your time and energy.

How do you know that any of these situations are truly times to quit and not critical moments before a breakthrough?

You just know. Something deep inside will tell you what work you are meant, and not meant, to do. Trust your instinct.

Tip #3: Hang Out in the Right Barbershop

A friend of mine said, "If you hang out in a barbershop, sooner or later you are going to get a haircut."

Which barbershop are you hanging out in? What kind of lives do the people around you lead? Are they positive, filled with humor, successful and creative? Do they constantly learn new things and improve their skills? Do they attract great partners naturally, without being pushy? Make a list of the qualities of people who bring out the best in you. My list of ideal partners includes things like:

- Approaches life with a healthy attitude and learns from mistakes
- Handles money well and isn't afraid to ask for what he or she is worth
- Treats others with dignity and respect
- Produces good work consistently
- Puts a priority on family life and does not work excessively
- Has a great sense of humor and laughs at mistakes
- Communicates openly and authentically

As you compile your own list, look around you and ask, "Do the people in my life exhibit these qualities? If not, how can I surround myself with people who do?"

Tip #4: Practice Forgiveness

We all make mistakes. Some of us make really big stupid ones (I use "us" very intentionally, as I continue to make some real doozies, even when I know better). Since we know they are part of the journey toward great work, learn how to do the following once you realize you screwed up: Understand why you did. The reasons may be:

- Didn't listen to your intuition
- Had too many things happening at once and lost control
- Didn't have the right partners
- Avoided an uncomfortable area

Grab the lesson. Ask yourself:

- What can I do next time to avoid this unfortunate result?
- How does this lesson position me for great success in the future?
- What is this situation trying to tell me?

Forgive and let go.

Do not let your period of embarrassment or despair drag on too long. Tell yourself, "You screwed up, you learned from it, and now it is time to move on. Everything is all right, and your whining is keeping you from doing the work you are meant to do."

Bottom line: Don't lose an opportunity, your wit, or your will by being a perfectionist. Life is too short!

Fling It on the Wall and See What Sticks

Much of what I just talked about is the *mindset* that will allow you to test your ideas without dying from humiliation.

The physical act of testing business ideas is really not a big deal.

- If you want to sell cookies, make some, put out a table on your sidewalk, grab a piece of paper and a Sharpie and write "Delicious, hot fresh cookies, 50 cents," and watch what happens.
- If you have an idea for an improved bicycle basket, get some cardboard, duct tape, and string and hang a prototype on your son's tricycle.
- If you have a great idea for a software product, invite ten of the smartest engineers you know, buy lots of Red Bull, and host your own Let's-create-it-test-it-launch-it Party (more on this later).

- If you want to be a life coach, start to have fifteen-minute coaching sessions with everyone you know. Your daughter's preschool teacher. The pharmacist. The guy at the bus stop. Don't worry about asking their permission; just turn on your mad coaching skills. If you are any good, they will be hungry for more.
- If you are going to write a series of best-selling self-help books that will shift global consciousness, go to wordpress.com and write three sentences of a really bad blog post in a really ugly-looking template. The longest journey begins with the smallest step.

You want to make testing and prototyping an integral part of how you grow your business. It won't just be the way you get your business off the ground, it will be the way your business continually grows and thrives.

Inside the Mind of an Entrepreneur

Rich Sloan is the cofounder of StartupNation, a resource-rich destination for aspiring and newbie entrepreneurs. Through his active online community, radio show, media appearances, and role as an angel investor, he probably gets pitched more business ideas in a week than most people hear in a decade.

Armed with specific business ideas from my blog readers, I interviewed Rich on how to go about testing and prototyping them. Here's one example:

BUSINESS IDEA

An assembly business service, assembling and installing play structures, barbecues, patio furniture, kids' toys, light fixtures, stereos, tools, just about anything that comes in pieces and troubles the average person to put together.

WHAT THE ENTREPRENEUR ALREADY HAS DONE

He's created a huge inventory of things that can be assembled. So he knows he can. He got a URL and a name and he drafted a plan in terms of hourly rates.

(continued)

WHERE HE IS STUCK

He thinks a lot of people need help but he doesn't know how to connect with his potential customer base. He's played with Google AdSense and he just doesn't know how to find people who need help and how can he get market demographics to figure out if it's viable. So what would be a way you would suggest that he could just start to test this a little bit to see if there's a market for it?

RICH SLOAN, STARTUPNATION

As for the viability of the service, people are often drawn to the self-assembly things because they are a little less expensive. And so one of the sensitivity points with what he's doing is absolutely going to be: Are people willing to pay for someone else to do this? Most of the time, people go into a purchase of something that needs to be assembled under the naïve assumption that what it says on the cover or label of the big box is true, which is "easy to assemble."

And I actually think that there's an attractiveness and an appeal to the place where the traffic is, the Home Depot or the Toys 'R' Us, whatever it may be. And there is a certain level of credibility that he will take on if his service is offered through those places. I also would say that the most compelling thing to me when I work with a contractor is knowing that other people have been satisfied. So I would further be willing to accumulate some number of initial customers at no fee whatsoever just to show off and acquire a testimonial.

A Prototype in Action

Ramit Sethi is the cofounder of PBwiki, the largest host of business and educational wikis in the world. As of this writing, the company employs twenty-five people and hosts over 500,000 wikis. But it wasn't always that way.

Ramit told me the story of how his company was launched in 2005, which is the ultimate example of quick testing and prototyping:

There is a thing called "Super Happy Dev House" where hackers come and work on something from evening all the way to the morning. David Weekly [cofounder] and others provided a group of programmers a bunch of Red Bull and a WiFi, and they sat down and started creating stuff. People talked to each other and got feedback. When morning came, we launched the project. It was a great way of quickly paring down what we had in the application and what we didn't.

Forty-eight hours after that initial overnight Red Bull–fueled product development session, 1,000 wikis were launched on the fledgling service.

Due to the publicity from relationships with well-connected bloggers that Ramit and David had cultivated for a long time and a clear "invite your friends" strategy with current users, the world spread about the new service.

And the numbers kept on going up from 1,000 to 5,000 and now (three years later) up to 555,000. Ramit says: "The key was putting out something really simple. In fact, if you look at the Internet archive, you can see how simple the Web page was. All you could do was sign up. It turned out people just wanted a really simple Web page that they can collaborate on."

The wiki idea was actually one of many that Ramit and David were evaluating. "In fact, we had about nine different pieces of software we were interested in that we put on a whiteboard. When PBwiki took off, that was when we said, 'All right. Forget the others. This is what we have to pay attention to.'"

Knowing that their product was bare bones and had lots of bugs, they made product improvement the number one priority. Product changes were made immediately.

We had a Gmail account that support questions would go to and we'd answer that. And then we'd be sitting in a room and talking about it or we'd be on IM because we didn't have an office. We'd make real-time changes and we would basically announce them right there and the changes would be incorporated into the product. It was a really pure time because there were two guys, product changes being made, feedback coming in, sketches made and designs launched. It's very quick. People love that, they love immediate feedback. They are willing to accept a lot of things if they get it.

In the true spirit of action over process, Ramit and David didn't have a big plan when they started.

> Our plan was: "Let's open up a Gmail account then, okay, that's it." People often confuse the idea of our start-up, thinking we had a big long-term vision. The reality was, we just created a wiki. And now, three years later, we've developed this very, very unique vision of collaboration for educators and businesses. But at the beginning often it's just "let's roll this thing out and see what happens." It's more of a curiosity.

The start of PBwiki has enough stories to fill a whole book. What I hope you take away from their start-up process is the power in trusting the prototype process.

Ghetto but It Works

RAMIT SETHI, PBWIKI

We have a sign up at PBwiki that says, "Ghetto but it works." The idea is: let's get something out fast. What we do is have tech demos in our morning meetings. We'll have an engineer who comes up with something overnight. He'll put up a tech demo and he'll say, "Okay, guys, I'm going to show you a tech demo but it's really simple. It's just a prototype." Right? But that takes courage to show a tech demo with a lot of broken bugs in it in front of your entire team on a projector screen. But they do it, and we applaud. Because this person spent the whole night creating a feature just to show us and some of the stuff doesn't work, the links are broken, sometimes you have to hit refresh or edit the code right there. But, guess what? It shows that someone took initiative and that they are not afraid to show this crazy idea they have because many of those crazy ideas end up in our product.

Visit Ramit's Web site: iwillteachyoutoberich.com.

Gain Experience and Credibility as You Test Your Ideas

Testing an idea to see if it is viable is one part of the business plan equation. Another is gaining real experience with clients, which will make the marketing and selling process easier. Olivia, one of my readers from Australia, sent a thought-provoking question that speaks directly to the testing/prototyping question:

> I've decided I'd love to do professional organising (only just emerging in Australia), and am reading lots of excellent books on the actual work/counseling and also marketing and business info. The biggest question is, since I've been a Personal Assistant, and that's the only thing I've ever done (18 years), how on earth do I break out of the mold of the old job, and find the guts to actually TAKE ON A FIRST CLIENT in my new field? I mean, to study and ponder and learn and prepare is one thing, but actually going out there and DOING it, I have no idea where to get the "nerve." This could be the difference to whether I take off or not. How do I go from *preparing* to *doing*?

This is such a juicy question because it highlights a number of challenges for first-time entrepreneurs:

If you are brand new in your field, "test drive" your service as a volunteer. Choose an individual or organization that would be an excellent case study and that would provide clear "before and after" results. Gain agreement from your client that if she is satisfied with the results, you may use her as a reference for future clients and would use her project as a case study for your marketing.

So in Olivia's case of being a professional organizer, she has a great opportunity to choose a client with a terribly messy office or closet. She can take a "before" picture, do the work, then do the "after" picture. If she does a stunning job (which I am sure she will) she can take a picture of her satisfied client and ask for a two-sentence testimonial. This will be great for her Web site or marketing materials.

Gaining Confidence

Find a mentor. There is nothing like hearing "stories from the trenches" from someone who used to be in your position and now has a thriving practice. You can get information, resources, and confidence from the right person, or group of people. You may also join a professional organization or community forum like StartupNation to get some ideas and support.

Getting Clients

Start by defining your niche. If you are concerned with just getting things going and taking on a few clients, start with defining your niche. That is the specific segment of people that you will target for your marketing efforts.

For just about anyone these days (well, anyone with something meaty to share and who likes to write), I would recommend starting a blog on your topic, since it is a great way to showcase your expertise, build community, test ideas, and develop a friendly relationship with potential clients.

In Olivia's case, since she mentioned that professional organizing was just getting started in Australia, maybe she could partner with a more established service professional such as an accountant to provide financial organizing services for their clients. Whatever niche she chooses, I would recommend starting in a targeted way, then as she gains exposure and experience, she could branch out to other groups.

Forget Strategy

DIEGO RODRIGUEZ, IDEO AND METACOOL

An innocuous typo I saw today got me thinking: what if we used a word called "startegy" instead of "strategy"? When faced with a blank sheet of paper, we tend to spend too much time engaged in discussions about strategy, otherwise known as "strategery," and too little time learning by doing. In this context, talking a lot about what to do and why is inappropriate because we don't know enough about context and constraints. When you're getting out into the world and starting things, guiding evidence has a way of surfacing in a way which doesn't happen within the cloistered confines of meeting rooms.

Revolutions don't just happen, they get started. *Startegy.*

Get Out of Your Mental Ghetto

San Francisco's Mission District is a lively Latino neighborhood, filled with activity, twelve kinds of chili peppers in outdoor markets, loud music, and killer restaurants. It is also home to two gangs: the norteños and the sureños. Each wears their designated color (norte = red, sur = blue) and stays within rigid boundaries of their neighborhood. If you are a young person with any remote affiliation to these groups (desired or not) and venture past these lines, the consequences are very violent, and sometimes deadly.

This context is important to understand how I could meet a young man named Dennis who had never been outside of the four-square city block he grew up in. He had never seen the Golden Gate Bridge, or Coit Tower, or the ocean. And he was fourteen years old.

Many people could look at his situation and think it was absurd. Of course he could have found a way to get out of his neighborhood. But logistics were not the real issue. What had created an imaginary electronic fence around his four-square block was a combination of fear and a false sense of security. He had seen many of his young peers fall to violence and was really terrified of the same thing happening to him. And he believed that if he just followed the rules and stayed within the "safe" boundaries of his neighborhood, everything would be okay. He had everything he needed to get by.

A lot of us get caught in the same mental ghettos with our professional affiliations.

- We huddle in online forums with our peers and convince one another that with a little bit more subject matter expertise or certification we will be ready to create a successful business.

- We attend conferences filled with people who all agree with us, and talk about practices, tools, and technologies that excite only us. (Participating on Twitter for a couple of months has led me to believe that there are more "Web 2.0/social media consultants" than there could possibly be businesses to support them.)
- We spend thousands of dollars in classes and workshops learning the next big coaching technique/marketing trick/SEO optimization that will magically make us successful.

What would happen if we just hung out with the people we want to serve?

By "hang out," I don't mean read a study on their behavior or conduct a structured focus group, I mean pull up a chair, sit with them in their natural habitat, attend their conferences, or pick up the phone and talk to them. Examples:

- If you are an accountant who wants to work with slightly zany, creative people, shred your "Accounting Trends 2008" conference tickets and hop a Volkswagen bus to Burning Man.
- If you are a software developer who wants to create time management software for busy moms, get off the Joel on Software forum and get to the grocery store at 5:00 p.m. and talk to twenty women with kids hanging off of their shopping carts.
- If you are a coach who wants to work with leading technology executives, save the money you would have spent on your "master double platinum certification training certificate" and attend the South by Southwest Conference in Austin, Texas.

It may feel as awkward and scary for you to do these things as it was for Dennis to cross the street at the edge of his "safe" zone. But, unlike him, you don't face a death threat. You have just as much to learn and discover outside of your mental ghetto as he did outside his.

What If You Crash and Burn?

I have highlighted some examples in this chapter of successful business launches that resulted from rapid testing and prototyping.

But what if the opposite happens?

- What if it doesn't turn out the way you imagined?
- What if no one likes it?
- What if no one buys it?
- What if someone else does it better?
- What if you have been wasting your time and should have done something else?

I don't want to minimize your frustration and pain, since it is not fun to fail at something you really care about.

But in the big picture, isn't it better to find out that your idea doesn't have legs before you have invested a lot of time, effort, and money? Won't that free you up to pursue other things?

As a culture, we revel in stories of early dejection that were followed by fame and fortune. Stories like these:

- After Harrison Ford's first performance as a hotel bellhop in the film *Dead Heat on a Merry-Go-Round,* the studio vice president called him in to his office. "Sit down, kid," the studio head said, "I want to tell you a story. The first time Tony Curtis was ever in a movie he delivered a bag of groceries. We took one look at him and knew he was a movie star." Ford replied, "I thought you were supposed to think that he was a grocery delivery boy." The vice president dismissed Ford with "You ain't got it, kid, you ain't got it . . . now get out of here."
- Tom Landry, Chuck Noll, Bill Walsh, and Jimmy Johnson accounted for eleven of the nineteen Super Bowl victories from 1974 to 1993. They also share the distinction of having the worst records as first-season head coaches in NFL history—they didn't win a single game.
- After his first audition, Sidney Poitier was told by the casting director, "Why don't you stop wasting people's time and go out and become a

dishwasher or something?" It was at that moment, recalls Poitier, that he decided to devote his life to acting.

These stories *should* fire you up.

The more you try, test, get beat down, get back up, laugh in the face of massive failure and maintain a spirit of curiosity, the better entrepreneur you will be.

Bestselling author, successful businessman, and marketing guru Seth Godin is thought of in most circles as a genius. But he has not been exempt from business failures, as he described in this blog post:

Failure as an Event

I try hard not to keep a running tally of big-time failures in my head. It gets in the way of creating the next thing. On the other hand, when you see failure as a learning event, not a destination, it makes you smarter, faster.

Some big ones from my past:

The Boston Bar Exam. My two partners and I spent a lot of time and money building this our last year of college. It was a coupon book filled with free drinks from various bars in Cambridge and Boston. The booklet would be sold at the bars, encouraging, I dunno, drunk driving. Lessons: Don't spend a lot on startup costs, don't sell to bar owners and don't have three equal partners, since one person always feels outvoted.

The Internet White Pages. This was a 700-page book filled with nearly a million email addresses. It took months to create and IDG, the publisher, printed 80,000 copies. They shredded 79,000 of them. Lesson: If the Internet Yellow Pages is a huge hit (it was), that doesn't mean the obvious counterpart will be. A directory that's incomplete is almost always worthless.

MaxFax. This was the first fax board for the Mac. It would allow any Mac user to hit "print" and send what was on the screen to any fax machine. We raised seed money from a wealthy dentist, built a working prototype and worked to license it to a big computer hardware company. Lessons: Don't raise money from amateurs, watch out for flaky engineering if you're selling a prototype, think twice before you enter a market with one huge player

(Apple knocked off the idea) and don't build a business hoping to sell out unless you have a clear path to do that.

I have a dozen more. The first wireless Sonos-like device. A nationwide game show using 900 numbers. A fundraising company that offered light-bulbs for sale to high school bands (lighter than fruit!). Not to mention classic book ideas like, "How to hypnotize your friends and get them to act like chickens." I'm not using hyperbole when I say that in 25 years, I had at least 20 serious career-ending failures.

I guess the biggest lessons are:

- Prepare for the dip. Starting a business is far easier than making it successful. You need to see a path and have the resources to get through it.
- Cliff businesses are glamorous but dangerous.
- Projects exist in an eco-system. Who are the other players? How do you fit in?
- Being the dumbest partner in a room of smart people is exactly where you want to be.
- And the biggest of all: persist. Do the next one.[3]

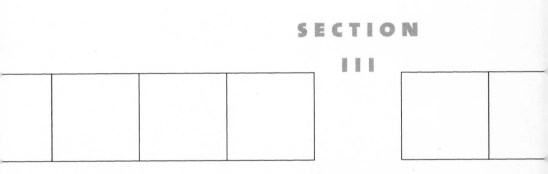

Make the
Money Work

12

Look Your Finances in the Eye

f you have always had a good handle on your personal finances, congratulations. This skill will serve you well in starting a business. I imagine that you already track your expenditures closely, know your net worth, and don't bristle at the thought of balancing your checkbook each month. You may skim this chapter to make sure you haven't forgotten anything, but most likely you can move on to the chapters on benefits, breaking the news you want to start a business to your spouse, or lining your ducks in a row.

If you are *not* naturally gifted when it comes to understanding and managing your finances, don't despair. Everyone has different strengths and weaknesses. That said, although you do not need to do all the money-related tasks of your business, *you do need to make sure they get done.*

Nothing will cause you more pain than ignoring the financial side of your business. Not horrible sales calls, crashed laptops, surly employees, or even bad press. When the financial side of your business is not working, life is miserable.

I don't speak in generalities. Right in the middle of writing this book, my husband's heavy equipment construction business in Phoenix, Arizona, formerly thriving with great profit, was hit by one the biggest economic slowdowns since the Great Depression. Clients who had always paid on time went sixty or ninety days overdue. Projects that were guaranteed to last for six months suddenly evaporated with one day's notice.

I had a tiny baby and toddler at home and was unable to do my full-time coaching and consulting work due to their pressing needs. (Try telling a tiny baby to hold off on eating or cuddling so Mommy can work!)

The market changed under our feet, and we were stuck paddling as fast as we could against gigantic waves of expenses with tide pools of income.

To say it was bone-chilling frightening is an understatement. I worried about paying the monthly expenses, and meeting the mortgage payment and providing a stable and happy home life for my kids. I would wake up at three a.m., sweating from anxiety. Meanwhile, I was writing a blog and book about quitting your job to start a business. Do you see the irony?

Thankfully, my husband weathered the storm, changed his market focus, formed a new joint venture with great partners, and is back on track.

I never want to live through a time like this again, and I don't want you to either. As we learned in our situation, some things like a perfect storm of (1) overoptimistic planning and equipment investment, met with (2) economic disaster (the meltdown of 2008) in (3) the hardest-hit industry (construction) in (4) one of the hardest hit parts of the country (Phoenix, Arizona) are difficult to predict.

But you can do some concrete things to make sure that you have a crystal-clear idea of where you stand financially so that you have the best chance of success in your new business. And if things start to get wacky in the economy or your personal life, you can quickly implement your backup plan so you don't put yourself or your family at too much risk.

Get a Clear Picture of Your Current Situation

Organizing your finances starts with getting a clear picture of where you stand today. Before you get too far with business planning, you want to identify if there are elements of your financial situation that you want to improve in order to start your business with your best foot forward. If it is not perfect, that is okay! The important thing is that you develop an understanding of where you are, where you want to be, and what you need to do to prepare to start your business.

Current Snapshot

Using a spreadsheet or personal finance software program (lots of examples to follow), capture the following information:

INCOME
- What are all your sources of current income?
- How many of these sources are predictable and recurring, like a paycheck or monthly payment on a rental property you own, rather than incidental like an occasional sale on eBay or a side consulting project?
- Have you loaned money to a friend or relative that you actually expect to get back?

EXPENSES
- What are your ongoing, fixed expenses, like mortgage, food, insurance, utilities?
- What is your average amount for discretionary spending like dining out, entertainment, gifts, clothes, etc.?

SAVINGS
- How much liquid cash do you have in traditional bank accounts or money market accounts?

INVESTMENTS
- How much do you have in investment accounts?

DEBT
- Total all of your outstanding debt including secured (mortgage, vehicles, etc.) and unsecured debt (student loans, credit cards, etc.). Include total debt and interest rates.

Define the Value of Your Employee Benefits

There are a lot of hidden perks from your employer, and you want to make sure to document all of the benefits you receive now that you would have to pay for out-of-pocket if you worked for yourself. Most human resource departments have a benefits adviser who can help you calculate your costs. One word of caution: if you are keeping your entrepreneurial plans really secret and don't trust your internal HR department to keep confidence, you can possibly get information directly from the benefit providers.

Item	Monthly dollar value if you pay for them yourself
Health insurance	
Dental insurance	
Retirement	
Sick pay	
Vacation pay	
Workers' compensation	
Life insurance	

Chapter 13 will give you lots of tools for shopping for benefits on your own, so you can adjust your numbers once you do more research on better-priced options. For now, in the case of health insurance, if you are in the United States, you can look up the COBRA payment number that you would pay if you carried your same health plan and paid for it yourself.

The Trick Is to Track

While you can use a plain old notebook and pen for scratching out a few numbers and making calculations, your life will be much easier if you choose a tool to automate tracking of your personal finances. The key to your financial health is having a consistent, up-to-date picture of your finances at all times, and a clear plan and path for the future.

The exact tool you use is not important. What is important is to do the following things:

- Set up a basic system that has all your major financial categories defined: income, expenses, savings, investments, and debt. This way, you can plug in new numbers when you are working on your business plan.
- Sign up for online banking. You don't want to have to worry about visiting a bank or staying on hold for twenty minutes every time you inquire into your accounts.
- Determine your strategy: if tracking your finances on a monthly basis yourself seems too overwhelming, hire someone to do it. The worst thing you can do is not do it at all.
- Automate as much as possible. You will have so many things to worry about when you start your business; spending four hours each month to manually enter your expenses line-by-line into a spreadsheet is not a good use of your time.

One of the most popular personal finance software programs is Quicken, made by Intuit, but there are a lot of other options available that you can see detailed at Read Write Web.[1]

Clean House

Once you get a clear picture of your current situation, you want to do everything you can to create a strong financial base for your new business. There are three components to this:

1. Clean up your credit.
2. Reduce your expenses.
3. Build up cash reserves.

Five Ways to Clean Up Your Credit Score

For the financial advice in this chapter, I leaned heavily on Lynnette Khalfani, financial expert and author of many books including *Zero Debt*, *The Money Coach's Guide to Your First Million*, and *Perfect Credit*. I respect Lynnette not just for her excellent advice, which she shares as a media expert on *Oprah*, CNN, FoxNews, and CNBC, but because she has personally recovered from $100,000 in credit card debt which she documented in her bestselling book *Zero Debt*.

She sees good credit as a huge boon for the small business owner, as it will allow you to easily set up accounts and get good rates on any necessary business financing. She says, "Whether or not you think it is fair, most financial professionals will judge your character and degree of responsibility by your credit score." Here are her suggestions for the five best ways to increase your score into the "very good" range of 760 to 850 points:

1. **Pay your bills on time.** 35% of your credit score is based on how well you pay your bills.
2. **Examine how much credit you are using of your allocated credit.** A portion of your score is how much credit card debt you have vs. credit available. Try to pay off your balances each month, and if not, pay more than the minimum payment.
3. **Do not cancel paid off credit cards.** A portion of your credit score is based on the average age of your credit accounts. So a mistake many people make is to pay off a credit card and close the account. This will erase this portion of your credit history, and could adversely affect your rating.
4. **Pay off credit card debt first.** Not all debt is the same. Mortgage or installment credit, like a car loan, is not as bad as revolving credit. Credit card debt is the worst. Try to pay that down as fast as you can, and see your scores improve.
5. **Watch your inquiries for new credit**. If you jump at the chance to save 10% off of purchases at a local store by signing up for their credit card, realize that lots of credit inquiries reflect poorly on your credit report. Ideally, you should only have one inquiry every 18 months.[2]

Reduce Expenses

It is easy to get used to "the lifestyle to which you have become accustomed." But when preparing for a big life change, you want to have a lean home operation. This is to reduce stress and give you more breathing room so that your business can really take root. There is nothing worse than having to make sales immediately in order to pay rent. This will make you frightened and desperate, not exactly qualities to help you win friends and influence people.

There are hundreds of ways you can cut expenses from your budget—be creative! And remember, you are not doing this to please some judgmental personal finance expert wagging her finger at you, you are doing it to get one step closer to building a business that makes you smile on Monday morning.

Build a Cash Reserve

Once you are clear where you stand and start cutting back expenses, it is time to build up a nice cash reserve. Experts recommend saving a range of three to six months of expenses, but if you are really motivated and risk-averse, you might want to save twelve months' worth of expenses.

For some of you, this may seem an impossible task, especially if you are struggling just to pay your bills. But I bet that with a little close evaluation, you will be able to save a bit each month. Don't consider this a make-or-break rule, just realize that if you don't have as much of a cash reserve, you should have a proven business idea (i.e., you are already making money on the side of your day job) and a very solid backup plan (like a boss who is willing to take you back, a great relationship with a recruiter, a rich uncle, or a very marketable skill you can draw upon that won't get you arrested).

The Number

Some people use this savings as a true reserve, and do not touch it. A good friend of mine is a longtime self-employed consultant and leads a very adventurous life. After doing some intense and large-scale projects, she builds up a cash cushion. Then she takes off chunks of time to scuba dive around the world and do volunteer work. When her savings hit $40,000, she goes back to work to fill up the pot. It is a nice model for her, because knowing that she will not totally deplete her savings, she actually enjoys her time off without guilt or fear.

Let Your Fears Guide You

Fears are not all bad! They can be a great way to ensure that your plan covers what it needs to. If you have a nagging fear about something that is not covered in your current plan, it is a good indication that you need to address it.

One of my blog readers shared some of his wife's concerns with me when he told her he wanted to quit his job to start a business. Her fears are listed below with some of my suggestions following. Use your professional network and trusted advisers to get the answers you need to whatever money fears pop into your mind.

HOW WILL I PAY FOR A MEDICAL EMERGENCY?

- Set aside a fund to cover the deductible on your health insurance plan.
- Become very familiar with the specifics of your policy so you know what is covered and what is not.

HOW WILL I REPLACE PAID TIME OFF?

- Unless you want to work 365 days a year (not recommended), you need to factor time off into your business model. When calculating your hourly rate, build in days off, and time to do marketing and administration.

HOW MUCH AM I REALLY GOING TO PAY IN TAXES?

- Talk with your accountant about different tax scenarios and specific taxes that relate to the self-employed.
- Set aside a percentage of savings to pay taxes each time you get paid by your client.

WHAT IF MY CLIENTS DON'T PAY ON TIME?

- Secure a business line of credit to use in emergencies when a client does not pay on time.

WHAT IF I GET SUED BY A CLIENT OR COMPETITOR?

- Talk to a lawyer about the appropriate type of liability insurance to ensure that you mitigate your risk.

Five Reasons You Shouldn't Have a Cushion
Before You Quit Your Job

While most financial experts and advisers I spoke to encourage people to have a substantial amount of money set aside in case of emergencies, Naomi Dunford of Ittybiz offered this contrarian advice:

Once upon a time, I wrote a post about the monetary benefits of having a financial cushion. And I agree with myself. From a purely money standpoint, you're an idiot if you don't have at least something tucked away for when all your clients die of smallpox.

But that's the money part of it. What about business-wise? As in, business growth–wise? From that angle, I don't know if it's the best idea. Here's why.

1. **Not having a cushion lights a fire under your ass.** From E-myth to StomperNet and everyone in between advises against analysis paralysis—what's the absolute BEST typeface to use on the logo? Should we go with blue or green? Does this job contribute to my future business goals?

   When you have no cushion, there's no time for that. That freelance gig you're dilly-dallying about bidding on? That's tomorrow night's dinner.

2. **You're forced to get creative.** If you want to market yourself—and since you don't have a cushion, marketing yourself would be a very good idea indeed—you have to actually think. Any idiot can buy a bunch of ads to get people to buy their service or check out their blog or order their book. But that's not where the good stuff comes from.

   When you have no money, you have to hustle. Your sole source of advertising might be the shirts you just had printed for fifty bucks. You might have to wear your cousin's bunny suit and stand outside the radio station holding a sign that pleads "Ask me what I do!" Hell, you might even have to get off your ass and talk to some real, live people and ask them for business.

(continued)

3. You're going to learn to focus. When you have a cushy start-up loan or a quadzillion months of savings in the bank, it's awful easy to get distracted. I mean, look at all there is to do out there! Flickr alone could kill a week.

But when you need work or exposure or sales, you focus like a laser. (Yes, Mom. A laser. In air quotes. From *Austin Powers*.)

When you need a check in the mail sooner rather than later, checking a blog to see if anybody responded to your witty and insightful comment doesn't exactly seem like the most efficient use of your time.

4. You don't lose the fire. When you're first starting out, you're burning to succeed. All you want is to get your hands in there and do it. You want to print those goddamn t-shirts by hand if you have to. Hanging around in your cubicle for 19 months until you feel you have enough start-up capital is soul-sucking. Your fire goes.

If your fire goes, soon enough those hand printed t-shirts don't seem like such a good idea anymore and you're signing the line for your fifth one percent cost-of-living raise in a row.

5. The sooner you start, the sooner you'll succeed. There's a great saying I love: "The best time to plant a tree was forty years ago. The second best time is today."

These are comforting words today because you don't have a tree. Don't cry over lost tree planting opportunities, I always say. (OK, no, I don't.) But do you think it would have been good advice forty years ago? Would you have said, "Well, maybe now's not the perfect time. I'll do it when I retire"? Not if you wanted the tree, you wouldn't have.

I have no doubt there are countless thriving businesses run by entrepreneurs who waited till the time is right, and I applaud them. I don't know much about them, though. I don't know much about them because they're not making the front page of *Fast Company*. They don't tend to launch on Tech Crunch.

The ones I know about, the ones with buzz and energy and excitement and soul, they're the ones who took the plunge and sold their stereo to pay for a bunny suit.[3]

What to Do While Still Employed

There are a few specific things you should do while still employed at your corporation. They include securing:

- Supplemental life insurance. To be really safe, you should have an amount of coverage that is about ten times your annual salary, to protect your loved ones. Most people don't invest in a high enough limit, and this puts your family at risk.
- Workers' compensation insurance. You want to get workers' compensation insurance before you quit your job.
- If you plan on making any changes to the deductibles on your health plan benefits, have all your family members take care of doctor appointments and procedures covered under your current plan.
- If you have money allocated in a health savings plan (HSP), make sure you spend it within the calendar year for which it is allocated. Check your specific plan to see how you can spend it—in many cases, it can be used for eyeglasses, prescriptions, and other items which can add up to quite a bit of out-of-pocket expenses.

Get Help

When weighing a big decision like quitting your job to start a business, you want to make sure you are as informed as possible about the financial implications of your decisions.

I recommend getting input and advice from the following professionals:

Financial Planner

A good financial planner will be able to help you look at the big picture of your finances and evaluate different options for meeting your goals. This person can help you:

- Define retirement goals
- Define education funding goals if you have children

- Evaluate options for types of self-employed retirement plans
- Define specific annual targets (e.g., you must fund your IRA with at least X dollars per year if you want to reach your goals)

Certified Public Accountant (CPA)

A CPA, together with a lawyer, can help you evaluate an appropriate business structure that gives you maximum protection and minimizes taxes. You can also get some good working numbers for how much you can expect to pay in taxes if you are self-employed for your working budget.

How to Find a Good Financial Planner

Small business expert and author of *Small Business Cash Flow: Strategies for Making Your Business a Financial Success* Denise O'Berry says there are two key areas you should focus on when selecting a financial adviser for your business: 1) your needs, and 2) fit for your business. She elaborates:

WHAT ARE YOU LOOKING FOR?

- **Geographical proximity.** Is it important that you work with someone who can meet you face-to-face, or are you comfortable with a virtual relationship?
- **Service level.** Are you schooled in all the different aspects of financial planning for your business and need only minimal direction, or do you require substantial advice and direction from an expert?
- **Paper handling.** Do you love poring over all the details of the financial papers of your business, or does the thought of doing so give you a headache?
- **Business size.** Are you more comfortable with a "big name" firm and their breadth of experience, or would you rather connect with a smaller, more personal firm?
- **Service fees.** Fees for service cover a broad range. Paying more does not equal better service. Consider your cash flow budget tolerance when making your selection.[4]

FINDING A FINANCIAL ADVISER WHO'S THE RIGHT FIT.

- Ask around. Tap into your network of entrepreneurial contacts to see who they use as a starting point.
- Interview carefully. Find out if the person specializes in businesses like yours. Each type of business has different requirements and needs. You'll also want to find out what they've done for others. Make sure they describe business results that are comparable to the ones you seek.
- Does it feel right? You'll want to make sure you connect with this person. Do they listen? Are they genuinely interested in you and your business? Can you envision having a long-term relationship with them?

Outsource vs. Abdicate

I am a big fan of outsourcing anything in your life that is not a core strength or a joy to do. As long as you focus your freed-up time to generate more revenue or opportunities, it is a good trade. Marcus Buckingham in the best-selling book *Now, Discover Your Strengths* says: "Whenever you interview people who are truly successful at their chosen profession—from teaching to telemarketing to acting to accounting—you discover that the secret to their success lies in their ability to discover their strengths and to organize their life so that these strengths can be applied."[5]

When it comes to your finances, you need to be careful to make sure that you don't outsource to *abdicate responsibility* for overseeing your money, but rather to *focus on more high-energy and high-return* activities. In my own case, I would rather give myself a root canal than spend hours hunched over a spreadsheet, but I do like knowing how my business is doing financially.

If you totally abdicate responsibility, you may open yourself to be taken advantage of by an unscrupulous person who will realize that you are insecure about and afraid of financial matters.

My dear Aunt Char, known to most of the world as Miss Beadle from the television show *Little House on the Prairie,* had such an unfortunate encounter when she was doing very well financially. She hired a business manager whom we will call "George" to look after all of her money and investments. At the time, she had a lovely home in Topanga Canyon in Los Angeles, a healthy check rolling in every month from the series, and plenty of money in the bank.

Because she wasn't comfortable handling financial details, she handed everything over to George, including power of attorney.

At first everything was great. She felt wonderful that her finances were taken care of so that she could focus on her acting career.

Then George developed a bad cocaine habit. All of her hard-earned money, assets, and home went up George's nose. It was surprising, devastating, and heartbreaking.

"He was a good friend who I trusted but I should have taken warning when I realized he was using 'recreational drugs' and that friends were trying to drop hints that all was not right. I could have avoided all this if I had done research on him and not just taken a friend's recommendation."

This case may seem a bit extreme, but believe me, variations on this theme happen every day.

You must oversee the work done by your financial advisers and managers. In particular, do the following things:

- Review your financial statements at the end of each month.
- Review money spent in each category in relation to monthly averages.
- Ask questions if you see charges you don't understand.
- If you feel your adviser is getting defensive about your questions or glossing over them, involve a trusted third party.
- Do not give over power of attorney to anyone but your most trusted close family members.
- Even if you do not get involved in the details of managing your money, learn financial basics. Know how to read an income statement and balance sheet.
- Identify a trusted third party with a strong finance background who can review financials periodically.

The Mental Side of Money

If you think that working for yourself is going to solve your lifelong problems with money, I hate to break it to you, it won't. Unless you address the underlying thoughts and beliefs that guide your financial behaviors, you are more likely to be in a *worse* financial situation if you work for yourself rather than as an employee.

If you make more money, you are likely to spend it. Think MC Hammer before he became a father of seven and a preacher. If you struggle with cash flow and getting clients, you are likely to panic and get further into debt. I was amazed to learn that Walt Disney went bankrupt.

So the biggest gift you can give yourself before starting your business is to understand your own thoughts, feelings, and beliefs about money so you can change any unhealthy behaviors that will get in the way of running an effective business.

Do You Define Yourself by Your Credit Score?

Some of the popular financial media figures have a lot of harsh words for those who have poor financial practices. They wag their fingers at "impulse shoppers" and use words like "irresponsible," "undisciplined," and "deadbeat."

I don't think people dig themselves into a financial hole because they do not want to be responsible. I think they do it because they feel insecure, overwhelmed, and afraid. It doesn't feel good not to be able to pay your bills.

A couple of years ago I conducted a telephone seminar on how to take back the power in your career for a group of employees in a nonprofit organization that was undergoing rapid change. We had just walked through an exercise about creating a vision of their ideal work, without the constraints of silly things like reality. I asked if there were any questions and got one from a very bright employee named Patrick.

"This is a great exercise for some people, but I can't even begin to define a vision of my perfect work."

I asked Patrick why it was so hard.

"I have lots of student loan debt and some credit card debt. Who could I possibly get interested to fund my dreams? I don't want to ask my parents to lend me money since they have done enough already."

What was *not* said on the phone was more powerful than what was said. Patrick is a smart, capable, caring, and perceptive young man who is already doing great things with his life. But he had convinced himself that since he was in a tough financial situation, he didn't have permission to even imagine what a perfect life would look like.

Since when did your credit score become the required pass to a better life?

The financial part of your life is one area where there is a public, accessible record of all your past behaviors and decisions, good and bad. Every move you make financially is carefully tracked and recorded. And as a society, we place a huge weight on this score, since to us it suggests a level of maturity, responsibility, and, I would argue, moral superiority. What if we tracked and scored a whole variety of other things in our lives?

GENEROSITY SCORE

Adds to good score: Listened compassionately to someone in need. Donated time, money, or items to worthy cause. Demonstrated love, compassion, and forgiveness on a regular basis.

Subtracts from good score: Never volunteered for anything. Ate all the cookies before your siblings got home. Held grudges and never forgave anyone for making mistakes.

RELATIONSHIP SCORE

Adds to good score: Dated only happy, emotionally healthy people. Spoke openly and honestly about feelings. Respected your partner and cared about his well-being.

Subtracts from good score: Dated drug-addicted drummer in heavy metal band. Spent endless years in a relationship that went nowhere. Blamed all of your unfinished emotional crap on your ex-wife.

DIET SCORE

Adds to good score: Ate balanced diet of fruits, vegetables, and grains. Didn't use excess sugar, salt, fat, alcohol, or unhealthy substances.

Subtracts from good score: Went on late-night Ben & Jerry's binge. Ate fast food and double chocolate lava cake with ice cream on the side. Fancied chips and salsa for dinner.

What kind of scores would you have in these other areas? If you are like me, you may find that it is impossible to be perfect in most areas of your life. But because there are not three agencies tracking your diet or relationship history and sharing the score with anyone who wants access, we tend to give ourselves more of a break if we are not perfect in areas besides personal finance.

People who have money struggles often face one or more of the following situations:

- **I have lots of debt and it is overwhelming.** Many people have the erroneous impression that people with huge debt are credit card–wielding shopaholics who have an insatiable desire for the perfect Manolo Blahnik shoe. And perhaps some of them are. But I find that the majority of people slowly and almost imperceptibly slipped into overwhelming debt by receiving a poor financial education, and using their credit cards for purchases they can't afford (including necessities like paying for college, room and board). This debt feels like a lead weight on your chest and creates a huge amount of fear.
- **I have a bad credit score because of mistakes that I made in my younger years.** Oh, the follies of youth. Some of us didn't understand the principles of money management or the pitfalls of getting access to credit cards too soon. We didn't realize that one late payment on a credit card could shoot interest rates through the roof, or that a lengthy delay on a payment would be reflected on our credit report for seven years. We also may have cosigned on a car or home loan for friends or relatives who were unable to pay and saw our credit scores plummet as a result.
- **I have excellent credit, my bills are all paid, and I have money in the bank. But I still feel poor!** Some people manifest their emotional relationship with money by never feeling fulfilled, no matter how much they make. They might have grown up without money and have an intense fear of poverty. Or they grew up wealthy and feel that if they don't continually bring in huge piles of cash they have no worth. People who don't have money or carry lots of debt can often be confused by this emotion since

these people have what they are looking for: financial stability. But to those who struggle with this issue, it is as scary and painful as being deeply in debt.

- **I feel uncomfortable asking for money for my services, whether it be negotiating my salary as an employee or setting an hourly rate as a free agent.** Our comfort level with charging for our services is often directly related to how we feel about ourselves and how well we understand the value we bring to our customers.

Being financially responsible is not about living up to anyone's standard of perfection. It is about respecting and valuing yourself, protecting your interests, and leaving many doors open for you to do whatever it is you want to do: travel, buy a home, provide for your children, or start a business. A good credit score is a great thing when you approach it from the right perspective.

Common Financial Patterns

Nearly every financial situation reflects one of three general patterns: seeing oneself as having less than enough, just enough, or more than enough money. The term "enough" is relative and highly individualized. For some people, having basic needs met is sufficient, engendering a sense of satisfaction and security; among others, no matter how much money they accumulate, the perception persists that they need more. This table illustrates these patterns and their main characteristics, as well as the accompanying thoughts, beliefs, emotions, behaviors, and relationship dynamics.

Financial Patterns	Less Than Enough	Just Enough	More Than Enough
Characteristics	Sense of need and lack Poor self-image A focus on the past, with worries about the future	Sense of adequacy Low self-image A focus on and concern about the future, with regrets about the past	Sense of abundance Healthy self-image A focus on the present, with positive expectations of the future
Thoughts	"I'm going to run out of money and there's no one to help me." "I wish someone would take care of me." "If only I could win the lottery." "I wonder who I can borrow money from." "I'll never get what I want." "I hate this financial struggle." "There must be something wrong with me because I can't make any money."	"If only I had a little more money, I could be comfortable." "I wish I knew how to get what I want." "I'll never have enough money to retire." "There must be something else I ought to be doing to get out of this rut."	"Life is good." "I'm doing a great job." "I like my life." "I'm grateful to be enjoying this abundance." "I'm really lucky." "I like sharing good fortune with others." "I appreciate everything I have."
Beliefs	"I'm not worthy." "There isn't enough for everyone." "There must be something wrong with me." "People like me can't make money." "I'm poor." "Money is the root of all evil." "It's not spiritual to have money."	"Wealthy people are not good." "I don't deserve luxury." "Luxury is bad." "I won't make good investment decisions, so having no surplus keeps me safe." "I'm not safe." "If I have surplus, people will want my money."	"It's an abundant world." "I have the right to have what I want." "It's okay to be rich." "Wealth is good." "I'm deserving." "I'm a good person." "I'm trustworthy." "There's enough for everyone." "Wealthy people can be kind and generous."

(continued)

Financial Patterns	Less Than Enough	Just Enough	More Than Enough
Beliefs	"It's noble to be poor." "If I'm poor, people will feel sorry for me."	"It's not safe to be wealthy." "If I'm wealthy, no one will like me." "Wealthy people don't go to heaven."	
Emotions	Needy, empty, alone, inadequate, unworthy, unsupported, defective, unfulfilled, depressed, sense of impending doom	Frustrated, unappreciated, invisible, bored, limited, blocked	Independent, satisfied, secure, joyful, generous, proud, respected, confident, connected, appreciated, accepted, acknowledged, loved
Behaviors	Chronic debting Late bill-paying Financial vagueness Check bouncing Dreams of having lots of money Tax avoidance Obsession with financial rescue dramas	Living paycheck to paycheck Periodic debting Occasional late bill-paying Bill-paying strategizing Keeping track of money grudgingly and sporadically	Solvent Skilled at money management Charitable Generous Curious about investments Adept at making rational investment
Relationship with Money	Conflicted Unstable Vague Struggling constantly Untrusting	Indifferent Vacillating	Comfortable Stable Caring Respectful Trusting
Relationships with Oneself and Others	Isolating People pleasing Having few intimate relationships Self-critical Needy Codependent	Having small circle of friends Yearning for more people contact Fearful of taking chances socially	Socially active Well supported by friends and associates Strong interpersonal skills Adept at networking

Financial Patterns	Less Than Enough	Just Enough	More Than Enough
	Uncomfortable expressing emotions Not good at setting boundaries Untrusting Withholding Controlling or controlled		At ease with people Good at setting boundaries Self-motivated

Source: From *Build Your Money Muscles* by Joan Sotkin

It might initially appear that people who view themselves as having less than enough money experience constant discomfort and those who see themselves as having more than enough live in joy and satisfaction. In reality, though, both financial patterns correlate with a wide range of emotional states. People who regard themselves as having less than enough money, although troubled financially, may enjoy the company of family and friends, participate in satisfying social activities, and experience success in nonfinancial areas of their life. At the same time, those who see themselves as having more than enough money might be dealing with family or work problems, feel unfulfilled creatively, suffer ongoing disappointments, or have relationship difficulties.

Facing and Fighting Financial Trolls

J. D. Roth has become one of the most respected "real life" financial bloggers who dispenses advice on his blog Get Rich Slowly. He offers advice for fighting "financial trolls":

COPING WITH EXTERNAL TROLLS

When I started Get Rich Slowly, I wanted people to like and agree with everything I wrote. Any time I received a negative comment, I took time to

(continued)

exchange e-mail with the person who left it. Here's an example of an actual criticism I once received: "I would love [this site] if only the privileged would acknowledge how lucky and privileged they are and how their 'advice' applies to only other privileged kids." I tried to carry on a conversation with the commenter, but nothing I could say would satisfy him—in his mind I was a rich jerk and nothing could change that.

- I realized that 95% of these people aren't interested in a rational exchange of ideas. They're external financial trolls. They have chips on their shoulders, they're clinging to preconceived notions, or they just want to argue. They're not worth my time.

Defeating most external trolls is straightforward. Because they're not internal, you can usually just remove yourself from the situation. Ignore the troll. Change the conversation. Leave the room. Hang up the phone. Do not argue . . . any time you argue with a troll, the troll wins. Do not engage the troll.

COPING WITH INTERNAL TROLLS

Internal trolls are more insidious than their external brethren. Because they are a part of you, eradicating them takes self-discipline. Examples of internal trolls include:

- Self-defeating thoughts and behaviors: "I can't do this—it's too difficult," "I'm not smart enough," "It's too much work," "I don't deserve to have money."
- Procrastination: "I'll start next week," "I'll worry about this later," "I can start saving next month—this month I'll buy an Xbox."
- Rationalization: "Buying just one pair of shoes won't blow my budget," "I'm out with my friends—I should join the fun," "I should reward myself for how well I've been doing lately."
- Barriers: "I don't know how to open an IRA," "It's too much bother to set up automatic deposits," "Sure I could call around for lower rates, but I don't like talking on the phone."

Conquering internal trolls can be non-intuitive. Most are a product of self-doubt, which is best combated through exercise, discipline, positive social interaction, and a healthy diet. Seriously. The following can also help:

- Talk back to yourself! It makes sense to avoid arguments with external trolls, but confronting internal trolls is an excellent tactic.
- Set financial goals. Review them regularly.
- Read success literature: personal finance books, self-development manuals, and biographies of successful people.
- Educate yourself. Learn about money. I resisted investing for a long time until I learned just how easy it was to open an IRA.
- Find a mentor, a coach, or an advisor. Learn from others.

I have much more trouble with internal trolls than I do with external trolls. They're a constant threat.

KNOW WHEN TO SEEK HELP

Some trolls are difficult to defeat. What do you do about a spouse who insists on sabotaging your financial security? How do you deal with your own compulsive shopping? Problems like these may require the assistance of a trained professional: an accountant, a lawyer, or a psychologist. The important thing is to deal with them. Until you defeat them, they'll only hold you back, preventing you from achieving success.[6]

In the End, Is It Really About the Money?

Money is a hugely important piece of your business puzzle. But it is not the only thing, and can be a distraction if you let it. Tim Ferriss says:

> There is much to be said for the power of money as currency (I'm a fan myself), but adding more of it just isn't the answer as often as we'd like to think. In part, it's laziness. "If only I had more money" is the easiest way to postpone the intense self-examination and decision-making necessary to create a life of enjoyment—now and not later. By using money as the scapegoat and work as our all-consuming routine, we are able to conveniently disallow ourselves the time to do otherwise: "John, I'd love to talk about the gaping void I feel in my life, the hopelessness

that hits me like a punch in the eye every time I start my computer in the morning, but I have so much work to do! I've got at least three hours of unimportant e-mail to reply to before calling the prospects who said 'no' yesterday. Gotta run!"

Busy yourself with the routine of the money wheel, pretend it's the fix-all, and you artfully create a constant distraction that prevents you from seeing just how pointless it is. Deep down, you know it's all an illusion, but with everyone participating in the same game of make-believe, it's easy to forget.

The problem is more than money.[7]

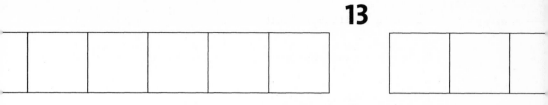

13

How to Shop for Benefits

I have to admit that of all the topics I talk with people about when they are pondering quitting their job to start a business, securing health benefits is the one that makes me want to poke myself in the eye with a pencil. Then I have to check my self-employed insurance policy to make sure that I am covered for vision care.

I think there are a number of reasons why it is such a difficult topic:

- There are horror stories from the media that tell of people losing everything in a medical emergency because of lack of insurance.
- There is an overwhelming amount of jargon and terms related to different types of insurance plans.
- The consequences of choosing the wrong plan feel very risky.

This chapter is definitely geared to U.S. readers since each country of the world has very different health care systems and structures.

Choose Your Approach to Researching Benefits

Like a lot of other topics discussed in this book, fear plays a big part in thinking about insurance. And like fear in other areas (Will I live in a van down by the river? Will my family and friends support me when I tell them I want to start a business?), the best way to deal with it is to deconstruct it in a straightforward and organized way.

Depending on your learning style and approach to research, I would imagine that you would fall into one of three main categories:

1. You are very excited to research insurance plans in great detail, create spreadsheets, and weigh a lot of the analysis yourself.
2. The whole prospect of researching benefits feels completely unpleasant and overwhelming (read: pencil in eye), and you would love it if someone just took care of it for you.
3. Somewhere in between the two extremes: you would like to be an active participant in the process, but would like expert help to make sure you make solid decisions.

The good news is that there are resources and support for any one of these approaches.

One of the helpful sources I used for this chapter is a book called *Get a Good Deal on Your Health Insurance Without Getting Ripped Off*, written by Jonathan Pletzke. Pletzke explains:

> I did not set out to write a book about health insurance. I was working on a different book which included a chapter about how to get your own health insurance. Once I dug in and started my research, I found that there was much more material than could fit in one chapter. While some of the materials can be found elsewhere, there is some very unique information that can only be found here: which includes a technique to compare all health plans "apples to apples," how to avoid being ripped off, and a simple yet comprehensive way to view all of the health plan information.[1]

I agree with Jonathan. There is far too much information related to securing health insurance to cover in one chapter of a book. So my short answer to each of the dilemmas would be:

1. If you have a preference for doing it all yourself, get Jonathan's book, read everything, do all the exercises, and get as much data as you can online. Make a decision, and then validate it with an opinion you trust from an expert broker.
2. If you just want it done, get a great broker and have him or her hold your hand through the whole process.
3. If you want to learn a bit and get it done, get Jonathan's book, read the relevant chapters, and get a good broker to help you choose a plan.

Or you could opt for a fourth, magic solution.

Magic Solution

Become a Canadian citizen.

Seems our friends to the north have a lot of things figured out when it comes to health care. My Canuck friend Tina Forsyth shared: "In Canada all our 'standard' health expenses are paid for—any doctors visits, surgeries, etc. So there are no worries around being able to pay for that as it is covered by our provincial health care plans."

Just so I wouldn't feel totally jealous, she added:

> What we don't have covered are "extras" . . . dentist visits, drug prescriptions, getting glasses, etc. If you are employed those are the kind of benefits that your company may give you, so you don't have to pay $200 to a dentist to get your teeth cleaned. The other thing normally covered with employee benefits that we have to pay for if we work for ourselves is life and disability insurance.

I share this scenario to give you a little bit of perspective and so you know that despite having excellent plans (if you are Canadian) it is just one of many factors to juggle when starting a business.

The important thing to remember is you have options, and there is a process.

So let's get to it.

How to Evaluate Self-funded Health Insurance

1. Define your ideal level of health, life insurance, and retirement benefits to ensure that you and your family are protected against risk.
2. Identify any personal issues that could affect your ability to get benefits (such as preexisting conditions).
3. Identify key partners or online resources that will help you in creating your plan.
4. Create a complete self-funded benefits plan that you can evaluate against your current corporate package.
5. Make a decision and sign on the dotted line.

Some Basics

The premise of health insurance is the same as for any other kind of insurance: fees vary depending on the amount of financial risk you are willing to assume versus the amount of risk the insurance company is willing to assume. Risk to you is a higher deductible. If you take on more risk, you will pay less. If you pay less, you will need to put money aside to offset expenses.

If you are smart about how you plan and weigh your risks, and adjust your savings plan accordingly, you can secure health insurance, even with preexisting conditions.

Benefits expert Paula Peck, who contributed to this chapter, had one of the ultimate "black marks" on her medical history: a diagnosis of cancer at age thirty-five, with (covered) medical bills that totaled upward of $650,000 after her treatment.

Yet with careful evaluation, shopping, and financial planning, when she became self-employed, she obtained good coverage at a reasonable cost.

Health Care Lingo

As you go through this chapter and see all kinds of terms thrown around, you may need a bit of clarification. The following is a glossary of health care lingo, written by Jonathan Pletzke for a series of articles about health insurance on StartupNation.

Navigating the health-insurance maze is a little easier if you understand the terminology. Here's a guide to most of the important terms you'll need to know as a small business owner:

- **Blue Cross and Blue Shield Association:** The national trade organization that links 38 independent regional health insurance companies in the United States. Some of the BCBS companies are not-for-profit. The association operates through a series of administratively independent franchises offering insurance plans within defined regions.
- **Catastrophic health insurance:** It protects you against the high cost of treating severe injury or long illness. These policies usually cover some, if not all, of your medical expenses above the maximum liability limit of another insurance policy.
- **Co-pay:** This is your out-of-pocket cost per doctor visit under the terms of your policy, often $5 to $25 for each visit.
- **Co-insurance:** Ever hear of an 80/20 or 50/50 policy? It's a policy with a "co-insurance" provision, and is typically less expensive than other policies. Essentially, you pay an annual deductible, then your insurance company pays a percentage of your expenses after that (e.g. 80 percent in an 80/20 policy). You pay the difference (20 percent in an 80/20 policy). This type of policy also has a lifetime maximum, which limits the amount the insurance company pays toward health-care expenses in your lifetime.
- **Deductible:** The amount you agree to pay out-of-pocket toward health care expenses each year. It's usually true that a higher deductible means a lower insurance premium.
- **Drug coverage:** Most policies have some prescription drug coverage, but don't assume it's there. Ask about it, and be sure you understand how the

(continued)

coverage works (e.g. Is there a co-pay, does it cover brand-name drugs, etc.).

- **Evidence of insurability:** Proof of a person's physical condition that affects acceptability for insurance or a health-care contract.
- **First-dollar coverage:** Insurance with no "front-end" deductible. Your coverage begins immediately for any covered benefit. It's common for many plans to provide first-dollar coverage for preventive care such as annual physical exams and immunization for children.
- **Guaranteed renewability:** Be sure that your health insurance cannot be cancelled after you become sick. You need "guaranteed renewability" in your policy.
- **Health Maintenance Organization (HMO):** A plan that covers visits to doctors in a network defined by the HMO. If you need to see a specialist or doctor outside of the network, you need a referral or approval from the HMO.
- **High-risk pools:** Thirty states operate these groups for the uninsurable. They guarantee to issue a health insurance plan, although at a higher cost.
- **HIPAA:** Primarily affecting the small-group and individual markets, the Health Insurance Portability and Accountability Act of 1996 (HIPAA) was designed to allow portability of health insurance between jobs. It also required the passage of a federal law to protect personally identifiable health information.
- **Medical underwriting:** Most individual policies are written against the specific medical status of an insured individual, while group policies (usually 10 or more employees) typically are not. Under this type of coverage, someone with a pre-existing condition or illness may not get coverage, or their coverage may be more expensive.
- **Out-of-pocket expenses:** Your portion of health-care costs that are not reimbursed by the insurer, including deductibles, co-payments and co-insurance.
- **Preferred Provider Organization (PPO):** A plan that covers visits to doctors in a network. If you go to a doctor outside the network, a smaller portion of your expenses are covered. The advantage of a PPO is the ability to

choose doctors without referrals or approval, which isn't the case with an HMO.

- **Pre-existing conditions:** For insurance purposes, a pre-existing condition exclusion must relate to a condition for which medical advice, diagnosis, care or treatment was recommended or received during the six-month period before an individual's enrollment in a new policy plan.

- **Portability:** A requirement that health plans provide you continuous coverage without waiting periods if you move from one plan to another. Portability requirements vary by state. In some, you get no credit for prior coverage and must wait, uninsured, during the entire pre-existing condition exclusion period.

- **Report card:** An accounting of the quality of services rendered by comparable providers over time. You can use report cards to choose a health plan or doctor, or check up on the overall effectiveness of your current plan or provider.

- **Risk pool:** A legislatively created program that groups together individuals—sometimes including entrepreneurs—who can't get coverage in the private sector.

- **Waiting periods:** The time an individual must wait to become eligible for benefits for a specific condition after overall coverage has begun.[2]

Understanding Current Coverage

Define Your Needs

Developing an understanding of your personal health and life insurance needs is an ongoing process. At different times in our lives we have different needs and are exposed to different risk factors, therefore our insurance needs change.

To start you need to have a full understanding of your current coverage and the costs. A common misconception is that the corporate benefit plan you enjoy only costs what you pay through payroll deduction plus a small corporate contribution. The fact is costs are often much higher for the corporation, which will impact you when you try to cover the cost yourself.

To understand your current costs, take an inventory of your current benefits and ask your employer for the actual costs.

Out-of-Pocket Expenses

Next you need to understand the cost of *using* the insurance.

- What are the co-payments for doctor visits, emergency care, hospital care, pharmacy, medical equipment, tests, etc.? What are the coinsurance amounts?
- Once you know the monthly cost of your health insurance coverage you need to evaluate how you use your insurance:

    How often do you go to the doctor?

    Are you undergoing treatment for a medical condition?

    How often do you go to the dentist?

    Do you have maintenance prescriptions?

    Do you need glasses/contacts?

- Pharmacy costs are probably the most volatile areas of concern. If your current coverage has a co-pay amount or a coinsurance amount it is critical to understand the true cost of the drug that you may be using. The difference between your current co-payments and the actual cost of drugs may prove to be rather shocking. The site www .pharmacychecker.com is a good place to at least get an idea of the cost. (It may not provide exact costs, but will give you an average price to work with.)

What Are Your Risk Factors?

Taking a personal medical inventory is critical to deciding which type of medical plan will best meet your needs. During this process you should evaluate yourself and your dependents.

Aside from a diagnosed condition, if you and your dependents are in relatively good medical condition then your medical risk should be low. If currently you or one of your dependents has an ongoing diagnosed condition then your medical cost risk could be very high.

It is very important when doing a medical inventory to understand your family history. For instance, if every aunt and uncle on one side of your family has had cardiac problems, then you are prone to have that condition.

Your medical history and your family medical history will also affect the pricing of any medical insurance you attempt to purchase.

Great Free Resource

If you are unsure what your health risks are, sign up for a personal health assessment at Health A-to-Z (healthatoz.com).

At this point you should have a good idea of how you currently utilize your health care coverage, and you should be able to identify what kind of medical risk you have and how much of that risk you can afford to pay for yourself and how much you may need to purchase insurance to cover.

You now need to dive in and evaluate all the different insurance plans available to you. This is a time when I highly recommend calling a professional broker.

Get a Broker

A health insurance broker, or "life agent" as they are sometimes called, is a critical piece of the health insurance equation. Even if you do most of the research yourself, it is smart to get the perspective of an experienced broker familiar with the nuances of providers and benefit plans. They might know of a lot more plans and options than you can find researching on your own, so you may want to contact them early in the process.

The job of a broker is to evaluate your needs, understand your tolerance for risk, and shop around for the best possible plan at the most reasonable cost. The insurance companies pay them, so their services won't cost you a thing.

What to Look For in a Broker

- **Track record.** Check to make sure the person has good experience in the field, and all up-to-date certifications and licenses.
- **Geographic expertise.** Each area in the United States is very different in laws, regulations, providers, and plans. So choose someone who understands the ins and outs of your particular geographic region.
- **Good references.** It is a great idea to ask for at least three references of people in your similar situation that they have helped. Ask about not only their results but the process of working with the broker. Were they easy to work with? Reliable, pleasant?
- **Broad perspective.** The broker who helped a blog reader secure insurance knew not only about individual plans, but also about how to choose the right organizational structure that might qualify you to start your own group plan at a much-reduced cost.

What Are the Options?

As you go through the process of identifying plans that may work for you it is important to ensure that your current providers are included in those plans. If you choose a plan that does not include doctors and providers that you are comfortable with, you are setting yourself up to be dissatisfied with the plan.

Do you have a primary care physician? Do you have specialists that you see on a regular basis? Is there a particular hospital that you prefer using? If you have dependents, who are the physicians that they regularly see?

For dental coverage, who is your dentist? And if you have dependents undergoing orthodontia care, who is their provider?

Make sure you share these preferences with your broker.

Types of Coverage to Evaluate

If you are happy with the coverage in your corporate plan, you can try to duplicate it on the outside, at the most reasonable cost possible. But if you are looking to expand and/or change coverage, you may want to evaluate the following categories, from Jonathan Pletzke's *Get a Good Deal on Your Health Insurance*:

- Wellness/Preventative
- Limited/Unlimited Lifetime or Annual Benefits
- Laboratory Work
- Pregnancy/Maternity
- Prescriptions
- Dental
- Vision
- Mental Health and Substance Abuse
- Alternative Medicine/Chiropractic/Acupuncture
- Accident and Life Add-ons
- International Coverage
- Home Health Care
- In Network or Out of Network Coverage

Some Special Considerations for the Self-employed

As you will see if you visit some Web sites and/or read Jonathan Pletzke's book, there is a lot of detail when it comes to insurance plans. And since each of you is different, it would be impossible to cover it all without boring you to tears.

But there are a few things I want to call your attention to when you are considering self-employment, just so you don't secure full-coverage medical and dental insurance and think you are done.

DENTAL AND VISION

For the most part dental and vision plans have annual limits per person. Dental plans will pay anywhere from $1000 to $3000 per person per year. Many vision plans pay around $500 per year including exams and glasses.

Depending upon your personal needs it may be cost effective to simply pay for these services without getting the coverage. However, one advantage of having a plan is you can take advantage of the contracted rate of the insurance company if you have the coverage.

This is an area where you need to examine your current usage and needs. Once again if you are considering self-funding this coverage, discuss it with your provider as they may be willing to give you a cut rate or the same rate as the insurance company.

One more possibility is that many individual medical plans will sell you dental, life, and vision coverage for a small fee.

SHORT- AND LONG-TERM DISABILITY

What would happen if you became ill or injured and were unable to work for an extended period of time? If you followed the recommendations in chapter 9, you may be saving from six to twelve months' worth of salary in an emergency fund.

But this money might not be enough to sustain you in the event of a health situation that would lay you up for an extended period of time. For this reason, it is good to consider a short- and/or long-term disability insurance plan.

Think about how much money you would need to get by if you were incapacitated, and check premiums with your broker.

LIFE INSURANCE

In chapter 9, I mentioned that many people are inadequately funded in life insurance, only paying for enough coverage to cover one or two years of their salary. Some people think about life insurance as an inheritance, a lump sum to leave to their kids.

Benefits specialist Paula Peck disagrees. She says: "The purpose of life insurance is to consider if your income is lost, how would your survivors be able to sustain the house? How would they pay off debts, and manage with the monthly expenses?"

If one spouse was not working and was taking care of the children, would he have to go to work and pay extra for child care?

Once you get an entire picture of your financial needs based on how you are choosing to fund your benefits, talk with your financial adviser to evaluate the appropriate amount of life insurance necessary to take care of your beneficiaries.

HEALTH SAVINGS PLAN (HSP)

An excellent idea for the self-employed who opt for high-deductible plans is to establish a Health Savings Plan (HSP). This can be a savings or money market account that you can contribute to tax-free, and utilize for any health-related expense. The fund can grow until you are sixty-five years old. It can be used for any health-related expense, including medical, dental, or vision care.

Think about this for a moment. Instead of paying extremely high premiums each month for full coverage and low co-payments, you can raise your deductible limits and put the money you would have paid to the insurance company in your HSP. If you don't have any health issues, your account grows over time. And if you need to use it, you will have the money set aside and available.

Your broker will be able to help you determine exactly what kind of plan you are eligible for, as there are some restrictions based on the type of coverage you have.

ASSOCIATIONS CAN OFFER INSURANCE OPTIONS

You may not realize that some of the professional associations you belong to can offer health insurance at better rates than you can secure on your own. These can be large organizations or small trade associations. Here are just a few examples. There are a lot more:

American Association of Retired Persons (AARP)
American Bar Association (ABA)
National Association of Self-Employed (NASE)
National Freelancers Union
Writer's Guild

WHATEVER YOU DO, DO NOT GO MORE THAN SIXTY DAYS
WITHOUT COVERAGE

In my research for this chapter, I learned that the worst thing you can do once you sever employment is to let health insurance coverage lapse for more than sixty days. When you do so, you lose your HIPAA rights to insurance coverage, which means your worst nightmare will come true: *you will lose your rights to guaranteed health insurance.* Although the guaranteed plan may be very expensive, it is guaranteed, so even if you have preexisting conditions, you can get health coverage.

So don't let it happen.

Fill out your COBRA paperwork and turn it in to your benefits administrator right away. By doing so, it does not mean you are obligated to pay for the COBRA program if you find a better and cheaper option, it just means that you lock in your ability to access it if necessary. If you go longer than sixty days without coverage, this may have a significant negative impact on your ability to secure coverage in the future.

If you blow the deadline, it cannot be fixed by a bit of sweet talk. It doesn't matter if you were out of the country, knocked out by the flu, or abducted by aliens.

No signed form by the end of sixty days, no guarantee of insurance. So just do it.

Making the Decision

It is a myth that you cannot buy health coverage any cheaper than you will receive from your employer. When your employer purchases health care coverage it is based upon the experience of the entire group, so if everyone in your company is in perfect health and never uses their medical coverage it could be very cheap. However, generally speaking probably at least 5 to 10 percent of your fellow employees have serious health conditions that drive the cost of coverage up every year. When you purchase an individual plan, your health and your family's health are the only underwriting factors.

The key will be to develop a very clear understanding of your needs, balance the premium versus deductible costs, and set up savings vehicles for whatever risk you choose to take on yourself.

If you are a spreadsheet ninja, you can gather all of your facts and figures, research and compare plans, and decide on your best option.

As for me, I made a beeline to a broker the second I quit my job. It simplifies so much, and they often have computer programs predesigned to handle all the different factors you are evaluating.

The Gigantic Disclaimer

I hope you have seen that while there is a clear process for determining what health insurance coverage you need and knowing how to secure it, you should view all sources of information—anecdotal, online, or in a book (like this one)—as just sources of information. As with anything important:

- Get more than one expert opinion.
- Read the fine print before you sign on the dotted line.
- Keep up with changes in policies.

I agree with the disclaimer in Jonathan Pletzke's book, which also applies to this chapter:

> This book is written for informational and educational purposes. Neither the author nor the publisher of this book is in the business of providing legal, financial, or other professional services or advice. As such, neither the author nor the publisher can be liable for your actions due to reading this book. You should contact competent professional advisors before making decisions about what is best for you. The author and publisher specifically disclaim any personal liability, loss or risk incurred as a consequence of the use and application, either directly or indirectly, of any information presented herein. Any similarity of fictional persons in this book to actual persons living or dead is purely coincidental.[3]

See, it is even scary to offer advice about benefits for those who are very knowledgeable. So do the sensible thing, educate yourself, and then check with the professionals.

Remember the basic rule of life (and especially Internet marketing): if it sounds too good to be true, it probably is.

Resources

- Healthinsurance.org
- NASE (National Association for the Self-Employed): www.nase.org
- BestHealthInsuranceBook.com (resources)
- PACE (Professional Association for Contract Employment): http://pacepros.com, http://www.healthinsurancefinders.com
- TheHealthInsuranceCenter.com
- Subject matter expert used for this chapter: Paula Peck, benefits consultant—paula.peck@sbcglobal.net

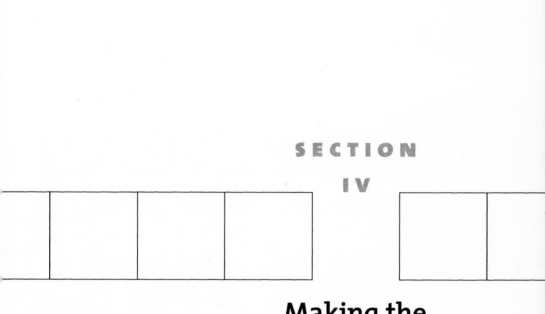

SECTION

IV

Making the
Leap

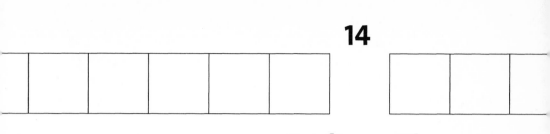

14

Dealing with Your Friends and Family

sat across the table from my client and studied his face as he talked. I could see small beads of sweat on his forehead. He swallowed hard.

I really am not sure what I am doing. After eighteen years climbing the corporate ladder as a sales and marketing manager, I want to be a freelance photographer. People who have known me for a long time think the idea is coming out of left field. My wife thinks I am crazy, and tells me to stop bothering her until I figure it out. Am I losing my mind?

One of the unexpected parts of moving from employee to entrepreneur is discovering that some of those around you are not ready, willing, or able to see you change. This can result in disagreements, fracturing or even ending long-term friendships and relationships. Here is why:

- **We usually form relationships around common bonds such as school, work, or community functions.** You might have a tight group of friends that helped you through the hell of medical or graduate school. Or you spent many hours in solidarity against an evil boss, griped about the lack of decent, eligible mates in the dating world, or watched your children grow up together. As you move away from these shared experiences, you may find that you don't have as much in common as you thought you did. And relationships fade.

- **Each person in a relationship assumes a specific role.** Maybe you have always been the kind and understanding friend who jumps into action when someone is in need, providing a shoulder to cry on, a truck to move furniture, or money to get out of a crisis. You may be the child who always made your parents proud, getting good grades, going to the "right" school, and getting a safe job. Your spouse may see you as a "rock," providing financial stability for the whole family. So if you decide to change roles, be prepared for some resentment. A true clue this is the case is when someone says, "What happened to the person I used to know? You don't act the same anymore!" They are right . . . and this is good!

- **You might be headed in a direction that freaks out your family and friends.** If you have always followed a safe and "respectable" path and suddenly contemplate doing something totally different, you may see some stunned reactions. Some friends may think that you have simply lost your mind. Others may be projecting their own insecurity on you by thinking, "If Ashok isn't satisfied with mundane suburban life, maybe I shouldn't be satisfied with my life either!"

- **As much as we all talk about wanting to be happy and fulfilled, when you actually are, it can annoy the crap out of those around you.** We bond with each other by our daily gripes. We start by sharing the depressing news in the paper with our spouse, then let the receptionist at work know how bad traffic was, then mumble quietly to a coworker about the stupid meeting we have to attend to start our day. And this is all before nine a.m. Can you imagine waking up and smiling at the day ahead of you? When someone asks you how you are, answering: "I am great, couldn't be better!" While eyeing you with suspicion, your friends may quietly check your bag for illicit drugs. Once they find you are on a natural high, they may tire of your positive demeanor and look for someone else to complain with.

How Can You Get Through These Tough Relationship Transitions?

Given what I just described, communicating with friends and relatives can be challenging. So let me give you the short version of this chapter:

You are crazy if you think you can convince all your friends and family that starting a business is a good idea.

Everyone has his own version of reality, a set of principles and values that may or may not be in sync with yours. No amount of information, communication tools, or techniques will influence someone who fundamentally disagrees with entrepreneurship as a viable employment option. Knowing this actually makes your job easier. Your task is not to sell your idea, it is to present it in a way that reflects your heartfelt intentions, and is clear, organized, and accessible.

With that in mind, there are four critical points:

- Common concerns about self-employment and their solution
- How to talk to your spouse about self-employment
- How to talk to your parents about self-employment
- How to filter useful feedback and toss the rest

Common Concerns

Family and friends can be a great source of support and love. They can also be ruthless critics.

While this is frustrating, there are actually some very good reasons why those you love may express fear or concern when you tell them you want to start a business. And it is not necessarily because they don't love you or because they want to see you forever bound to your drab, lifeless cubicle. To better understand their concerns, review this:

Concern	Reason for Concern	Solution
1. Your business idea doesn't make sense.	**They don't understand your business idea because you haven't explained it in a way that makes sense to them.** You may be totally enthusiastic about developing a computer program that fixes a critical flaw in a major software application, but this could be too technical or meaningless to someone else.	**Simplify your business description,** using terms and analogies that anyone can understand and relate to. This is a good thing to do in general, as most people you meet won't have a clue what you are talking about either.
2. Your business idea is not viable.	**They don't have enough information about your business to decide if it sounds viable or not, so they assume that it isn't.** You may have been planning and researching your new business venture for a long time and feel very familiar with both the business idea and the opportunity for success. But if you haven't shared this information with those you love, they may assume it doesn't exist.	**Share your business plan,** demonstrating the information and research that you have done to back up your idea. What, you haven't done any analysis or business plan? You should have more concerns than skeptical family members. See chapter 9 for information about business plans.
3. You will lose your shirt in your new venture.	**They have deep fears about risk and money that don't have anything to do with you personally.** A client mentioned that his spouse was terrified about losing financial stability if he went out	**Ask a lot of "what, why, where, when, and how" questions in a very open and nonjudgmental manner.** For example, ask "What in particular are you afraid of? Why do you feel this way? When did you feel something

Concern	Reason for Concern	Solution
	on his own. He was frustrated about this, since he felt he had a very viable business idea and a solid plan. When I asked him about his wife's background, he told me that her father had quit his job and started a very unsuccessful string of entrepreneurial ventures, adding stress and tension to the family. That is where the real heat of her emotion was coming from.	similar in the past? What would you need to know or experience to dissipate this fear?" The key here is to ask questions and *listen*, not refute each point. Once you get to the root of the concerns, you can decide if they are valid for your situation.
4. Your idea has lots of holes in it.	**They have a different communication style.** You might perceive your friends and family as unsupportive because they ask lots of critical questions about your business plan. But maybe that is just how their brains are wired, and they must ask the questions in order to understand and support your idea.	**Adjust your communication style.** Don't react negatively to critical questions. Use the same questioning techniques as described in #3. Pay attention to how the person processes information and give them the resources and time to digest it. If they are highly analytical, you may want to give them some detailed information about your business idea or plan. If they are big-picture and results-oriented, stay brief with your description and focus on impact, results, and rewards. The DiSC Profile™ is a great tool for understanding different communication styles. (See sidebar for more information on DiSC™.)

(continued)

Concern	Reason for Concern	Solution
5. You don't have what it takes to be a successful entrepreneur.	**They have seen you start and stop many projects in the past and are not confident that you have the follow-through skills to pull off the marathon of entrepreneurship.** I don't know if I totally agree with Dr. Phil that past behavior is the best predictor of future behavior, since I have seen many people make significant changes in their lives. But in the last ten years, if you have demonstrated that you enthusiastically started remodeling projects and then lost steam with holes in the wall or a half-painted room, if you join a gym and never go, if you get enthused with new hobbies every month and never take them anywhere, you may have some problems with follow-through.	**If you think that this endeavor is totally different, explain why.** Share why you think it is not just a fleeting idea, but something that you are willing to invest a lot of effort and energy in for the next couple of years. Practice the art of discipline and follow-through by sticking with projects to completion. You may also want to stay in your "day job" a bit longer than other people while you develop and test your business idea to ensure that it maintains its same appeal and value after months of hard work.
6. You are risking too much for your dream.	**They don't know what the exit strategy or backup plan is.** Leaving a job to start a new business may seem to some like jumping off a cliff. It is not a point of no return. Every new entrepreneur should be able to describe an exit strategy if the venture fails, or takes longer than	**Create an exit strategy.** Determine things like: How much money you are willing to spend without return How much time you will allocate to see if your business idea will be successful Alternatives for generating income Strategies for getting a

Concern	Reason for Concern	Solution
	anticipated to get off the ground.	job if you need to jump back in the world as an employee
7. You will change.	**They are afraid you will ignore or leave them if you get too happy and successful.** This may seem crazy and counter-intuitive, but it is a real fear for some people. This feeling is usually based on their own insecurity. But it is based on truth too: you may find that as you change, some relationships will not survive.	**Reinforce your love.** Talk about what the relation-ship means to you. Carve out time for your relationships as you are working on your business plans.
8. You are selfish.	**They are bitter that you get to have fun and be creative while they sacrifice their own happiness for a safe path.** This can be particularly tough with spouses, as they may have to sacrifice some of their own flexibility, lifestyle, or job satisfaction while you get your business up and running. Parents may carry a chip on their shoulder that "we sacrificed our happiness in order to give our kids a good life," and feel you should do the same for yours.	**Encourage them to share their dreams with you.** Not everyone wants to start a business, but they do have dreams and ambitions. Encourage your friends and family to take risks, and then support them. If you are in a relationship, get clear on timelines for each of your interests, and be sure that each of you is making sacrifices to support the other's happiness. If they see how you are willing to adjust and change to support them, they will be more likely to support you.

(continued)

Use DiSC to Strengthen Your Message

The DiSC Profile is a tool that describes different communication styles and gives tips on relating to each. I have used it for over ten years in all kinds of environments and found it to be exceptionally helpful for tailoring messages to different people. To take the assessment online, see www.escapefromcubiclenation.com/disc. Otherwise, look for clues here:

If your family member or friend:	Stress these things in the conversation:
• Is motivated to solve problems and get immediate results • Tends to question the status quo • Prefers direct answers, varied activities, and independence Then they are most likely the **Dominance** profile	• Bottom-line results • Excellence and winning **Example:** "While I need to use $10,000 of savings to start up the company, I will pay it back in one month and net an additional $50,000 by April 1. I should be the #1 independent trainer in my market by early 2009."
• Is motivated to persuade and influence others • Tends to be open, verbalizing thoughts and feelings • Cares about the "greater good" and big ideas Then they are most likely the **Influence** profile	• Benefit to large groups of people • Excitement of opportunity **Example:** "While I need to use $10,000 of savings to start up the company, I am really excited by the impact it will have on our community. I will be able to train 50 leaders, impacting the lives of at least 500 families."
• Is motivated to create a stable, organized environment • Tends to be patient and a good listener • Prefers participating in a group rather than directing it; also prefers listening more than talking Then they are most likely the **Steadiness** profile	• Financial security for the family • A structured process with clearly defined steps **Example:** "I realize that spending $10,000 of savings to start a business sounds like a very scary thing. But I have carefully weighed the risks and

If your family member or friend:	Stress these things in the conversation:
	made a three-month plan to ensure we are safe in case things do not go as anticipated. If, after three months, we don't feel comfortable moving forward, I have a job lined up with the same salary and benefits as my current position."
• Is motivated to achieve high personal standards • Is influenced by data and facts more than feelings • Prefers environments with clearly defined expectations Then they are most likely the **Conscientiousness** profile	• Strong and reliable research • Objective data **Example:** "I know that $10,000 is a lot of savings to spend. But I spent three months testing my business idea with my target market, analyzing the competition, and running different financial models in my business plan. I am willing to test my assumption that I will convert 10% of new prospects into paying customers. If it doesn't work after ninety days, I will go to Plan B" (said while handing them the backup research document).

There will be some relationships that do not survive your change from employee to entrepreneur, and that is okay. If you lose someone dear to you through this process, keep these things in mind:

- **Honor the history you have together.** It can be perplexing and painful to lose connection with people you love deeply. But it will solve nothing to get angry and say something hurtful that you will regret. If you are able, tell your friends how much you appreciate all the years you had together. If you aren't talking, write the words down in a journal, or say them in a silent reflection.

- **Trust that "your people" will show up for this new phase of life.** There is an awkward stage of transition where some of your old friends may not be available anymore, and you don't have any new friends to support you. This is a very lonely place. Trust in yourself, and keep moving on your path toward your right life. When you least expect it, new, wonderful people will appear to support and encourage you.

> I have a hard time letting friendships and relationships go, even when it has become clear that that is the natural course of things sometimes. But you are right—in my heart I know I am headed in the right direction at the moment, even though that makes it difficult, even with some family members who would prefer I stay in a rut similar to theirs so they will have someone to commiserate with.[1]

Armed with an understanding of the most common concerns about self-employment and some tips for communicating your message effectively, now it's time to tackle two of your most significant and difficult relationships: your spouse and your parents.

Getting Your Spouse On Board

At age forty, Matthew Scott appeared to have it all. The vice president of sales for a successful medical devices company, this former Special Forces military commander had done all the right things. He married his seventh-grade sweetheart and had three beautiful children. He had a fancy house in San Diego by the beach. Work took him all around the globe. He was well paid and well respected. What he lacked, however, was a sense that his life had any meaning. So without warning, he told his wife he was going to take off to figure things out.

His wife, who had stood by him for military deployments overseas, stressful sales jobs, and a travel schedule that took him away from home for weeks at a time, was perplexed by his decision.

> I blew my first attempt at following my "calling" with my wife. I told her how unhappy I was in my work and something was missing in my life and headed for the coastline to "figure it out." Well, as you can imag-

ine when your forty-year-old husband says this you would freak out and imagine the worst. I could not understand why she was so concerned about me doing this and began to internalize my own head-trash of thinking she was ungrateful and did not want to jeopardize our so-called great life with my fancy title and big house. Boy, was I a putz![2]

What Matthew forgot, as many stressed-out corporate employees do, is that it is very easy for spouses to mistake career despair for relationship despair. For this reason, it is critical to communicate early, often, and openly with your spouse about your desire to start a business.

You never start a business by yourself; whether they want to or not, your spouse and children start it with you. Unlike a business partner who can bow out if things get tough, your spouse and children are in it for the long haul. Your success or failure has very concrete and scary impacts on things like level of personal debt, credit rating, child care, and quality of family time.

So start communicating early about your desire to start a business. You will set precedent with your first conversation. To do it well, follow these guidelines:

How to Break the News to Your Spouse That You Want to Quit Your Job

- **Choose a low-stress moment when you have time and energy for a long conversation.** It is not fair to drop a major bombshell when you won't have time to discuss it. Don't talk about it right before bed or in the morning before heading off to work, as this will just stir up questions in your spouse's mind.
- **Choose the best setting for your conversation.** I find it is a lot easier to have a deep, meaningful conversation with my husband when we are up and moving around. We have had some of our best conversations on long walks or drives. Because you should be concerned about your spouse's preferred communication style and not your own, choose the place that he feels the most comfortable with.
- **Minimize distractions.** Get your kids a sitter and turn off your cell phone and BlackBerry. Don't go somewhere like your favorite local café where you will be interrupted by lots of friends. You need complete focus in this conversation.

- **Explain why you are so excited about starting your own business.** Make sure your spouse knows all about why this idea is so compelling to you and why you are excited about it. Don't just talk about the business idea, talk about what it would mean to you personally to get enjoyment from your work. Would you have more energy? Would you watch less TV? Want to help around the house more? Become a nineteen-year-old sex machine? (Okay, okay, now you're going overboard.)

- **Explain the consequences of *not* following your dreams.** Everyone processes job stress differently. Some people have a high tolerance for staying in an unhappy or stressful work situation if it means bringing home lots of money. Others have very low tolerance and develop health problems including depression, high blood pressure, weight gain, anxiety disorders, and low energy. Make sure your spouse understands the consequences for you if you are unhappy with your work.

- **Ask lots of questions.** Your spouse may say something like "If you quit your job, we will lose all financial stability!" Make sure you really understand what he is talking about and ask, "What in particular are you concerned about? What amount of money in the bank would make you comfortable that our expenses are covered? What is it about me being self-employed that makes you the most nervous?" You may find after asking a lot of questions that the original reasons he gave are not the real, emotionally charged reasons. The real fears are things like "If you get really happy and successful, you may leave me!" or "If you do what you love, I will have to sacrifice all my happiness for you!" or "If you start your own business, you will destroy our family, just like my dad did."

- **Reciprocate.** Ask your spouse how he is feeling in his work life. What would make him more happy and fulfilled? What big dreams does he have? How can you help him reach his goals?

- **Take the advice to heart!** Don't view this conversation as a one-way sales call. Your spouse may have some very valid reasons for his resistance, and you should carefully listen to and reflect on what they are. All of us know a family member, neighbor, or work colleague who blew the family savings on day trading or a harebrained get-rich-quick scheme. Make sure you aren't that person. Even if you don't agree with all of your spouse's concerns, acknowledge and respect them.

- **Make a plan to continue the conversation.** You will definitely not resolve all your concerns in one sitting. Plan on spending more time discussing the issues until you both feel comfortable with the plan.

If you follow these guidelines, you are likely to have a rich, useful discussion. Just make sure you don't commit these faux pas:

How NOT to Talk to Your Spouse About Self-employment

Over the phone. This conversation needs to be live and unplugged. You simply cannot discuss such a meaty issue unless you are face-to-face.

By e-mail. Using the impersonal medium of e-mail to talk about a deeply personal topic may be frustrating to your spouse. If both of you are busy and in front of e-mail all the time, it is fine to follow up with specific links, tips, and articles once you have had a good initial conversation about your interest in starting a business. But don't start it that way.

In the middle of financial stress. You will fan the flames of fear if you talk about leaving your job right when you are stressing out about bills or facing a huge property tax or tuition bill. Try to pick the most stable financial time to talk about this issue. If your financial life is continually in flux, you may want to address that issue first by reducing expenses and paying down debt as you will need a bit of wiggle room in the months you are starting up your business.

In front of your kids. Although I do think it is good to share your plans with your kids, don't raise the topic for the first time over family dinner. Depending on their age, your kids may get upset if they hear you and your spouse disagreeing and stressing about money. They want to know that no matter what happens their life will be secure, so plan to have a conversation with your kids once you and your spouse have a mutually acceptable plan.

Once you have your initial conversation, make regular communication with your spouse a priority. Create a plan to address the concerns raised in your first conversation and follow up. Your spouse will want to see you persist with your business idea and stick with it, despite obstacles. They also want to see that you respect their opinion and treat them as a full partner. To create an environment for effective communication and minimized conflict, clarify the following things:

Key Things to Clarify with Your Spouse as You Build Your Business

- The type and amount of information your spouse wants about the business
- The role (if any) he or she wants to play in the new business
- How you will make joint financial decisions
- Mutually agreed upon timeframe for testing the viability of the business
- Exit strategy, with specific alternatives and responsibilities for both parties

These practices really do work when there is a solid relationship to start with. Matthew, whom I introduced earlier in the chapter, followed all of these good communication practices (after his initial bungling!), and his story ended well. He and his wife discussed career change options at length. They spent six months choosing the best place to raise their kids and moved from San Diego to the Oregon coast. They articulated and designed an ideal life together. Matthew started a very successful practice as a coach and consultant. Their marriage and life are good. Their kids are thriving.

Not all stories end this way. I don't mean to scare you. But when you start to make major changes in your life, any weaknesses in your relationship are amplified. It is like dropping a brick on the exact line of a bone fracture.

What Happens If Your Spouse Is Totally Resistant and No Amount of Heartfelt Conversation Will Garner His Support for Your Dream?

This is where I must bow out and refer you to a more competent adviser like a couples counselor. If your spouse or significant other is totally uninterested in your happiness, it sounds like there may be some bigger challenges in your relationship. Successful entrepreneur Francine Hardaway found this out the hard way:

> I lost a husband to my entrepreneurial dream. When I quit my nice safe professorship to start my first company, my professor husband (who was my department chairman) decided I was going to be a failure and lose all our savings, impacting our financial future. He found himself another girlfriend and left me (in that order).
>
> But I made enough money to be the major support of our children, and he evolved into the one who took them to the library and the dentist. We worked it out and remained friends, but my risk tolerance was so different from his that we couldn't stay married.[3]

Getting Your Parents On Board

If you thought spouses were resistant, just wait until you tell your parents that you want to quit your stable corporate job to start a business.

You may be one of the lucky ones like me who have parents who enthusiastically support anything you do, even if it includes traveling by yourself to Rio de Janeiro to study martial arts, starting a business with no experience, or running off to Arizona to marry a Navajo medicine man. There is not much I could do that my parents wouldn't support unless it made me unhappy or broke a law.

Or you could be like Peter W.:

> My dad arrived in the U.S. as an immigrant from Germany. He escaped just as the Nazis were taking power. He spent his whole life working hard in mind-numbing but stable jobs so that his kids could have better opportunities than he had. Self-realization and personal development are not part of his vocabulary. I am scared to death to tell him that I want to quit my comfortable job as a software engineer to start a photography business.

Peter faces a very common challenge that is exacerbated by the following characteristics of parents.[4]

- Parents can push your buttons like no one else on the planet.
- They grew up in an era when the work contract was very different from what it is today (both the literal and figurative contract, including expectations between employer and employee).
- No matter how old you are, your parents see you as a child.
- Their biggest concern is for your safety.

So when speaking with your parents, follow all the advice you have read thus far including:

- Choose the right place and time to speak to them.
- Provide the right information communicated in the way best suited to their communication style.
- Do not get defensive. Ask questions to understand their concerns.

But pay attention to these common traps in parent-child communication:

Common Traps When Discussing Your Career with Your Parents

- **Thinking they understand what you are talking about.**
  Anyone who has tried to explain "Social Media," "Web 2.0," or blogging to an elder relative may recognize the vacant stare and look of puzzlement on their face. Even nontechnical people your age can get confused. My husband has grown up in the low-tech environment of the construction industry and rarely touches the computer except to play Solitaire. The first time I talked about my blog, he thought I said "blob." I can just imagine the image that came to his mind of a gigantic, gooey dark creature that oozed its way through the city streets, slowly gobbling up people and cars.
  Solution: *Reduce any and all jargon.* Talk about your business concept in a very simple way that anyone from a seven- to a seventy-year-old can understand. "Mom, having a blog is kind of like sitting down and writing a letter to someone every day. But instead of it being delivered to only one mailbox, the same letter gets delivered to a thousand. And if someone likes what they read, they write me back right away."

- **Thinking they understand that you have changed since your failed lemonade business in fifth grade.**

  Try as we might, it is so hard to break the stereotypes that our parents have about us based on what they saw when we were growing up. "You could never stick to one thing, Martha, you were always distracted in your studies," or "Bob, how in the world could you start your own business? Remember how painfully shy you were in high school? Your mom had to go to the prom with you!" Even if they don't come right out and say it, you can feel their disapproval based on their body language or tone of voice. My friend Desiree and I talk about the "The Tone" that our moms use with us occasionally on the phone. They don't have to say a word, it is just the way they say "hmmmm" that lets us know they don't agree with what we are saying. Now that we are moms too, we are carefully perfecting our Tones.

  Solution: *Change your expectations.* You will never be able to convince your family you have outgrown your innate shyness, so stop trying. Show results by your actions. If you get too frustrated in a conversation, smile and change the subject quickly. The worst thing you can do is argue your point. You will never win, and will most likely revert to acting like a ten-year-old.

- **Thinking they understand the changing job market.**

  Some parents are perplexed by the fact that the average person now has seven careers in a lifetime. They grew up in a world where the best career security was finding a good job in a good company and staying until retirement. Lots of job changes were seen as being irresponsible, unstable, and a sign of a poor work ethic.

  Solution: *Come armed with a nice "elevator speech" about today's job market so that you can help them see that you are not outside of the norm.* "Twenty-five percent of women in their mid-forties are successfully starting businesses, Dad," or recite the "seven careers per lifetime" statistic above. If they still don't get it, let it go and change the subject.

  I once told my dad I wanted to start a small business. As he was shaking his head he looked me square in the eye and said "don't do it." I'm still stuck in the cube and whenever I start planning a venture that thought goes through my head. I'm not sure if he discouraged me because of who my partners were at the time or if he didn't want me to suffer the "pains" of business ownership. (Jim S.)

Calming Techniques

If, despite your best efforts, conversation with your parents becomes strained, use these calming techniques:

- **Breathe deeply and relax.** When you feel the conversations get intense or heated, take a deep breath and stop talking. Then follow the next strategy:
- **Laugh.** If you step back from your personal situation for a minute, you can find the humor in it. Imagine that you are writing a television script about a crazy family. Observe the funny dynamics in your dialogue and laugh from your belly.
- **Commiserate with a beloved sibling.** Siblings are the only people in the world who truly understand your relationship with your parents. If you have a rough time, call your favorite sibling and give your unedited debrief of the conversation. Commiserate together, share an encouraging word, and move on.

The Final Step: Keep the Useful Feedback and Toss the Rest

I hope your conversations with your friends, spouse, and parents go well. You are likely to come away with a lot of feedback that will be helpful as you refine your business idea, evaluate your finances, and assess the needs of those you love. But you also may be overwhelmed with criticism, or feel frustrated with those who aren't supportive. You may even hear some insulting, judgmental, and unfair characterizations that make you feel like you are seven years old. At this point, you need to take the feedback and put it through a filter.

Exercise

1. Imagine you have a large, metal tray with a screen bottom, much like you would use to pan for gold.

2. Take all the feedback you have gotten from family and friends and sift it through the screen using the following criteria:

WHAT STAYS
- Specific questions about your business idea that would also concern your target market
- Useful considerations about managing your personal finances
- Insight into your personality; strengths and weaknesses that you feel are accurate
- Valid concerns about relationships with those you love

WHAT GOES
- Judgments about your skills or character that you know aren't true
- Critique of your business idea from those who know nothing about your field or target market
- Generalized fears like "no one ever makes money being self-employed" or "no one in our family is cut out to be a businessperson" or "Latino males do not start a dance company" or "Asian girls do not manage a punk record label"
- Belittling comments that make you feel two feet tall

You can love, respect, honor, and adore your friends and relatives, but you can't make them approve of your decisions. If you are happy about the direction of your own life, that is all that matters. In general, most people would rather see you doing something that makes you happy rather than trudging miserably through your life.

But if they are *all* resistant, don't despair.

You can always find people who don't need convincing or cajoling to embrace your idea. They have been in your shoes. They "get" entrepreneurship and are ready to support you as soon as you find them.

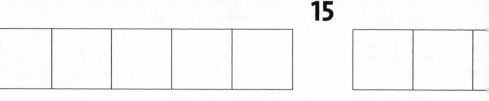

15

Line Your Ducks in a Row

few months ago, after I tucked the kids into bed, I went to my iMac and prepared to start my evening's work. I immediately noticed that my Outlook e-mail was running really slow, but because I run Parallels software in my Mac environment (which basically allows me to run both Mac and Windows at the same time), I figured I would just restart and everything would be okay. (Admit it, you do it too!)

The whole computer was running slow, so I did a manual shutdown, then I restarted. But instead of my main screen coming up quickly as it usually does, I got a pale gray background with a flashing question mark inside a folder icon.

I knew this wasn't good.

After a few more attempts at restarting, I shut it down and went to bed. If I am cranky, a good rest helps, so maybe my computer felt the same. It had been a couple of busy weeks, so maybe it just wanted the night off.

The next morning, it was more of the same. A couple of times I was able to get to my hard drive, but it was exceptionally slow, and by the time I was able to access a folder to start the backup process, my whole system would freeze and the restart process would repeat.

So after spending an hour with tech support on the phone, I drove my ill iMac to the Apple store.

The "Genius" (their term for in-store technical wizard) behind the support desk poked around and said, "It appears you have a bad hard drive." Followed by "But you do have your files backed up, right?"

Herein lies the lesson on the importance of lining your ducks in a row before starting a business.

No, I didn't have my files backed up. I did a weekly backup to an external drive on my old PC, but when I got my shiny new iMac, somehow I was blinded by a combination of slick marketing messages, which promoted the Mac environment as being much more stable than Windows, and good old-fashioned stupidity. I thought, "It is a Mac, it won't crash! I'll figure out a backup plan later. Now, I am much too busy."

One of you aspiring entrepreneurs should start a virtual business where as soon as someone utters such a thought, a large, concentrated electrical shock strikes him or her in the forehead. Such thoughts should not be allowed to cross the minds of seasoned professionals such as myself, but alas, they do.

Having a solid backup process in place is one of a few areas that you want to make sure you have down before you launch your business. The scenario could easily be one of the following:

- You didn't get a patent on your great product idea and a competitor snatched it out from under you.
- You never separated your personal and business banking and suffered a horrendous audit from the IRS.
- Your house flooded in a big storm and you lost critical paper files and expensive computer equipment that was not insured.

My story has a happy ending: I was able to recover all files and, most important, this book manuscript. But it taught me an important lesson about the kinds of ducks that must be in a row before starting your business.

Which Ducks Should Be in a Row?

There are a million questions to answer when you are thinking of starting a business:

- Should I set up my business as an S Corporation or an LLC? (Two examples of U.S.-based business structures)
- Do I need liability insurance?
- Should I make people sign a nondisclosure agreement if I share details about my product or business model?
- Should I set up my books on a cash or accrual basis?

These are all great questions for which I have a singular response: *Don't follow my advice, talk to a professional.*

I certainly have opinions, but this is very different from understanding the details of your business and the myriad of (always changing) laws and regulations that govern it. Many an unhappy entrepreneur has gotten into hot water because they "followed Uncle Bill's advice" instead of investing money in a lawyer (nothing against Uncle Bill). StartupNation describes the "big four" professionals every entrepreneur needs to run an effective business:

Your Professional Advisory Team

1. A lawyer
2. An accountant
3. A banker
4. An insurance specialist

These professionals can ensure that you set up a solid foundation for your business. Often, entrepreneurs try to "bootstrap" everything and only call in an expert when they are in trouble. Investing in the right professional advice early on can save you headaches, or worse, in the long run.

Since most of the "big four" have high hourly rates, to get the most out of your investment, be very prepared for your meeting and come with specific questions. If you can describe the nature of your business, your target market, and your products and services in a succinct way, they will be able to get you the information that you need more quickly.

How Do You Find These Professionals If You Don't Know Any Personally?

Ask successful businesspeople in your field whom they recommend. We found our very competent accountant by asking our trusted insurance agent.

- Search for professional directories like the American Institute of Certified Public Accountants or the Small Business Law Firms.
- Contact your local Small Business Association and ask for referrals.
- Search for members in your local Better Business Bureau.
- Ask members of your tribe! Do you remember how I was encouraging you to connect with smart, positive, successful people in chapter 7? They will be an excellent source of information and referrals, especially if you are active in social media environments like LinkedIn, Twitter, or Facebook.

I realize that cash flow is king when you are starting a business. It can be painful to write a big check to a professional when you may want to use the money to develop a prototype or invest in marketing. In the long run, however, you will be happy that you set things up the right way. No one should endure the heartbreaking loss of someone stealing your intellectual property, face the agony of huge tax adjustments in favor of your government when it is discovered that your accounting was inaccurate, or deal with the frightening experience of a lawsuit that puts your personal assets at risk.

Must-dos

There are a few things that you must take care of to make sure you stay out of hot water.

Legal Matters

- Get the appropriate business licenses and certifications to operate in your geographic area.
- Explore whether you need to trademark, patent, or copyright any of your intellectual property including brand name, products, or writing.
- Identify a business structure that will give you maximum personal protection and professional advantage, like tax breaks and good deals on insurance.
- Determine whether you need any legal documents when you share business ideas, such as nondisclosure agreements (NDAs).

Each region, state, and country has unique rules and regulations, so there is no way to give blanket recommendations for best practices. A lawyer well versed in your business should give you expert guidance in what to do or not do.

Financial Matters

- Establish separate banking accounts for your business. In most cases, you will need to have your business name and license already in order to open a business bank account, so take care of that first.
- Select an accounting system that tracks business expenses only. In chapter 12 there were all kinds of suggestions for personal finance tracking systems and programs. You want to make sure to totally separate your personal and business expenses, and the best way to do this is to have distinct tracking systems. If you have no knowledge of or interest in accounting, you may choose to outsource this function from the beginning (more on outsourcing in a minute).
- If possible, secure a business line of credit. This can be for emergency use only, but it follows the basic guideline of finance—it will be much easier to get credit when you *don't* need it rather than when you *do*. This is even more true in the current climate of tightened credit markets.
- You may also want to secure a business credit card to use for business-only transactions. This is especially important if you do a lot of traveling.

Insurance Matters

- In chapter 13 we talked about personal health insurance, life insurance, and short- and long-term disability. Depending on your business, there are other forms of insurance you need to evaluate.
- You need to do an assessment with an insurance broker to identify the particular risks in your business. It will vary widely if you have a retail location, if you serve clients in your home office, if you own expensive equipment, or if you operate in a litigious market. I remember being shocked when I was asked to provide two million dollars' worth of liability insurance for a large corporate client. At the time I was designing training materials, and my first thought was "I need to make a pretty horrendous typo to warrant a two-million-dollar policy!" The truth is you never know what exposure you may have.
- For this reason, it is advisable to connect with an insurance broker who covers small business. There are a lot of different options to choose from, so ask your broker what applies to your particular situation.

Will Make Your Life Easier If You Dos

Cash Flow Planning

When you're first starting your business, you're understandably most concerned with marketing your services so that people can find you and with selling your services. The first time you close a sale, you will feel like dancing a jig since it's one of the most memorable points in your business history. Very quickly, however, you'll begin to realize that the act of a customer *signing an agreement* with you is very different from the act of *receiving a check* in the mail, which you can deposit in your business account. Obviously, this applies mostly to service-based business where you invoice for your work, not a product business where you have all sales automated on the Web and where people must pay first before receiving your product. But these kinds of businesses still can be affected if a big customer wants to purchase a large volume of your product and you can't process it via your regular e-commerce site. So what you must do is to carefully think through your cash flow assumptions and check them out with your clients or customers. Then, you need to create mutually agreeable terms.

Let's look at an example of an information technology consultant who's been hired by a large company to assess and evaluate its IT infrastructure, make some recommendations for improvements, and then oversee the transition to a new environment. A project like this usually has multiple phases.

When estimating the total cost of the job, you can figure out how long each part will take and come up with the total amount for the project. When you set up your billing, however, you must take two things into consideration—what are the natural points in the project that you can bill on, and what are the terms and accounting cycles of your client. Many large corporations have notoriously long payment cycles—paying forty-five or sixty days after receiving an invoice. If you choose to bill at monthly milestones that could mean that you won't see a cent of your hard-earned money in your bank account until three months after starting the project.

So for large projects, you might consider billing for a portion of the project up front. Some people charge as much as 25 to 50 percent of the project cost up front. And bill the rest in regular increments, usually as significant portions of the work are completed and approved by the client.

To manage your cash flow in general, here are some guidelines:

- **When you're in the final stages of the sales process, ask about the financial terms and conditions of your client.** This may affect how you write your final proposal.
- **As part of your joint agreement, clearly state what your terms and guidelines are for payment.** One very common problem in the consulting world occurs when your client drags at the timeline of the project by involving a lot more people in the decision-making process than was originally agreed upon. So include stipulations in your billing agreements that say things like "If the scope of the project has changed and it is mutually agreed upon, we may bill for partial completion of a milestone."
- **Follow invoicing and contracting guidelines to the letter.** You may have invoices kicked back that don't meet corporate standards and this can delay things by weeks. So read the information that they send you and make sure you do everything, including the way you format your invoice and who you send it to and when you send it, exactly how they tell you.

- **Get to know your contact and accounts payable personally and treat them as the wise and powerful people they are.** Do not, and I repeat, do not act condescending and bullying if you're frustrated at the payment process. Every accounts payable person I have ever worked with has been very organized and efficient. But if they sense you're being a bully, they will delight in losing your invoice. You should never be rude with anyone in any capacity in your client company—that's just part of being a decent human being. But especially, don't piss off the people who cut your check. You will regret it.

- **Just as you should have a good relationship with accounts payable, make sure that you have a good relationship with the decision maker in your client project who has enough authority to approve and change financial transactions.** So you may work with their project manager for most of your project, but you may need to work with their manager if you get stuck with the delayed payment. So meet these folks up front and know who it is that has the authority to make these decisions.

- **In the case of a large sale—large-scale product sale—make sure you don't ship all of your product without seeing any cash.** Either have cash-on-delivery terms or at least ask for a percentage up front.

- **Plan out your own cash flow from a worst-case scenario.** You don't always know what a company is really like in their payment cycles until you start working with them on a regular basis. Make sure you have savings available or secure a business line of credit in case you need to float for a period of time before being paid.

- **Do your research on a company before committing to a large project.** If you see some danger signs that they're experiencing cash flow problems themselves, or have problems with other vendors, you may not want to consider working with them. I have never *not* been paid for work I have done but I have waited over four months for a check from one client. My husband, who has a construction business, was cheated out of $7,000 from a contractor who went bankrupt and then disappeared. It's painful to not get paid for work you put your heart into. So I sincerely hope that it never happens to you.

I hope these guidelines have given you something to think about when planning cash flow for your business. Remember not to make the assumption that just because you made the sale, the money is already in the bank. The money is in the bank when the money is in the bank.

Documenting

Tips to Set Up Business Processes on the Fly

If you are just launching your business, chances are, setting up business processes and infrastructure is the last thing on your mind. Usually, you are more concerned with things like:

- How in the world will I get new customers?
- Will my business idea work in the real world, or am I deluding myself?
- Was I insane to leave my "stable" job and put my family's financial future at risk?

If you keep your focus and work diligently, these fears will generally dissipate. But you may quickly become overwhelmed with the sheer volume of details related to keeping a whole business afloat by yourself.

One of the best ways to make sure you are efficient with your time from the start of your business is to adopt the practice of only going through the excruciating process of gathering information or crafting communications once.

You will find that in the start-up phase of business, many of the vendors, government agencies, potential customers, media contacts, and partners want the same kind of information about you and your company. So instead of digging through file folders and your "sent" e-mail, here are four suggestions for setting up quick and dirty business processes and organizing your information for easy access:

1. **Create a "General Company Information" cheat sheet.** This can have things on it like:

   - **Legal identity information**—your business name, when you were established, when you were incorporated (if different), official contact information, tax ID numbers, trademark registration info.
   - **Contact information for your key business partners** like your accountant, lawyer, insurance agent, and banker. Make sure to add the complete contact information of name, address, phone, fax, and e-mail.

- **Current supplier contact information for credit applications.** If you are applying for credit the first time, often they will ask for references to ensure that you have a track record of paying people on time.
- **Client references.** Prospective customers may want to talk to some past clients to be sure you are who you say you are and will meet their needs. Just be sure to check with these references to see if it is okay to have someone contact them. As a general rule of thumb, I don't like to give out the same name more than three times, lest I waste the time of a satisfied customer.
- **Policy information for insurance.** This can include coverage for life or liability insurance. Make sure you note what the total value of the coverage is.
- **Financial information about your company.** This can include current revenues, projected sales, profit margins, and, for bank and credit applications, personal net worth.
- **Major business assets if your company requires major equipment.** Write down the name and description of the equipment, year, make and model, purchase price, and date of purchase.

2. **Create e-mail templates for common inquiries.** If your marketing is in order, you will get inquiries from prospective clients that say things like "please tell me about your services." I have a very basic e-mail template that I send out to people who inquire about my services that describes the process of coaching in a few bullet points, outlines basic services, and encourages them to sign up for an introductory session. Any time you notice that you are sending the same general e-mails to many people, create a quick template to save time. These can be for things like:

- Company background for prospective clients
- Explanation of standard billing procedures or processes
- General agreements for joint venture partners
- Media inquiries (see #3 for more on this)

3. **Whip up a "media page" if you plan on courting the press as part of your marketing strategy.** A media page (or media room) should have the following information to make it easy for the press to contact you and see if you are the expert they are looking for:

- **Brief bio** that describes what you do and what qualifies you to do it. This is not the place to say things like "enjoys listening to Journey songs and doing yoga on the beach," since most media contacts really don't want to get to know you that well. Do include things that make you unique and press-worthy. It can be appropriate to include personal information like marital or parental status, if that would be relevant to your status as an expert (I chose to mention that I am married with kids, as much of my target market struggles with issues of supporting a family while starting a business).

- **Media appearances.** These can be online and offline media appearances in print, radio, and television. It helps to put the most noteworthy toward the top, since one of the best ways to be characterized as an expert is to be featured in a prominent mainstream news source. Include the name of the publication or media outlet, title of the story, and date of publication. If you want to link to the story itself, that is fine, but not totally necessary when you first get up and running. Be careful when displaying video clips on your site (such as from TV appearances) since you can run into copyright issues if you don't get permission first.

- **Story angles.** Help the media think up newsworthy articles by suggesting story angles based on your expertise.

- **Interview questions.** Outline the major types of questions that are of critical interest to your target market. This can save the reporter time, and make sure that you get to reinforce key messages as part of your brand and company mission.

- **Contact information (again).** Even though you have the contact information up front, put it at the bottom. Reporters are busy, busy people, so the easier you make it for them to contact you, the more likely they will. Final tip on that—call the media RIGHT BACK. They are often under last-minute deadlines, and will quote whichever expert gets back to them first.

4. **Start a bare-bones operations manual for common business processes.** This doesn't have to look great or have a huge amount of detail. Just start by capturing the basic steps required to execute key business activities such as:

- Bringing on a new client ("Send welcome e-mail," "Send agreement in the mail with prepaid envelope," "Enter contact information into Outlook").
- Starting a new project ("Send billing procedures confirmation to accounting contact," "File final version of proposal in project file," "Enter project milestones into calendar").
- Purchasing a new piece of equipment ("Update general business info sheet with information," "Add equipment to insurance policy," "File warranty paperwork").
- Conducting a presentation, event, or workshop ("Book event location," "Send confirmation notice to participants," "Book catering six weeks in advance").

With any of these quick and dirty business infrastructure tips, you can go crazy making them look pretty or technically flashy. A common trap for new entrepreneurs is to take too much time with internal processes and not enough time on external processes like marketing or pressing flesh with prospective customers. So while you could spend forty hours creating a beautiful database to house your general business information for the next five years, don't—at least at this point. Instead, spend forty minutes creating a Word document, then enhance it later. When the big bucks are rolling in from all your new clients, you can hire someone else to make everything look great and function perfectly.

As a final note, an added benefit of documenting these basic processes from the beginning of your business is that it will be much easier to delegate tasks to assistants and partners as you grow. I have known many entrepreneurs who grew substantial businesses with all key information in their head, and nothing on paper. When they were totally overwhelmed with work and ready to outsource to others, it took lots of time and effort to hand over tasks.

Smart Outsourcing

Some entrepreneurs have a hard time asking for help, preferring to do everything themselves, from computer software and hardware installation to billing to licking stamps.

I firmly believe in the principle of not re-creating the wheel. If there is someone who has done (well) what I am attempting to do and can sell their expertise in the form of coaching, education, or instruction, I am more than happy to purchase it. I believe what Marcus Buckingham and Donald Clifton preach in their book *Now, Discover Your Strengths*, which is that we should stop spending lots of time and energy learning skills to prop up our weaknesses and instead should focus on building and leveraging our strengths.

The only problem with using lots of outside resources, of course, is that this can get rather expensive, if you don't have any criteria for deciding when, who, and how to use them.

When to Use an Outside Resource

The mantra I used to use in my corporate training and development work was "just in time learning." What this means is that you are much more likely to pay attention to, absorb, and integrate skills if you learn them just before or during the time that you will apply them. So the best time to learn presentation skills is just before you have to deliver a real presentation. In these circumstances, not only will you be very interested in what you are learning because you know you will need to apply the knowledge immediately, but you will be emotionally invested in mastering it because you will be demonstrating it in a live situation, with real people.

Whom to Use

If you are hiring a coach or an expert, there are some obvious and not-so-obvious criteria to use, including:

- **Expertise**. It goes without saying that you should hire someone who has the knowledge and skills to help you solve your particular problem. For some people, certifications and credentials are very important (such as an advanced degree from a reputable institution, or training in a particular methodology). For others, knowledge based on real-world experience is more important. Know your own preferences and screen for someone who meets your criteria.

- **Experience.** Someone can be very knowledgeable, but not have the experience of applying this knowledge in real-life situations with real clients. So be sure to ask whom they have worked with in the past and the different kinds of situations they have faced.
- **Results.** You are actually not buying the time with your expert, you are buying the results of your time together. So be clear about the results you are looking for, and ask if they have obtained similar results with others in similar situations.
- **Rapport**. This is really, really important. You must feel trust, ease, and comfort with a person you are working with, particularly if you are dealing with sensitive issues like financial matters or personal fears or blocks. Even though a colleague may rave about a particular program, product, or coach, make sure that they are a fit for you.

In Order to Know What Is Best for You, Ask Yourself the Following Questions

- What is my preferred learning style? Am I auditory (learn by listening or reading), visual (learn by watching), or kinesthetic (learn by doing)? Do I learn best one-on-one or in a group? Am I able to tune into a virtual learning environment (like a teleclass, webinar, or group coaching program) or do I need face-to-face interaction?
- What motivates me to get things done? Is it clear information, support from a buddy, group interaction and dialogue, peer pressure, or threats and intimidation? (In which case you may want to hire the bully who tormented you in high school to come sit in your office and call you names when you really want to get something done. Some desperate times require desperate measures.)
- Is this task one that I want to be doing myself on an ongoing basis in my business (in which case a learning program may make sense), or is it something I would much rather someone else worry about and complete (in which case you might outsource it immediately)?

Lifehacking

For those of you not glued to the Internet like I am, *lifehacking* is a term that is used to describe tips and downloads for getting things done. Gina Trapani is the editor of Lifehacker.com, and says this:

> Every day, you have dozens of opportunities to get work done faster, smarter and more efficiently—with the right shortcuts. Contrary to what some "gurus" will tell you, there's no single, life-changing secret to working less and living more. The reality is that small changes practiced over time yield big results.
>
> There are hundreds of simple techniques and small adjustments you can make to the way you work that will help you get done and get out the door with a clear mind and a clean slate. Armed with the right know-how, you can put tech tools to work for you and be more effective, efficient, and on top of your game than ever before.[1]

Trapani literally wrote the book on lifehacking techniques, in addition to the hundreds of updates on the blog each week.

For the best way to understand which parts of your business you can "lifehack," look at the table of contents of Trapani's *Upgrade Your Life:*

- Control your e-mail
- Organize your data
- Trick yourself into getting done
- Clear your mind
- Firewall your attention
- Streamline common tasks
- Automate repetitive tasks
- Get your data to go
- Master the Web
- Hone your computer survival skills
- Manage multiple computers

Looking at this list, you may think that it only applies to hard-core technology workers who have twelve computers in their basement and whose idea of a good time is to write code. Actually, even the most hands-on crafty person can benefit from employing lifehacks.

Thinking back to Mignon Fogarty's (Grammar Girl) comment in chapter 6, that the most surprising thing about building a business around a passion is how little time you spend working on that passion once it grows into a business should motivate you to explore lifehacking.

Upgrade Your Life has hundreds of extremely practical tips on everything from setting up e-mail message rules to organizing your digital photos. Here is a sample that I bet will save you two hours a week at a minimum if applied effectively:

The One-Minute Rule

When you've begun an e-mail processing session, start at the oldest message you receive and work up. Follow the one-minute rule: if a message will take less than one minute to process and respond to, do it on the spot. One minute doesn't sound like a lot of time, but in reality a whole lot can happen in 60 seconds. Dash off quick answers to questions, follow up with question on request, and knock down any "Sounds good" and "Let's discuss on the phone, when's a good time?" and "Received the attachment, thanks" type of messages. If you think that a message needs a lengthy, complicated response, consider taking it offline and making a phone call instead.

Most of your new messages will fall under the "can respond in less than a minute" umbrella, so go ahead and answer them.[2]

If you outsource as much as possible and then apply really smart and organized lifehacks to your work, you will find that you are extremely productive.

Get the Most from Your Time as a Corporate Employee

I have given a lot of thought to the idea of what it means to be entrepreneurial. An obvious answer is when you own your own business and generate your own income. But another definition could be to take full ownership and responsibility for your work experience, no matter how you are getting your paycheck.

This philosophy can be extremely helpful for those of you who are in a place where you need to work for another year or two or five either to more fully develop your business plan or to bank up enough cash to go out on your own.

It is very easy to bash the Corporate Man and complain about how hard it is to get things done inside a large bureaucracy. I fully realize that there are some very unattractive things about working in a cube, otherwise I would never have taken the entrepreneurial path, or written this book.

However . . . there are some great entrepreneurial behaviors you can practice while employed in a corporate job:

1. **Say "I choose to work here."** Why is this so hard to say? Every time you utter the term "they made me do this," you are telling a lie. No one can make you do anything without your permission. If you didn't choose to work as an employee, you wouldn't work there. Assume responsibility for your employment choices and feel a bit more swagger in your step.

2. **Always know the two things you want to learn each quarter.** If your goal is to open an import-export food business and you work for a large computer company, see what you can learn about distribution channels and global tax laws from people in your own company. Maybe you will have to do lots of presentations to get funding and partners for your new venture. Identify the best presenter in your company and see if you can tag along to a presentation so you can take notes. The next time you do a presentation, ask if she would be willing to give you feedback about what you do well and what you could improve.

3. **Learn about the business of your company.** Do you know all the factors that go into your company's profitability? What are the five-year strategic goals of your company and what are the threats in the market to realizing these goals? What keeps your CEO up at night? Who are your company's prime customers and what do they care about? I don't care if you are an engineer, a marketer, or an accountant, you could learn truckloads about running a business from the one you are in. How do you find this information out? Ask! (CEO included.)

4. **Build your network.** It can be much easier to build relationships with a diverse group of people while you are an employee at a company rather than sitting at your home office. Get to know your vendors, colleagues, business partners, and customers. Don't fall into the bad habit of lunching alone at your desk all the time. When you have the opportunity to go to a conference or business gathering, go! Talk with interesting people and make sure to get their business cards.

5. **Take a risk.** This can be something small, like volunteering to give a presentation at the next staff meeting, or as big as proposing a radically different way to complete a task or process. If you are in sales, take a big leap . . . don't use PowerPoint at your next customer meeting. After you get through hyperventilating, you may actually find that you have a much better customer interaction. And here is one of my favorite suggestions: invite the person you absolutely can't stand to lunch. If you are a salesperson, this may be the curmudgeonly engineer who always heckles you at presentations. If you are an engineer, maybe it is the smooth-talking person from HR who you feel is completely clueless. Maybe it is the person in finance who refuses to pay your expense reports if you have a $.01 discrepancy. The only ground rule is that you must only ask non-work-related questions at lunch. Find out what kind of books, movies, and music this person likes. What do they do in their spare time? After they get over the shock of realizing that your lunch proposal is sincere, you may find out some surprising things about your perceived "enemy."

The more you focus on learning as much as you can in your corporate job, the more powerful you will feel. And the more powerful you feel, the more likely you will transfer this confidence into doing something about your business idea. Whining is fun sometimes and venting relieves pressure, but if that is all you do in your corporate job, you are missing great opportunities to learn how to be more entrepreneurial.

Plans B, C, and D

No matter how careful you are about your business planning, there is no real way to know if you will be successful until you actually cut the strings and start your business.

Hopefully you have been saving money and have a well-thought out approach to what you are doing. But if not, what is the worst that can happen? What if your new business fails miserably and you have to make a living another way?

Here are five suggestions for creating some solid, viable backup plans.

1. Maintain an excellent relationship with your former coworkers. They can either hire you as an independent contractor, or refer you to others in their network. Or they could hire you back as an employee! You don't need to be afraid of this option—it could be used on a temporary basis while you bank up some more money or gain the necessary experience to really get your business off the ground.
2. Make sure you have up-to-date and professional profiles on LinkedIn and Facebook. Keep your eyes on opportunities and nurture your professional relationships.
3. Get to know some great recruiters in your field of expertise. When you have good rapport with recruiters, they will keep you in mind for new opportunities, and can help you find work quickly.
4. Think creatively about how you might use your skills to generate income. Perhaps you have a valuable and rarely used skill that can bring in some income in a pinch.
5. Depending on your assessment in chapter 8, you may choose to relocate to a much more affordable place to live in order to free up some breathing room to develop your business.

The Lecture

I feel pretty strongly about the importance of making sure you have key parts of your business in place in order to protect yourself, your family, and your business assets. If you design the backbone of your business in a smart and secure way, you will get to focus your time on the good stuff: making a difference, making meaning, and making money.

16

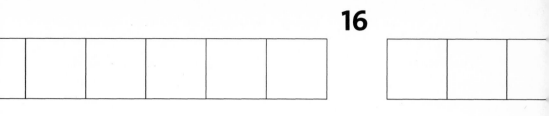

When Is It Time to Leave?

ouldn't it be great if you could gather the passion and resolve from Tom Cruise's character in *Jerry Maguire,* grab Flipper the goldfish in a plastic bag and ask, "Who is coming with me?"

If you haven't seen the movie, you missed an impassioned speech from a disgruntled employee, steeped in principles of decency and decrying the greed and heartlessness of the corporate world.

Poor Jerry. Or is it poor Tom and Jerry?

The character demonstrates a common mistake made by corporate employees: You wait too long. You lose your mind. And you do stupid things.

It works in Hollywood, but I'm hoping your exit is a little more understated.

If you are serious about weighing your decision to leave the corporate world, I suggest you take one last look at all the things we talked about in this book.

As I said way back in the introduction, *hating your job is not a business plan.* So how do things look?

What's in Place?

I wish there were a secret formula to ensure that the business idea you have been madly brewing in your mind is going to generate enough income to compensate for your current salary as an employee, if not much more. That would make me a very rich woman. Unfortunately, there are many, many factors that go into determining business success. One person can have a great, well-researched business idea that seems destined for success on paper, but whimpers out due to a poor sales and marketing effort. Someone else can have an airtight marketing plan that skyrockets exposure and generates lots of interest, but implodes due to poor operations planning or cash flow management.

Napoleon Hill, in his 1937 book *Think and Grow Rich*, names six basic fears that hold us back from success: fear of failure, fear of poverty, fear of criticism, fear of old age and ill health, fear of loss of love, fear of the unknown.

Quitting your job to start a business pretty much hits every one of these fears, so is it any wonder you are taking this process seriously?

Read over this checklist and see how prepared you feel.

Chest-Bursting Enthusiasm

In order to birth your business idea, you are going to have to have a tremendous amount of energy and stamina. When you are totally enthusiastic about an idea, you don't have to worry about "staying motivated" or "dealing with procrastination," concerns voiced by many prospective entrepreneurs. Here are your enthusiasm checkpoints:

- When you think about your idea, do you get a big smile on your face?
- Do you think about it all the time, whether or not you are working on it?
- When you think about it, do you feel *physically* good?
- To use a Martha Beck term, does the idea of starting your business feel more "shackles on" or "shackles off"?
- If you had your daily expenses taken care of, would you work on the idea anyway because it is so exciting to you?

- Do you see how this business fits into your overall life plan? Would being successful in this business give you the kind of life you want? Would you be happy *while doing it,* not just once you were making money?
- Have you looked your fears in the eye, dissected them, and separated the lizard variety from the legitimate ones?

A Solid Business Case

Passion without a business model or viable market is a sure road to perdition. Business case checkpoints:

- Have you spent time developing and defining your idea?
- Have you prototyped and tested your idea with real people in your target market?
- Have you made sales, or signed up people on your mailing list, or gotten them to download your trial product?
- Do you have a viable business model? Is it based on sound principles or pipe dreams?
- Are you willing to change strategies immediately if things don't go as planned?
- Can you identify your competitors?
- Can you describe what makes you different, more effective, or more appealing?
- Could your business survive if the market radically shifted?
- Do you have a truly useful product or service?
- Do you have all the right business processes and infrastructure in place to execute your business idea?
- Have you consulted with professionals to make sure you won't get sued, audited, or arrested?
- Are you prepared for various disasters, natural and otherwise?

An Eager Market

You know that your business cannot serve everyone in the world. Who, exactly, do you want to serve? Do they have deep, important problems that your product or service will address? Will your product or service make them money, save them time, build their brand, or improve their health? Do you know this or are you just making it all up? Market checkpoints:

- Can you define your target market in clear and specific terms?
- Do you know where they congregate in person, online, in associations, or in the media?
- Have you spent lots of time with them?
- Do you know what they crave?
- Do you know what will happen to them once they buy your product or service?
- Do you know what they care about deeply?
- Do you know how they like to communicate?
- Do they have access to cold, hard cash to pay you for your services?
- Are they the kind of people who would be fun to hang out with, regardless if you were doing business or not?

A Money Plan

As I mentioned in chapter 12, if you don't manage the money side of your business, you are destined for misery. Financial checkpoints:

- Are your personal finances organized and tracked in a systematic way?
- Have you improved or are you improving your credit score?
- Do you have six to twelve months of living expenses saved?
- Do you know how much money it will take to get your business off the ground?
- Do you have the money to get it off the ground?
- Are you up-to-date with your taxes?
- Do you have a process in place for managing finances, or an outside resource that will do it for you?
- Have you talked with a financial planner about the implications of your change in employment status?
- If you are really close to retirement, have you thought through the costs/benefits of quitting before fully vesting in your plans?
- Do you have solid Plans B, C, and D that you can activate if things don't work out as planned? (Remember, they never do.)

A Marketing Plan

You may know exactly who you want to work with, but if you can't actually talk to them, how can you expect to make any sales? It may take a good, long while for you to build a relationship with mutual knowledge, respect, and trust, so you must get started right away. Marketing checkpoints:

- Have you chosen a marketing model and are you implementing it step by step? (Duct Tape Marketing, Action Plan Marketing, and Michael Port are all great models.)
- Have you started an official opt-in mailing list?
- Do you communicate with your list at least once a month?
- Do you have a functional Web site that clearly nudges people to do what you want them to do? (Sign up for your list, download your product, join your community, etc.)
- Are you doing a handful of marketing activities consistently each month like writing articles, blogging, speaking, participating in online forums, or inviting interesting people to lunch?
- Do you have a clear referral program in place for happy customers?

A Healthy Approach to Sales

I worked with salespeople for years and am convinced they are born with special (some say mutated) genes. Excellent, ethical salespeople are totally excited by the sales process. Most first-time entrepreneurs, on the other hand, feel like throwing up at the thought of asking prospects for money. The fact is that you are going to have to talk to lots and lots of people about your product or service. If you are deathly afraid of asking for money, you must get over it. Selling checkpoints:

- Do you know what problem your product or service solves?
- How does it add specific value to your customers?
- Are you a good investment for other people's money?
- Do you know what your sales process is? Do you lead your prospects through it or wait for them to take the lead?

- Is your enthusiasm and vision for your idea stronger than your fear and terror of selling it? (Hint: all you need is a 51 percent to 49 percent ratio for it to work.)
- Are you willing to talk about your idea with people every day for the next 1-2-3-4-5 years?
- Do you sincerely care about solving your customers' problems?
- Do you have a good sense of humor?
- Can you get over criticism, even if it is undeserved?
- Would you feel proud to sell your product or service to your most trusted mentor?
- Do you know how to ask for a sale?

Time to Create the Business

It takes time to get your business up and running. If you have to continue working as an employee while you develop your business, create a project plan and carve out time in your schedule to make steady progress. You may need to forgo activities that make you happy such as evening television, golfing weekends, or excessive volunteering. The time will need to come from somewhere, and it is not a good idea to use lots of time from your day job to plan your business. Time checkpoints:

- Have you cleaned up and organized your work space?
- Do you have efficient processes in place for managing your e-mail, tracking projects, and accomplishing tasks?
- Do you have the appropriate technology in place to run your business effectively?
- Have you wiggled out of any nonessential obligations?
- Have you identified strong outside support like virtual assistants, personal assistants, and business partners so you can focus only on what you are best at?
- Do you know the major milestones you have to accomplish to get your business off the ground?
- Do you have the time to do them?

Support from Your Family

Starting a business is a very emotional experience, and you will need all the support you can muster from those closest to you. I gave you tips for talking with your spouse and loved ones in chapter 15. How did the conversations go? Family checkpoints:

- If you have a partner or spouse, do you have a mutually agreed upon life plan?
- Have you listened at length and without judgment to the concerns voiced by your spouse?
- Have you shared your business plans and checked for understanding?
- Do you know what the hot buttons are for your spouse? (Time, money, social status, etc.)
- If you know you don't have support from your family, are you willing to live with the consequences of moving forward anyway?
- Have you factored time with your family into your business plans?
- If you have kids, have you talked to them about what you want to do?
- Do you have mutually agreed upon metrics like amount of money in bank account, length of time to get business off the ground, amount of hair you are willing to lose before pulling the plug?
- Have you explicitly and mutually defined the role your spouse will or will not play in your business?
- Have you clearly discussed the risks he or she will assume if you are married? (Credit rating, cosigning for equipment or contracts, etc.)
- Have you scheduled regular conversations with your partner to see how he or she is feeling?
- Do you have an elevator speech that is not technically a lie that you can pull out at the holidays, on the phone, and during trips to Mom and Dad's that makes a good argument for your business idea?

Support from Your Tribe

If you have grown up inside corporate environments, many of your friends may not be experts in entrepreneurship. I cannot tell you how many times I relied on experienced mentors when I started my business—they saved my life many times. There are general online forums for entrepreneurs like StartupNation, specialized forums like MyMicroISV, and some advice for finding a mentor in this book. You don't need to know everything about your new business, but you should know people who do.

- Have you significantly expanded your personal network?
- Did you sign up for LinkedIn, Facebook, and Twitter?
- Do you have at least one mentor, mastermind buddy, staunch advocate, technical expert, and friend at your fingertips?
- Do you know where members of your tribe hang out?
- Are you well known in the places your tribe hangs out?
- Do you regularly and willingly help others, share information, and provide resources without being asked and without expectation of reciprocation?
- Have you found a way to remove Negative Nellies from your life?

A Mixture of Faith and Mistrust in the External Market and a Backup Plan

I have now lived through two significant upheavals in the financial markets as a business owner: Silicon Valley in 2000 and Phoenix, Arizona, in 2008. What I learned by living through the busts is that nothing lasts forever (both the good and the bad). If your business success depends on the economy staying the same for the next five years, you are doomed to intense moments of panic and possible financial ruin. Work on worst-case scenarios, and always think of your exit plan. Market checkpoints:

- Have you learned as much as you can about the market you are operating in?
- Do you regularly read information about your market?
- Have you identified competitors who are successful in your market?
- Have you studied what they do?
- As I mentioned in the Money section, do you have a Plan B, C, and D?
- Do you have a positive mindset and constructive thoughts about your new venture?
- Are you willing and able to look on the bright side of the most stormy market condition, even if it means radically adjusting your plans?

Turtle Steps

If this list is overwhelming, is there a way you can chip away at it bit by bit?

Keep in mind a few things:

1. **If you can make a huge sum of money without too much planning in your first year in business, do it.** Don't let me or anyone else stop you.

2. **Faster is not always better.** There are really great things that result from taking the time to plan and launch a business. For people who have a lower risk tolerance (financial and otherwise), slow and steady growth can be a lot less scary and more rewarding than an all-or-nothing hundred yard dash.

3. **If you think it is easy to make a huge sum of money your first year in business, you may want to test your assumptions.** Real-world testing is the best: launch a small product, do a consulting gig or two, try to get some new clients on the side of your day job. I hope I am wrong and #1 applies to you. But I would rather temper your optimism with realism than watch you fall on your face and lose more than you need to in your first year out.

Learn from the Pros

One of the best ways to prevent failure is to learn from those who have done it already. Here is what Guy Kawasaki said about his own journey:

Five Most Important Lessons I've Learned as an Entrepreneur, by Guy Kawasaki

This is my last posting for my friends at Sun Microsystems, and I'd like to leave you with something to remember me by: a list of the five most important lessons I've learned as an entrepreneur.

1. **Focus on cash flow.** I understand the difference between cash flow and profitability, and I'm not recommending that you strive for a lack of profitability. But cash is what keeps the doors open and pays the bills. Paper profits on an accrual accounting basis is of no more than secondary or tertiary importance for a startup. As my mother used to say, "Sales fixes everything."

2. **Make a little progress every day.** I used to believe in the big-bang theory of marketing: a fantastic launch that created such inertia that you flew to "infinity and beyond." No more. Now my theory is that you make a little bit of progress every day—whether that's making your product slightly better, increasing your skill in one small way, or closing one more customer. The reason the press writes about "overnight successes" is that they seldom happen—not because that's how all businesses work.

3. **Try stuff.** I also used to believe that it's better to be smart than lucky because if you're smart you can out-think the competition. I don't believe that anymore—this is not to say that you should strive for a high level of stupidity. My point is that luck is a big part of many successes, so (a) don't get too bummed out when you see a bozo succeed; and (b) luck favors the people who try stuff, not simply think and analyze. As the Chinese say, "One must wait for a long time with your mouth open before a Peking duck flies in your mouth."

4. **Ignore schmexperts.** Schmexperts are the totally bad combination of schmucks who are experts—or experts who are schmucks. When you first launch a product or service, they'll tell you it isn't necessary,

can't really work, or faces too much competition. If you succeed, then they'll say they knew you would succeed. In other words, they don't know jack shiitake. If you believe, try it. If you don't believe, listen to the schmexperts and stay on the porch.

5. **Never ask anyone to do something that you wouldn't do.** This goes for customers ("fill out these twenty-five fields of personal information to get an account for our website") to employees ("fly coach to Mumbai, meet all day the day you arrive, and fly back that night"). If you follow this principle, you'll almost always have a good customer service reputation and happy employees.

I hold these truths to be self-evident and hope you can use them to kick butt and change the world.'

The Cosmic Joke

You know the funny thing?

There will be someone who checks every single box in this summary chapter and still will not make enough money to support himself.

And there will be someone who does none of it, who quits her job on a whim, makes up a product or service in a burst of inspiration and flings it out in the world to great financial reward.

What I have found, and what I offer, is that business success is not the real reason to undertake this adventure.

Nothing will teach you more about yourself. Nothing will stretch you and challenge you and confound you like running your own business. Nothing will bring you to your knees in agony, and in joy, like trying to create something out of nothing.

So the questions become:

- Will I be a better, smarter, more compassionate human being for having attempted this, regardless of the outcome?

- What will make me a little bit less like the guy in the "Cat's in the Cradle" song?
- Will the world be a little bit better because of my efforts?

Make Meaning

GUY KAWASAKI, *THE ART OF THE START*
The truth is that no one really knows if he is an entrepreneur until he becomes one—and sometimes not even then. There really is only one question you should ask yourself before starting any new venture:

DO I WANT TO MAKE *MEANING*?
Meaning is not about money, power or prestige. It's not even about creating a fun place to work. Among the meanings of "meaning" are to:
- Make the world a better place
- Increase the quality of life
- Right a terrible wrong
- Prevent the end of something good.[2]

My Parting Advice

If you took this process seriously, you just did a whole lot of work.

You excavated your soul. Found your muse. Read books. Surfed blogs. Worked late nights. Had tough conversations. Cut back, cleaned up, scrimped and saved. Planned, tested, failed, adjusted, and tested some more. Put yourself out there in the world like you never have before. You gathered reinforcements. You planned, and hoped, and evaluated.

Now you are here, peering over the edge.

This is it.

No amount of data, checklists, spreadsheets, focus groups, analysis, or information is going to tell you if it is the right time to quit your job.

It is a leap of faith. You can choose to take it or not.

If you choose to leap, congratulations. Welcome to the other side. I have been waiting for you.

If you choose to stay, I support you. When you are ready, I will still be here.

What is your plan? Let me know. Come join the conversation at www .escapefromcubiclenation.com.

ACKNOWLEDGMENTS

There were days writing this book when I felt like I had a thousand hands at my back, pushing and encouraging me to move forward. In fact, this was true: my blog readers are the heart and soul of my work, and for this I am thankful to all of you for your generosity, friendship, advice, and encouragement.

A select group of 150 people took a step further and volunteered to be bothered with frequent e-mails with questions ranging from "What does it feel like to be stuck in a cube?" to "What are your biggest worries about securing benefits?" Escape from Cubicle Nation Advisory Council, you are a gift and I am eternally grateful for your detailed recommendations and feedback.

My Twitter buddies endured eight weeks of nonstop questions. Thanks for your great advice, humor, and late-night support.

My clients are some of the bravest people on earth, navigating personal fears and business challenges with gusto and grace. I am so honored to know you and work with you. Thanks for your trust and support. I have already seen, and will continue to see, great things from all of you.

Staunch allies (in no particular order) include Marilyn Scott-Waters, Lisa Evans, Matthew Scott, Andy Pels, Brooke Castillo, Philippa Kennealy, Andy Wibbels, John Fritz, Ramit Sethi, Sophfronia Scott, Havi Brooks, Naomi Dunford, John Dodds, Robert Bruce, Bob Walsh, Michelle Woodward, Meadow De Vor, Tina Forsyth, Nathan Bowers, Colleen Wainwright, Jonathan Fields, and Glenda Watson-Hyatt. Thanks for pulling me back from the brink many times and for being such exemplary friends, smart people, and human beings.

I am not embarrassed to admit that I am a devout fangirl of my High Council of Jedi Knights, which includes Guy Kawasaki, Seth Godin, Rich Sloan, Andrea Lee, Tim Berry, Kathy Sierra, Hugh MacLeod, Garr Reynolds, Bob Sutton, Srikumar Rao, Lynnette Khalfani, and John Jantsch. Your work inspires me so much and pushes me to do my very best while serving my tribe with an open heart.

Suzanne Falter-Barns, you were so right—developing a killer brand is the secret to the universe. Thanks for your perfect advice and teaching.

Martha Beck, I know you understand more than anyone the magical mystery tour that happened when I aligned my deepest purpose with my right work. The fact that I get to work with you and be your friend after admiring your work for so long is a testament to the message of this book.

My editor, Emily Rapoport—what can I say? You made this happen. The fact that you made an author out of a scrappy blogger speaks to your faith, capacity, and willingness to take risks. I am truly blessed to work with you. Joelle Delbourgo, my agent, you gave me the exact advice I needed with just the right combination of strength and support. I am exceptionally glad to be a Penguin/Portfolio author and will wear the brand proudly.

Barb, Mary Jo, Kris, MaryAnn, and Leslie, you made the first decade of my business a true joy, and for this, I will be eternally grateful. Skip, Mark, and Peter, thanks for your trust and willingness to share business with me!

Suzanne and Laura, you made my transition to Arizona and all the wildness that ensued a true hilarious adventure. I love you both. Desiree Adaway, my best friend on the planet, my life is permanently better because of you. Dear departed Carlos Aceituno, your life inspires me. All my capoeira "kids," you are always with me. Cecilia, your loving care of Angela is a tremendous blessing.

Ed, Madelyn, Todd, and Trisha Smith, your support and generosity are truly awe-inspiring. Thank you for your belief in Darryl's business and our family.

Mom, Larry, Gretchen, Gary, Brian, Rose, Dad, Dee, Mom Slim, Gerri, Ronnie, Cilla, Dean, Steve, Rose, Monte, Patty, Maria Jose, Jimmy, and all my nieces and nephews, you are my strength and pride.

And my precious family, Darryl, Jeffery, Joshua, and Angela, you are in the very center of my heart. Your love made this book happen. I am the luckiest woman in the world.

Chapter 1

1. Dilbert.com Mission Statement Generator, http://www.unitedmedia.com/comics/dilbert/games/career/bin/ms_verb.cgi.
2. Paul Graham, "You Aren't Meant to Have a Boss," http://paulgraham.com/boss.html.
3. Jacob and Wilhelm Grimm, *Kinder- und Hausmärchen*, 1st ed., translated by D. L. Ashliman (Berlin, 1812), vol. 1, no. 21.
4. Kathy Sierra, "Brain Death by Dull Cubicle," Creating Passionate Users, February 20, 2006, http://headrush.typepad.com/creating_passionate_users/2006/02/brain_death_by_.html.
5. Timothy Ferriss, *The 4-Hour Workweek: Escape 9–5, Live Anywhere and Join the New Rich* (New York: Crown Publishers, 2007).

Chapter 2

1. Martha Beck, *Steering by Starlight* (Emmaus, PA: Rodale Press, 2008).
2. Martha Beck, *Finding Your Own North Star* (New York: Three Rivers Press, 2001).
3. Barry Moltz, *Bounce! Failure, Resiliency, and Confidence to Achieve Your Next Great Success* (New York: Wiley, 2009).

Chapter 3

1. William Bridges, *Transitions: Making Sense of Life's Changes* (New York: Perseus Books, 1980).
2. Julia Cameron, *The Artist's Way* (New York: G.P. Putnam's Sons, 1992).
3. Christine Kane, "How to Create a Vision Board," christinekane.com, February 1, 2007.

Chapter 4

1. Jonathan Fields, *Career Renegade: How to Make a Great Living Doing What You Love* (New York: Broadway Books, 2009).

Chapter 5

1. "Lichens of North America," www.lichen.com.
2. Ibid.
3. Marci Alboher, *One Person/Multiple Careers: How the Slash Effect Can Work for You* (New York: Business Plus, 2007).
4. Michael E. Gerber, *The E-Myth Revisited* (New York: HarperCollins, 1995, 2001).
5. Jonathan Fields, "For the Last Time, Blogging Is Not Passive Revenue," Awake at the Wheel Blog, March 24, 2008, http://jonathanfields.com/blog/for-the-last-time -blogging-is-not-passive-income/.

Chapter 6

1. Kathy Sierra, "Help Your Users Kick Ass," Creating Passionate Users, June 2005, http://headrush.typepad.com/creating_passionate_users/2005/06/kicking_ass_ is_.html.
2. Hugh McLeod, gapingvoid.com.
3. Tim Berry, personal interview.

Chapter 7

1. Seth Godin, *Tribes* (New York: Portfolio, 2008).
2. Jason Alba, personal interview.

Chapter 8

1. Personal conversation with Paul Hyatt.

Chapter 9

1. Tim Berry, *The Plan as You Go Business Plan* (Irvine, CA: Entrepreneur Media, Inc., 2008).

2. Tim Berry, personal interview.
3. Ibid.
4. Denise O'Berry, *Small Business Cash Flow: Strategies for Making Your Business a Financial Success* (Hoboken, NJ: Wiley, 2006).
5. John Jantsch, Duct Tape Marketing Blog, September 3, 2008, http://www.ducttapemarketing.com/blog/2008/09/03/i-dont-have-time-for-marketing/.

Chapter 10

1. Tom Asacker, "Flash of Branding Insight," A Clear Eye, March 18, 2008, http://www.acleareye.com/sandbox_wisdom/2008/03/the-flash-of-br.html.

Chapter 11

1. Anne Lamott, *Bird by Bird* (New York: Random House, 1995).
2. Seth Godin, *The Dip* (New York: Portfolio, 2007).
3. Seth Godin, "Failure as an Event," October 2008, http://sethgodin.typepad.com/seths_blog/2008/10/failure-as-an-e.html.

Chapter 12

1. Read Write Web, http://www.readwriteweb.com/archives/banking_20_money_management_in_the_cloud.php.
2. Lynnette Khalfani, *Zero Debt* (South Orange, NJ: Advantage World Press, 2004).
3. Naomi Dunford, "5 Reasons You Shouldn't Have a Financial Cushion Before Quitting Your Job," Ittybiz, August 2008, http://ittybiz.com/financial-cushion-before-you-quit-your-job/.
4. Denise O'Berry, *Small Business Cash Flow: Strategies for Making Your Business a Financial Success* (Hoboken, NJ: Wiley, 2006).
5. Marcus Buckingham and Donald O. Clifton, *Now, Discover Your Strengths* (New York: The Free Press, 2001).
6. J. D. Roth, "Facing and Fighting Financial Trolls," Get Rich Slowly, January 16, 2007, http://www.getrichslowly.org/blog/2007/01/16/facing-and-fighting-financial-trolls/.
7. Timothy Ferriss, *The 4-Hour Workweek: Escape 9–5, Live Anywhere and Join the New Rich* (New York: Crown Publishers, 2007).

Chapter 13

1. Jonathan Pletzke, *Get a Good Deal on Your Health Insurance Without Getting Ripped Off* (Chapel Hill, NC: Aji Publishing, 2007).
2. Jonathan Pletzke, "A Glossary of Terms for Small Business Owners," Startup Nation.com, http://www.startupnation.com/articles/1393/1/health-insurance-lingo.asp.
3. Pletzke, *Get a Good Deal on Your Health Insurance*.

Chapter 14

1. Joanne Bamberger (Pundit Mom), http://punditmom1.blogspot.com/
2. Matthew Scott, personal interview.
3. Francine Hardaway, personal interview.
4. Clearly, there are some parents who are not healthy and do not have your best interests at heart. They may intentionally do things to sabotage your success or make you unhappy. If this is the case, move forward with your ideas without sharing them, to keep your emotions and self-esteem intact.

Chapter 15

1. Gina Trapani, *Upgrade Your Life: The Lifehacker Guide to Working Smarter, Faster, Better* (Hoboken, NJ: Wiley, 2008).
2. Ibid.

Chapter 16

1. Guy Kawasaki, "Five Lessons on Starting a Business," August 18, 2008, http://www.sun.com/solutions/smb/guest.jsp?blog=five_lessons.
2. Guy Kawasaki, *The Art of the Start* (New York: Portfolio, 2004).

Office Space (movie, 1999)

Bloggers and Their Blogs

Marilyn Scott-Waters, The Toy Maker
Bob Walsh, 47hats
Kathy Sierra, Creating Passionate Users
Rich and Jeff Sloan, StartupNation
Gary Vaynerchuk, TV.WineLibrary.com
L. P. Neenz Faleafine, Pono Media
Sohaib Athar, Really Virtual
Ramit Sethi, I Will Teach You to Be Rich
Jonathan Fields, Awake @ The Wheel
Elizabeth Gordon, Flourishing Business
Hugh McLeod, Gapingvoid
Dr. Srikumar Rao, Are You Ready to Succeed
Leo Baubata, Zen Habits
J. D. Roth, Get Rich Slowly
Lea and Jonathan Woodward, Location Independent

Books

Timothy Ferriss, *4-Hour Work Week: Escape 9–5, Live Anywhere, and Join the New Rich*
William Bridges, *Transitions: Making Sense of Life's Changes*
Martha Beck, *Finding Your Own North Star*
Barry Moltz, *Bounce! Failure, Resiliency, and Confidence to Achieve Your Next Great Success*
Byron Katie, *Loving What Is*
Julia Cameron, *The Artist's Way*
Anne Lamott, *Bird by Bird*
Dan Clements and Tara Gignak, *Escape 101*
Jim Collins, *Good to Great and Built to Last*
Rich and Jeff Sloan, *StartupNation: Open for Business*
Marci Alboher, *One Person/Multiple Careers*
Seth Godin, *Tribes*
Jason Alba, *I'm on LinkedIn, Now What???*
Lea and Jonathan Woodward, *X Marks the Spot: The Indispensable Guide to Living and Working Wherever You Want*
Lea and Jonathan Woodward, *Creating a Location-Independent Business*
Jonathan Pletzke, *Get a Good Deal on Your Health Insurance Without Getting Ripped Off*
Skip Miller, *ProActive Selling* (a former client!)
Rich Karlgaard, *Life 2.0: How People Across America Are Transforming Their Lives by Finding the Where of Their Happiness*
Richard Florida, *The Rise of the Creative Class: And How It's Transforming Work, Leisure, Community and Everyday Life*
Richard Florida, *Who's Your City*

Financial

QuickBooks; quickbooks.com
Fresh Books; freshbooks.com
Peach Tree; peachtree.com
Mind Your Own Business; myob.com
Microsoft Accounting 2008; http://office.microsoft.com/en-us/accounting/default.aspx
Less Accounting; lessaccounting.com
MyBizHomePage.com—a resource page for QuickBooks users

Infrastructure

getdropbox.com
sugarsync.com
jungledisk.com
www.apple.com/macosx/features/timemachine.html

Creating a Business Plan

Tim Berry, *The Plan as You Go Business Plan* (www.planasyougo.com)

Jim Horan, *The One Page Business Plan* (www.onepagebusinessplan.com)

Laura West, *The Joyful Business Guide*™ (www.joyfulbusinessguide.com)

Guy Kawasaki, *The Art of the Start*

www.businessplanpro.com

www.paloalto.com/marketing_plan_software (marketing plan, powered by Duct
   Tape Marketing)

INDEX